D0116492

A NEW COVENANT WITH NATURE

1996

2.00
10/25/19

A NEW COVENANT WITH NATURE

NOTES ON THE END OF CIVILIZATION AND THE RENEWAL OF CULTURE

RICHARD HEINBERG

A publication supported by
THE KERN FOUNDATION

Quest Books
Theosophical Publishing House

Wheaton, Illinois ◆ Madras, India

Copyright 1996 by Richard Heinberg

First Quest Edition 1996

All rights reserved. No part of this book may be
reproduced in any manner without written permission
except for quotations embodied in critical articles
or reviews. For additional information write to

The Theosophical Publishing House
P.O. Box 270
Wheaton, IL 60189-0270

A publication of the Theosophical Publishing House,
a department of the Theosophical Society in America

Library of Congress Cataloging-in-Publication Data

Heinberg, Richard.
    A new covenant with nature : notes on the end of civilization and the
renewal of culture / Richard Heinberg.
      p.   cm.
    Includes bibliographical references and index.
    ISBN 0-8356-0746-1
    1. Human ecology.   2. Civilization, Modern.   3. Social change.   I. Title.
GF50.H45   1996
304.2—dc20
                                              96-19678
                                                CIP

6 5 4 3 2 1 * 96 97 98 00 01 02

Printed in the United States of America

For Janet

CONTENTS

ACKNOWLEDGMENTS

 I WOULD LIKE TO take this opportunity to thank Brenda Rosen, my editor at Quest Books, for her friendly encouragement at every step of this project, and for the understanding and skill with which she honed it. I'm also indebted to the rest of the staff at Quest for their cheerful help in transforming *A New Covenant* from manuscript to book.

I would also like to express my appreciation to Helena Norberg-Hodge and Sierra Club Books for their permission to quote extensively from *Ancient Futures: Learning from Ladakh.*

The ideas in this book were first developed and set forth in my monthly four-page *MuseLetter.* My subscribers often provide helpful feedback, and I am always grateful for their support and input. For subscription information or to contact the author, write:

MuseLetter
1433 Olivet Road
Santa Rosa CA 95401

Foreword

THE NOTION THAT MODERN mass society is sick is not new. From their first encounters with westerners, indigenous peoples saw the dysfunction of the encroaching world. One of the most incisive expressions of this unsettling vision appears in a short story by Choctow-Cree writer Gerald Haslam. "Hawk's Flight" is the story of an Indian boy whose entire village is destroyed by American soldiers, who witnesses the wanton murder of his parents and relatives, and now awaits his own execution. As he does, the boy watches. He sees a sickness he has never witnessed before: "Hawk found himself feeling a strange kind of pity for these hopeless creatures who possessed no magic at all, no union with Earth or sky, only the ability to hurt and kill . . . . They were sad and dangerous like a broken rattlesnake."

Within a generation of the events described in "Hawk's Flight," across the Atlantic Ocean, Sigmund Freud saw the same broken rattlesnake. The year was 1939, and Freud stood at the pained edge of Nazism's rise. "May we not be justified in reaching the diagnosis that, under the influence of cultural urges," he wrote in his now infamous *Civilization and Its Discontents,* "some civilizations or some epochs of civilization—possibly the whole of mankind—have become 'neurotic'?" Writing in the aftermath of the Holocaust and Hiroshima, R. D. Laing asserted that our "socially shared hallucinations, our collusive madness in what we call sanity," while his colleague psychoanalyst Erich Fromm asked, "Can a society be sick?" and answered: "That millions of people share the same form of mental pathology does not make those people sane."

In the early 1980s—after Vietnam, in the midst of El Salvador, and as Reaganism was furthering the reach between rich and poor—psychohistorian Paul Shepard took up the task of social diagnosis once again. In his ground-breaking *Nature and Madness,* Shepard revealed how as westerners became more removed from the natural world, our child-rearing practices decreasingly answered our evolutionary expectations for nurturing and independence; hence, a systemic, collective mental illness came into being, an illness that expressed itself in the very structure of the individual psyche, in cultural assumptions, and in the structure and policies of social institutions.

In *My Name is Chellis and I'm in Recovery from Western Civilization,* I take the notion of dysfunctional society one step farther, applying the diagnosis of post-traumatic stress disorder to the whole of civilization and translating the principles of individual recovery into guidelines for social change.

And now there comes Richard Heinberg. And none too soon—as the General Agreement on Tariffs and Trade loosens the last restraints against social insanity, thrusting transnational corporations into positions of global control that would make Alexander the Great and Adolph Hitler envious. Heinberg is one of the new holistic thinkers, his terrain ranging from anthropology and history, through ecology and global politics, to include psychology and spirituality. In his latest offering, *A New Covenant with Nature,* he adds his voice to the most important conversation taking place today. What is wrong with modern civilization? he asks. How can human beings participate in the survival of life? What can those of us who live within the dictates of corporate-dominated civilization do to enhance justice and ensure sustainability?

In his answers, Heinberg manages the nearly impossible with the clarity of a Paleolithic pool and the agility of an aikido master. To take mass society's pulse, he uses the very tool it most esteems: human rationality. Questioning such deeply-embedded institutionalized concepts as the evolution of consciousness, progress, money, war, private property, institutionalized religion, and consumerism, he concludes that society is suffering from post-traumatic stress disorder.

With an eye towards healing, Heinberg calls upon native cultures and the indigenous heritage of non-native peoples to serve as the baseline for authentic human sanity. This is an approach that increasingly makes good sense, and by taking it, Heinberg joins such thinkers, activists, and social healers as Helena Norberg-Hodge, Satish Kumar, Vandana Shiva, Subcommandante Marcos, John Mohawk, Oren Lyons, and Kirkpatrick Sale. From the perspective of trauma recovery, such an approach constitutes what is called "conjuring the future self."

Although I am of European American heritage, I have lived these recent years in an indigenous Chicano village in northern New Mexico. Most of my neighbors look upon the dominant society—these days making itself known to them through radioactive fallout, Wal-Mart, "Melrose Place," tourism, and real estate—as a tragic assault, and the most often-heard conversation in the village is about how things used to be. This perspective is a profound relief for me; it is also a challenge. Despite a lifetime spent nursing my "future self" by peeling away the dominant society's assumptions, my own assumptions are daily disarmed. Once a vaquero, riding an old mare with a handmade leather saddle, summed up the world situation in a single sentence: "The down-to-earth people are finishing," he said sadly. Down at the village store, my anti-globalization politics (which might take me forty-five minutes to explain) have been reflected back to me: "She is against the chain stores." Once the storekeeper, with great thoughtfulness, asked me, "Do you think that regular people should use a FAX machine?" (Heads up: regular = indigenous.) And of a ten-acre piece of desert land that came up for sale, a chili farmer told me: "That land is good for nothing. Except maybe putting a house."

Fortunately for us all, not everyone aiming to disarm the assumptions of mass society needs to live in an indigenous village; to launch the same questioning mind, we can read Richard Heinberg's *A New Covenant with Nature*.

Continuing and enriching the work of previous social diagnosticians, Heinberg offers a stark perspective. By concluding that modern society is both traumatized and traumatizing, he does not skirt the severity or complexity of the problems facing humankind today. Instead he causes those of us who live within mass society to reflect deeply about who we have become. Heinberg, however, goes beyond most of his predecessors. He offers a social vision for the future—unabashedly proposing withdrawal from mass consumer society into sustainable, bioregional community.

The challenge is, of course, monstrous. It means literally applying the means of healing pioneered by post-traumatic stress disorder specialists: examining the multitudinous shattered fragments of consciousness, culture, and livelihood that have so tragically been lost through the march of massification. It means finding ways, seemingly impossible ways, to unite the fragments into the whole of creation. And it promises to take us through the painful remembrance of forgotten ways, the profundity of generations-old grief, the adamancy of protest against untenable doings, the exhilaration of rediscovery, reconnection, and creativity, and the risk of manifestation.

Heinberg knows all this, and with a clarity that honors the complexity of challenge, he writes this book to launch and sustain our collective questioning, our collective recovery, and our collective manifestation.

Heal the rattlesnake.

Chellis Glendinning, Ph.D.
Chimayó, New Mexico

INTRODUCTION

IMAGINE YOURSELF IN THE AREA where I live—the vicinity of Santa Rosa in northern California—as it was a few centuries ago.

The people here are members of the Pomo nation. They are relatively short and round-faced and wear no clothing except in winter, when men don a cloak and women a skirt made of shredded redwood bark. They are a peaceful people who build their circular, communal huts in nearly five hundred villages in an area bounded by the Pacific Ocean to the west and the Coast Range of mountains to the east, the Russian River valley to the south and Eel River and Clear Lake to the north.

In each Pomo village everyone is related. An elder settles disputes and attends to the spiritual needs of the people. Every village has its dance house, as well as a sweat house which is used daily for both healing and ceremonial purposes.

The people easily obtain food from the surrounding countryside; their diet includes acorns, sunflower seeds, beans, hazel and buckeye nuts, manzanita berries, bulbs, roots, tubers, fish, and deer. Everyone learns early in life how to build a house, how to gather food, and how to treat common ailments with local herbs. Average life expectancy is not long by modern standards, but that is due largely to the high rate of infant mortality. Elders often reach ages of seventy, eighty, and more. Cancer and heart disease are extremely rare, as are degenerative diseases.

Life is relatively easy for the Pomo: no one has to work more than three or four hours at a time to supply basic survival needs, and the rest of the day is devoted to talk, laughter, play, ceremony, and handicraft (the women make beautiful coiled and twined baskets). These people are proud and happy, and while they maintain generally friendly relations with other native groups in the region, they are content to live out their days within this relatively small geographical area, traveling only rarely beyond its natural boundaries. They know their land intimately—every stream and hill, and every species of herb, tree, bird, frog, fish, lizard, insect, and mammal.

Now imagine the scene shifting to the city of Santa Rosa in the present. There are far more people living here today (125,000 in the city itself), and they have a vastly greater impact on the land. Nearly everywhere they have built—or are in the process of building—houses, office buildings, and roads. Streams have been rechanneled, hills leveled, flood plains drained, and forests logged.

The people obtain most of their food from supermarkets; few know how to grow or gather it. Though the local economy is still somewhat tied to agriculture (Sonoma County is known for its fine wines), most food is imported from far away.

Likewise, few people know personally how to build a house: they rely on professionals to construct their dwellings, and the materials are nearly all imported and toxic. Houses tend to be large and elaborate, and in most cases are inhabited by only one family. A modest house in Santa Rosa costs the equivalent of seven years' wages for the average worker. Many people cannot afford to own a house, and a few cannot afford even to rent one; these unfortunates live on the streets or in old cars.

Nearly everyone has a car—a typical new one costs a year's average wages—but few know how to repair them, and no one in Santa Rosa builds them.

Political leaders are elected by the people, but few of the people have ever actually met one of their leaders.

For everyone, life requires a constant supply of money, which is used to obtain all goods and services, including entertainment. The money the people use is created thousands of miles away by a process few understand, and is stored and transferred by way of computerized bookkeeping entries. Most people earn money by working at a job eight or more hours a day, five or more days a week. Some people in Santa Rosa are so wealthy that they don't have to work at all. But life is hard for others, particularly those with low-paying jobs and children to feed.

Santa Rosa has modern hospitals filled with expensive, up-to-date equipment. Life expectancy has increased greatly compared to that in past decades, but rates of cancer, heart disease, and environmental illnesses are worrisomely high and rising.

Most of the music, dances, and ideas current in the city come from far away via magazines, radio, and television. Nearly everyone watches television many hours a week; the images they see reinforce their desire for more manufactured consumer goods (products that are available in identical forms nearly everywhere in the world), and therefore for more money.

The people of Santa Rosa travel a great deal. In fact, only a minority of residents were born here. Out of necessity, people spend most of each day attending to human systems of money, transportation, and communication. They study road maps, store catalogs, and telephone directories, but they spend comparatively little time getting to know the land where they live. Few people can trace the boundaries of the local watershed or name more than a dozen or so indigenous plant or animal species.

The differences between the Santa Rosa of today and the Pomo village of five centuries ago are profound. To what extent have human lives been improved by all this change? The surviving Pomo people may be permitted to doubt whether the passage of time has brought unmitigated progress, since their ancestors—most of whom suffered horrible deaths from diseases brought by the Spanish and other European settlers—were never given a choice of whether to maintain their old pattern of life or adapt to the invaders' ways. That decision was made for them. But it would be equally simplistic to say without qualification that people were better off in the old days: they may have lived with less stress then, but they had fewer comforts and conveniences, less knowledge of world geography and politics, and fewer opportunities for travel. It is popular in academic circles these days to adopt an attitude of neutrality or relativism regarding cultures—to assume that every culture has its unique strengths and shortcomings, which on the whole tend to balance out. Since human culture is an unfathomably complex phenomenon, say the cultural relativists, it is foolish to try to judge one way of life as fundamentally superior to another. Who, after all, is knowledgeable and impartial enough to do the judging? But when we consider the impact of culture on the land and wildlife in a given place, such as Santa Rosa, an impartial stance becomes difficult to maintain. Once this gentle land was thriving; now it is being paved, eroded, and polluted at a furious and dangerous pace.

It seems that between the first and second temporal snapshots something has gone terribly awry in the relationship between people and nature. And in this regard Santa Rosa is little different from other places; everywhere the story is essentially the same. As biologist Peter Raven put it at the 1987 meeting of the American Association for the Advancement of Science, "We are killing the world." What has gone wrong? And what can we do about it?

ॐ

It was in late childhood that I first began to realize that the society around me was on a reckless track. I recall being infuriated by the insipid materialism and commercialism of America in the 1950s. As I learned a little about history, I began to regard war as more evidence of crassness and stupidity. Why did people allow their governments to behave like schoolyard bullies? It seemed that the fate of the planet was in the hands of raving idiots.

Meanwhile, it was clear that the world was in a whirlwind of change: Every year brought new products and inventions (like lasers and microwave ovens), social controversies (such as those surrounding the civil rights movement), and cultural phenomena (like the Beatles). It was all exhilarating, yet disturbing. The only certainties were change itself and the general direction in which it was headed—toward anything that was *more, bigger,* or *faster.*

In 1964 my high school geography teacher, in one of her frequent sardonic asides to the class, mentioned something about awful consequences that would follow if America were to get mired down in a conflict in Southeast Asia. At the time, I attached little significance to her warning: Asia meant nothing more to me than words and pictures in a book. Only a few years later, most young men of my generation were either in Vietnam or trying desperately to find a way to avoid being sent there. I was one of the lucky ones: I had a high draft lottery number and was never called. Instead, I went to college and joined the antiwar movement.

The Vietnam War was an education for many of us—but a very different education from the one we were receiving in school. Our textbooks led us to believe that America was the wisest and kindest of nations. Our country, we were told, was a torchbearer of freedom. Yet in Vietnam our government seemed to be championing a puppet dictatorship and ignoring the wishes of the people. The war appeared to be the creation of the very military-industrial complex that Eisenhower, in his last speech as president, had warned against—huge transnational corporations that were largely financed by Pentagon contracts; that increasingly controlled government policy; that were interested only in raw materials, markets, and profits; and that routinely destroyed indigenous cultures around the world in order to enrich themselves.

Once the debate over Vietnam had torn the mask of civility from the empire culture in which we were living, many of us began to see that it was riddled with all sorts of contradictions and inequities. It became apparent, for example, that the way of life to which we had become accustomed was polluting and exhausting the natural environment; that women and people of color were being routinely exploited; that the rich were continually growing richer and the poor poorer. This was difficult information for any young person to absorb. What to do about it?

Since I had grown up in a religious family, my first reflex was to look for spiritual solutions to the world's problems. Perhaps humanity was acting in selfish, cruel, and shortsighted ways because it needed enlightenment. The wickedness in the heart of the worst industrial polluter or political terrorist exists in my heart too, I thought, if only in essence. If I cannot expunge envy, hatred, and greed from my own soul, then I have no real basis for blaming others for their shortcomings; but if I can, then perhaps I can provide an example.

For the next twenty years I studied Buddhism, Taoism, and mystical Christianity; lived in spiritual communities; and explored New Age philosophies, therapies, and trainings. It was a time of growth and learning for which I shall always be grateful. But eventually I realized that spirituality isn't the full answer to the world's problems. I often met people whose dedication to God was unquestionable, but who had adopted an authoritarian or intolerant attitude, or who glossed over economic and social dilemmas that couldn't easily be framed in the context of their etherial worldview. After two decades of waiting for the formation of a "critical mass" of enlightened pioneers to spearhead the evolution of humanity into a New Age of universal harmony, I began to realize that in reality the world was worse off than ever.

Meanwhile my investigations of comparative religion were leading me toward the study of tribal societies—such as those of the Native Americans, Africans, Aboriginal Australians, and Pacific Islanders. These nonindustrial peoples, many of whom had ancient Earth-based spiritual traditions, didn't (at least, until time of contact) share many of the problems of the First World. Their cultures may have been imperfect in their own ways—the natives of Papua New Guinea, for example, routinely practiced human sacrifice—but in terms of environmental destructiveness they were far less ruinous than the industrial societies of the twentieth century. Their patterns of existence were sustainable, while ours is not. As I researched tribal peoples it became apparent to me that their social and ecological stability derived not just from their religions, but from all the details of their ways of life.

Simultaneously, I began to see that the insanity of the modern world is not due simply to a lack of morals or spiritual awareness, but is embedded in every aspect of our collective existence. Our destruction of the natural environment, our horrific wars, and the spread of poverty throughout both the Third World and our own First World cities cannot be fully halted by a government regulation here or a new invention there. They are inherent in the overall pattern of existence we have adopted.

I gradually came to see that what we eat, how we think and live, and the kinds and quantities of resources we use all imply a certain contract or covenant with nature, and that every culture makes such a covenant by which its members (mostly unconsciously) abide. Humankind and nature exist in a reciprocal balance: just as people shape the land to their needs, land and climate also affect people—leading them not only to rely on locally and seasonally available foods, but to entertain attitudes toward life that spring from their adopted patterns of subsistence. Desert pastoralists tend to have consistent and predictable mythologies, forms of social organization, and worldviews, no matter what continent they live on; and the same can be said of coastal fishers, arctic hunters, and tropical horticulturists. Moreover, historical hindsight and cross-cultural comparisons suggest that some covenants with nature are more successful than others. Civilization—the pattern of life that involves cities, lifetime division of labor, conquest, and agriculture—represents a uniquely exploitive covenant in which humans seek to maximize their control of their environment and minimize its constraints upon themselves. In the past, many civilizations have fallen because of their unrealistic demands on soil, water, and forests, leaving deserts in their wake. We are presently living in a society whose patterns of reliance on nature appear to be leading to similar ends. But in this case, because our civilization has become global in extent, we may seriously impair the biological viability of the entire planet before our institutions finally sputter and die.

Along the way, a voice in my head raised objections: *Aren't you merely romanticizing primitive cultures? If you actually had to do without all of the conveniences of modern life you'd probably be miserable. Anyway, we can't simply go back to living the way our ancestors did. We can't "uninvent" the automobile, nuclear reactor, or computer.* This voice refuses to shut up. Sometimes its arguments appear irrefutable. But as yet it has offered no alternative solution to the great underlying crisis of our civilization—the fact that we are presiding over a worldwide biological holocaust. The voice of "realism" merely says that the crisis is somehow inevitable, perhaps an evolutionary necessity.

But of course there *are* alternatives, there *are* solutions. The path away from our predatory industrial-electronic civilization need not be an attempt to imitate the lifeways of the primitive peoples. We cannot all become

Pomos. But we *can* relearn much of what has been forgotten in the march of "progress." We can regain the sense of responsibility to land and life that indigenous peoples have always known. Even if we cannot now envision all the details of a post-imperial culture, we can at least speak of it in general terms, discuss the process by which it might come into being, and take practical steps toward its realization.

This book is a collection of notes and observations stemming from the core realization that *the processes of coming into a healthy relationship with the natural world and of rediscovering and renewing human culture are identical.* The book has grown out of meetings with Native Americans, New Zealand Maoris, and Aboriginal Australians; readings in history, anthropology, economics, and comparative religion; and years of living in experimental communities. It has two purposes: to trace the historical events that have led us to equate "progress" with the destruction of the natural world, and to outline the process of cultural renewal. One way or another, we must evolve a new covenant with nature, and much depends on our ability to forge this covenant more consciously and deliberately than was the case in any previous civilization. To do this, it is essential that we understand our past covenants, and our present one.

Of course, one book cannot by itself create a new human culture. That is the project of many lives over many generations. But each of us, in our way, can contribute to that great project, and it is my hope that this book will help to galvanize and focus our efforts.

ᢀ

Part I of this book explores human culture and the origin of civilization. What are the terms of humanity's various covenants with nature? How did we arrive at the present one?

Part II looks at the anatomy of cultural transformation. Each culture consists of ways of knowledge, spiritual beliefs and practices, economic activities, and forms of social organization that evolved in response to a particular climate and geography. Our task in creating new, life-affirming cultures must be to renew and reintegrate all of these fundamental cultural activities so that they together form a single taproot reaching deep into the heart of both the soil and the human soul. Various chapters explore the arts, economics, systems of governance, science, and technology, both as symptoms of our present estrangement from nature and as gateways to a new cultural integrity.

Part III explores the dangers and opportunities of the time in which we live—a period that some native prophets have referred to as the Great Purification.

PART I

CIVILIZATION

RECONSIDERED

1 | OUR COVENANTS WITH NATURE

 IN ORDER TO UNDERSTAND *why* modern Western electronic-industrial civilization is so destructive to the natural environment, we somehow have to distance ourselves from it. As long as our thoughts are shaped from cradle to grave by the society in which we have grown up, it is hard to have an objective view of it.

An obvious way to gain perspective on the culture of one's birth is to study other cultures—and the more different from one's own, the better. I have found the cultures of the Native Americans, tribal Africans, Pacific Islanders, and Aboriginal Australians to be excellent teachers in this regard.

It is no exaggeration to say that people who live in different cultures live in different worlds. While there are some universalities to the human experience (all humans eat, use tools and language, and instinctively smile and grimace to indicate pleasure and displeasure), the variety of strategies human beings have adopted to solve the basic problems of existence is astonishing.

Consider the problem of deciding who should marry whom. While those societies influenced by Christianity have adopted monogamous customs, many others have sanctioned polygamy. And among polygamous societies, both *polygyny*—the practice of one man having more than one wife (common, for example, among traditional Arab peoples) and *polyandry*—in which one woman has more than one husband (practiced by the Tibetans and the Inuit) have been known, as has group marriage (which, according to Julius Caesar, was favored by the ancient inhabitants of Britain). In India, parents have traditionally arranged for their children to be married at around the time of puberty, whereas in modern Europe and America, it is assumed that only mature men and women should marry, and that they should do so by their own choice. In societies where it has been customary for a man to choose his wife, he might do so by capture (as in Aboriginal Australia), purchase (as in West Africa), or consent (as among most North

American Indian tribes). However, among the Fulani of Niger, it is the woman who chooses her husband: at a special festival men dress and paint themselves, hoping to be selected by a bride.

Every culture is unique. But when we compare cultures systematically, we begin to see patterns. Anthropologists have found that groups of people who get their food in similar ways (whether through fishing, farming, or foraging) tend to have other things in common as well.

Each way that people have found of obtaining food implies a covenant with nature. In each instance, humans must take something from the Earth—whether it be a manioc root, a sheaf of wheat, or a rabbit—in order to survive. How they treat the Earth in return determines whether it can continue to support them.

When we die, we return to the land as compost. All of life is an exchange, one great round of eating and being eaten. But for humans the terms of that exchange are quite variable. What shall we take, and how much? What shall we give back to the Earth or to the gods? Many societies address these questions explicitly in their creation myths, which speak of the gifts of the gods and the reciprocal obligations of humanity (as in the Genesis passage in which God gives the first people "every tree that is pleasant to the sight and good for food," and enjoins them to "dress the garden and to keep it").

This chapter explores the five primary covenants with nature that human beings have adopted during the past few thousand years. For now, I will leave open the question of why people have occasionally abandoned one covenant and adopted another (that will be the subject of chapters 2 and 3).

GATHERING AND HUNTING

The oldest and most basic way human beings have derived sustenance from their environment is by collecting wild edible plants or hunting wild animals. This is presumably how everyone lived thousands of years ago. The exact point in prehistory when food plants first began to be cultivated is a matter of some controversy; but even after that fateful transition, much of the world's population continued to gather or hunt. (I assume, by the way, that gathering preceded hunting, since most other primates are vegetarians.)

Most gathering or hunting societies tend to undertake periodic migrations in response to seasonal variations in their food supply, and to travel in small groups of about twenty to fifty individuals. Because they are nomadic, they find it impractical to accumulate material possessions. Individuals are virtually self-sufficient and enjoy considerable personal autonomy. As a rule, there are no chiefs who can enforce their will over other individuals in the group. Moreover, among most food-gathering societies, there is relative equality between women and men. The two sexes usually celebrate religious rites separately and have distinct fields of responsibility: by and large, it is the women who gather (usually supplying between sixty and eighty percent of the group's food), while the men hunt. For most such groups, basic survival activities require only fifteen or twenty hours of attention per week; the rest of their waking time is devoted to music, art, storytelling, play, rest, and ritual. Even survival activities partake of an all-pervading attitude that is at once ceremonial and playful.

Child rearing among the food gatherers tends to be indulgent and permissive in the extreme during infancy and up to puberty, when there is a distinct break marked by a ritualized initiation, after which young people take on full adult responsibilities.

Gathering and hunting societies tend to have a magical view of the world—everything is alive and capable of being influenced or communicated with. Land, weather, animals, and plants are all included in a complex but unified system of myth and ritual.

Foraging constitutes a simple and direct covenant with nature, one which entails minimal interference with the environment. People essentially take only what is immediately available to them, and only as much as they immediately need, the way other animals do. They understand that they are part of a larger whole, and that their well-being is determined by vitality of that entire system. Gatherers and hunters perform ceremonies for the increase of the animals and plants on which they depend, and in most instances make a conscious effort to avoid depleting the environment by over-hunting or over-harvesting.

While foragers are completely at the mercy of nature, they tend to regard their surroundings as benevolent. Typically they have no sense of lack, but feel instead that they live in the most abundant of worlds.

Today only a tiny fraction of one percent of the world's population still subsists by gathering or hunting. Until only a few centuries ago, gatherers and hunters freely roamed North and South America, Australia, and southern and central Africa, and there were small bands as well on some of the Pacific islands and in Asia. Gradually, however, these lands were appropriated either by their more culturally "advanced" neighbors, or by agents of colonial powers, so that nearly all of the indigenous foragers have been forced to take up other means of subsistence. This process has repeatedly resulted in hideous examples of exploitation and genocide.

Nevertheless, during the nineteenth and twentieth centuries anthropologists were able to record some of the details of the lifeways of hunters and gatherers, of whom the most thoroughly studied were the Aboriginal Australians, who serve as an excellent case study.

Until this century, the Aborigines lived for most of the year in the open, sheltering themselves only from the most intense or persistent cold, heat, wind, or rain. In harsh weather they might build small huts of branches and grass, or shelter themselves in caves or under rock overhangs; otherwise, they were content to sleep around a campfire under the stars. Despite living on a continent that is mostly desert, they found food with little difficulty: even the inhabitants of the dry central region had access to dozens of edible species of wild plants and animals. Early European explorers consistently remarked on the Aborigines' tendency to praise the lushness and productivity of their country, their lack of anxiety about food and water, and their belief that life was naturally plentiful and easy.

Each band of twenty to fifty individuals identified itself with a specific locality—varying in size—which it knew in exhaustive detail. However, these people did not regard themselves as "owning" the land; it would be more accurate to say that the land owned them: They felt they had a sacred obligation to keep and maintain it, in both a spiritual and a material sense. This obligation took the forms of specific taboos against over-hunting, as well as periodic ceremonies to revivify plant and animal species and the terrain itself.

The people did not leave the land entirely untouched; indeed, over the millennia their presence left an indelible mark. The activity that most altered the landscape consisted of burning dry grass to flush game. This produced brushfires that eventually changed the ecology of the continent. Forested areas diminished in size and many Eucalyptus species evolved in such a way that they now *require* periodic fires in order to reproduce. A new natural balance was achieved, one in which humans played an active part. According to Australian anthropologist W. E. H. Stanner,

> The vegetation suffered severely and, in consequence, plants and animal populations must have changed radically over millennia of occupation, enforcing new human adaptations, but there can have been few countries where more than 1000 generations left so few physical

traces. After a place had been left for long unvisited only thinned-out timber around a pool, a grass-grown midden, or abandoned stone-tools might suggest human habitation.[1]

The Aboriginal Australians used tools that were, by our modern standards, few and seemingly crude. Yet these tools served the people's needs with elegance and economy. Stanner again:

> Their material equipment might better be described as brilliantly simplified than "simple" or "primitive." . . . For example, in the rigorous environment of central Australia, where aridity put the highest premium on mobility, excess weight and complexity of equipment would have raised needlessly high the effort-costs of life. A single implement—the spear-thrower—was developed, with great ingenuity, to serve multiple purposes. It could be used as a container for liquids, as part of a fire-saw, as a scraper or adze or chisel, as a shield and even a musical instrument. A man could clasp in *one* hand his spears and a device which not only increased their force and range but also met a range of needs for which special implements otherwise would have had to be carried.[2]

Women and men had different functions in Aboriginal society and they celebrated many of their rituals separately. Child-rearing was left largely to the women, though men took an active role in the initiation of young boys. Infants were carried and breastfed for two to four years, and children were allowed an unrestricted freedom to explore and play.

A combination of constant lactation among mothers with small children (which lowered female fertility), plus high infant and child mortality, resulted in the maintenance of a fairly steady level of population over thousands of years among the indigenous Australians. Now that the Aborigines have been forced to adopt a more settled way of life, their population is growing rapidly.

In all, the Aborigines enjoyed a pattern of existence that was far different from the image of constant privation and misery that most civilized people tend to assume must characterize life lived apart from cities, markets, roads, houses, and elaborate technologies. Rather, in the words of Stanner, the Aboriginals

> . . . not only lived well but sweetened existence by spirited pursuits of life in no way concerned with mere survival. . . . [Their] least-cost

routines left free time, energy and enthusiasm to be expended—as they were, without stint—on all the things *for* which life could be lived when basic needs had been met: the joys of leisure, rest, song, dance, fellowship, trade, stylized fighting, and the performance of religious rituals.[3]

HORTICULTURE

This second contract with nature, characterized by the domestication of food plants and the use of a simple digging stick or hoe for cultivation, implies a deep commitment to the world of vegetation. It is only by staying in—or regularly returning to—one place that a horticulturist can sow, tend, and harvest a crop. Here, the soil, the heavens, the seasons, the gardener, and the plant itself are all participants in a magical seed sacrifice from which new life arises.

The most basic form of horticulture still practiced is *swidden*—which is sometimes pejoratively referred to as "slash-and-burn"—gardening. Swidden is pursued in forest environments, such as Amazonia and New Guinea, where native peoples traditionally clear an area of trees with axes and fire, plant gardens there for a few years—that is, until the soil becomes depleted—and then move on. Until recently, scientists regarded this procedure as destructive and inefficient. New studies suggest the contrary, however. In the best cases, swidden horticulture imitates natural cycles in the environment, substituting a harvestable diversity of edible plants for the diversity of forest plants that ordinarily grow. Native horticulturists in the Philippines, for example, may plant 150 varieties in a single three-acre plot. Rain forests produce notoriously poor soils, but burning the trees releases stored nutrients into the soil. Burning, together with dense and careful intercropping, makes swidden far more productive than conventional modern agriculture would be, given the same environment. Moreover, the method turns out to be ecologically sound as well: secondary forest quickly reclaims the clearing once it is abandoned, and native gardeners typically allow their plots to lie fallow for many years before reusing them. The biggest drawback, from a modern perspective, is that only about 70 people per square mile can be supported this way.

Because horticulturists tend to build semi-permanent dwellings (unlike nomadic gatherers), they are free to accumulate more possessions. They can make and use heavy tools and pottery that would overburden a hunter or a gatherer. Moreover, while gardening requires more work, it yields more food from less land than does gathering. Therefore large, extended families can afford to stay together in growing communities. In doing so, however, they have to invent complicated clan systems in order to avoid inbreeding.

Particularly in the simplest gardening cultures, women tend to hold prominent roles in the community. Having been the plant gatherers in foraging societies, women were probably responsible for the initial domestication of food plants. They were, thus, closer than men to the means of production within the community. Not surprisingly, therefore, it is among horticultural societies that we find the highest incidence of three related practices: matrilocal residence (young couples living near the bride's closest relatives); matrilineal descent (children belonging to the kin group of their mother); and matrilineal inheritance (property passing through the female side of the family, so that a child always inherits from the mother).

Simple horticultural communities tend to be among the most peaceful of all human societies. Indeed, early Neolithic horticultural groups seem to have lived virtually without warfare: their towns were unprotected, they had no weapons of war, and their artwork never included images of violence between people—though some of these groups apparently practiced ritual human sacrifice. Surviving simple horticultural societies tend also to be highly egalitarian and to raise their children permissively. There are exceptions to these generalizations, however: Most of the swidden horticulturists of New Guinea are both warlike and patrilineal.

Religion in horticultural societies often revolves around symbols of an Earth goddess, and around seasonal festivals connected with the cycles of planting and harvest. With the permanent, sedentary group comes the tendency for the submersion of the individual in the collective, and while among gathering and hunting peoples religious rituals emphasize personal attainment of vision and power, horticulturists' rites aim to infuse the entire group with vitality.

As a covenant with nature, horticulture represents a radical departure from foraging. Planting implies an active shaping of the environment to meet human needs. It permits more people to live in a given area of land, but it involves more work. Horticulturists therefore tend to have less of a feeling of abundance. In return for their harvest, many traditional gardeners perform a sacrifice—whether a symbolic seed sacrifice or a blood offering—and hold seasonal festivals by which they seek to maintain the balance of light and dark in the world.

While many cultures in southeast Asia, the Pacific Islands, and South America still practice traditional horticulture, self-sufficient gardening as a way of life is today nearly as threatened as gathering and hunting. The subsidized importation of food grown by industrial agriculture makes horticulture "uneconomical" over the short term, and in many cases, tribal lands that have been swidden-farmed for centuries are being bought or appropriated by multinational corporations for logging or mining purposes.

The Hopi of northern Arizona are an especially resilient horticultural people. They consider themselves the first inhabitants of America, and their village of Oraibi is unquestionably the oldest continuously inhabited settlement on the continent. The word *Hopi* means "peace" or "the peaceful ones," and indeed, but for some sadly violent episodes brought on by the European invasion, there are few peoples on the planet who have been less warlike than the Hopi.

Most Hopi villages cling to six-hundred-foot-high escarpments along three mesas that rise abruptly from the desert plain. Traditional houses are built from sandstone from the mesas, chinked with pebbles and mortared with mud. Often houses are linked together into pueblos—the Hopi equivalent of apartment complexes.

Traditional Hopi government consists of councils of elders. Religious and ceremonial knowledge, rather than material wealth, constitute signs of status. Both men and women can attain status of this kind, though their fields of responsibility are different; and both women and men are responsible for planting, irrigating, and harvesting crops.

The Hopi grow unique varieties of beans and corn. They plant their corn deep—eight to twelve inches—so that it has access to residual moisture from winter storms until the summer rains come. No corn varieties other than the one they have cultivated for untold generations can withstand such deep planting. Hopi lima beans are also uniquely adapted to their desert environment. These traditional gardeners are careful to maintain genetic diversity within each variety, planting small, large, and misshapen seeds without distinction; in this way they avoid the genetic vulnerability of modern crop monocultures.

The Hopi closely observe the seasonal path of the Sun and time their intricate yearly round of dances, celebrations, and ceremonies to the solstices and equinoxes, as well as to the natural social rhythms of planting and harvest. The Hopi religious ceremonies are lengthy and involved, and even after decades of careful study by anthropologists, few non-Hopi have much understanding of their real significance.

Since the arrival of Europeans, the Hopi have resisted many pressures for change—including Spanish missionaries' insistence that they convert to Christianity. Inevitably, however, European-American culture has had its influence. When oil companies found promising reserves on Hopi land, they urged the U.S. government to obtain leases from the tribal council. Knowing that the Indians would be unlikely to grant the leases, Bureau of Indian Affairs officials created representative electoral systems for the Hopi, who mostly ignored the elections. The tribal government put in place by the small minority who did vote quickly signed the leases. Then, beginning in 1942, the reservation began to be mined for uranium, and today many open-pit and underground uranium mines sit abandoned, unreclaimed, and highly radioactive. Still, there are many traditional Hopi who are determined to keep to the ways of their ancestors—who long ago foretold the arrival of the "white brother" and an eventual catastrophe that would swallow up the materialistic culture that he would bring with him.

ANIMAL HERDING

Some groups with previous knowledge of horticulture or agriculture whose environment is too arid to permit settled cultivation come to rely primarily on domesticated animals for food production. Herd animals like sheep, goats, camels, and cattle can survive on land that is unfit for farming, but they need plenty of space and must be moved periodically to new pasture.

Historically, the domestication of animals goes back at least ten millennia, perhaps much longer. Like planting, it has brought the human race both benefits and costs. Goats and sheep were domesticated in the Middle East; pigs and chickens in southern Asia; cattle in central Asia and Europe; turkeys in Mesoamerica; and llamas, alpacas, and guinea pigs in South America. Collectively, these animals have provided meat, eggs, and milk—plus hides, wool, feathers, antler, and bone, which could be used for tools, clothing, and ornaments. The larger animals have also supplied labor: horses, donkeys, burros, camels, cows, and water buffalo were harnessed to plows and carts. This paved the way for large-scale agriculture and represented the greatest technological revolution since the use of fire and until the yoking of wind, water, and steam many centuries later.

The benefits that flowed from the herding of animals came at the price of new diseases like bubonic plague, smallpox, tuberculosis, measles, whooping cough, mumps, and chicken pox; and parasites and microbes including lice, fleas, ticks, worms, scales, and fungi. Every infectious disease known among humans has an animal counterpart, and animals can therefore sometimes act as hosts. As gatherers or hunters, humans had only passing contact with animals; as herders, they lived closely with large flocks that were often tightly packed together in corrals or barns—sleeping with them, grooming them, and helping them give birth. As a result, human societies that learned to keep domesticated animals became subject to epidemics on scales previously unknown. Until the arrival of Europeans, the North American natives had no domesticated animals except the turkey and dog; the Australians and Pacific islanders had none. Following the European invasions, diseases struck these indigenous groups, killing up to 90 percent of their populations.

Throughout history, herders have always been at odds with planters. This is partly because of the inherent conflict between pastoralists' need for unobstructed grazing land and farmers' habit of erecting fences to protect crops. But the enmity is also due to herders' tendency to bring diseases with them. Anthropologist Jack Weatherford has suggested that the final and worst plague Moses brought against the Egyptians may have been an animal-borne disease that killed the children of the sedentary Egyptians while passing over the children of the pastoral Hebrews, who had already developed some resistance to it.[4]

Social relations among pastoralists often reflect the relative harshness of their surroundings. When their environment is friendly and things are going smoothly, people tend to tolerate diversity and dissent, and to be permissive with their children. In times of crisis, however, people look to a strong leader to take charge, and the charismatic individual becomes a hero. In these circumstances, the strict disciplining of children and the suppression of dissent may seem necessary for the cohesion and survival of the group.

Pastoral nomads are, in a sense, people who have learned to live in a permanent state of emergency. They are both survivors and survivalists, and with their crisis mentality they tend to dominate other groups with which they came in contact. Their family life is often severely patriarchal, and the position of women in pastoral society is usually quite low. Communities are small, but they are usually stratified and complex. Pastoralists are often fiercely warlike, and they routinely subject their children to corporal punishment.

Perhaps because they are nomads, pastoralists have a keen sense of individualism. But compared with their foraging forebears, herders are more concerned with the domination and control of nature. Virtually all pastoral societies worship masculine sky gods; their mythologies often revolve around war epics; and their moral philosophies frequently depict life as a battle between the irreconcilable polar forces of good and evil.

The terms of the covenant with nature which animal herding constitutes are severe. People's survival is dependent upon the well-being of the herd or the flock, which must constantly be fed and protected. Because most pastoralists live in prairie or semi-desert environments that offer few other sources of nourishment, there is little margin for error.

While hunters see game animals as magical beings belonging to the gods, pastoralists regard their flock animals as property. The herder may care for his animals, but they are no longer equals, but dependents. Part of nature has been taken and subjugated. In return, herders may offer their sky gods occasional animal sacrifices. The obligations of humanity are often seen in terms of the keeping of strict divine injunctions having to do with cleanliness (perhaps to minimize animal-borne disease), obedience, and moral rectitude.

In some respects, life in the modern world is becoming easier for pastoral nomads: access to supplemental foods and to health care have expanded their chances for survival. However, animal herding requires open land, which is becoming more scarce nearly everywhere. As a result, animal herding as a way of life, like food gathering, hunting, and traditional horticulture, is on the decline worldwide.

Like most pastoral nomads, the Samburu of Kenya have adopted a severely functional view of the world. There is little room in their lives for anything that does not serve the purposes of survival.

The Samburu manage to keep dairy herds (which need more water and grazing land than do beef cattle) on what amounts to semi-desert land— no mean feat. They eat meat occasionally, but rely primarily on milk from their cows, which must be kept constantly in a reproductive state. Since the animals need a steady supply of grasses, the Samburu move them frequently. In addition, they must keep their herds safe from predators (primarily lions and hyenas) and drive them to and from water every second or third day. Male leaders need to know the land in great detail, as well as the climate. They must know the location of water and must constantly calculate times and distances, planning herd movements to take advantage of seasonal grazing opportunities and to avoid undue stresses on the animals. These heavy responsibilities can be borne only by elders who have spent decades learning from experience. The elders carefully watch the Moon and the positions of the stars, and use their knowledge and skills to predict periods of drought and hunger.

Drought is a significant part of life for the Samburu. A dry period falls between each rainy season and the next, and the severity of the dry spell determines the depth of hunger the people will suffer. Samburu elders recognize three levels of drought, the worst of which occurs about every hundred years and results in the deaths of many cattle and people.

The Samburu are a deeply religious people. They call their deity *Nkai*—which is also their word for rain. When elders meet, they ask one another about family, livestock, and land. Replies are always accompanied by a slight bow of the head and a supplication: *Nkai, Nkai*.

AGRICULTURE

While horticulture (from the Latin *hortus*, meaning "garden") is practiced on a small scale, often by women working with hoes in tiny plots near the home, agriculture (from *ager*, meaning "field") implies a far larger-scale and more intensive mode of production—and hence a new contract with nature. The technological key to the transition from one mode to the other is the plow.

With plows, often pulled by draft animals, full-time farmers can produce a surplus of food, thereby sustaining large communities. Thus agriculture can lead to the creation of market towns, then cities, which ultimately can band together to form states. With larger concentrations of population come greater division of labor, together with increased social needs for the keeping of records and for extensive and reliable systems of transportation and communication. Writing, large-scale trade, and the complex cultural achievement we call civilization all spring from the plow's deep furrow.

In nearly every case agriculture leads to social stratification: at the top of the social pyramid is a ruling class (usually less than one percent of the population) surrounded by retainers (officials, soldiers, and servants). The urban population also includes priests (professional, full-time religious officials), merchants, and artisans; while beyond the city walls live peasants (so defined by their payment of rent in exchange for the right to till the land). Most agrarian societies are organized along either autocratic or feudal lines. In autocratic societies (examples of which have included ancient Egypt and Mesopotamia), a central authority controls the state; while in feudal ones (such as pre-imperial China and medieval Europe), power is held by scattered nobles who often fight among themselves. Agrarian societies nearly always maintain armies, and in most—especially the larger ones—there is nearly incessant warfare.

While in the simplest horticultural societies women control the means of production, in agrarian ones men tend to do more of the field work and women are relatively powerless economically and subordinate socially. In horticultural communities, women can carry infants with them as they work in the garden. In agrarian society, nearly all the main activities are incompatible with child-care responsibilities. Women are useful mostly as breeding machines, and so tend to be regarded as property. Children are trained for life as members of a rigid class system—as peasants, warriors, administrators, or rulers.

The religions of agrarian peoples reflect the overall class structure: Not only is the priesthood vertically organized, but everyone worships a hierarchy of deities that serves as a cosmic prototype for the pyramiding of society. In agrarian religions humanity is almost never conceived of as a part of nature (as it always is among food gatherers), but as separate from, and often superior to, or even opposed to nature.

As a covenant with nature, agriculture represents yet another step away from the reciprocity and directness of humanity's original food-gathering contract. Farmers must clear their land of trees and whatever else is already growing there, introduce plants different from indigenous species, remove "weeds" (indigenous species trying to reestablish themselves), and fight off "pests" (animals or insects that wish to eat what has been planted). And unlike horticulturists, who do this on a small scale and who often plant many varieties within a given plot, farmers sow large fields with a single variety. While swidden gardeners move frequently, farmers tend to stay in one place more or less permanently. Where local rainfall is insufficient or widely variable, they build irrigation canals. The combination of over-irrigation and permanent cultivation can result in the gradual degradation of soils over large areas. For farmers, nature becomes as much an adversary as a source of nourishment. The wilderness or jungle—which, to the gatherer or hunter is a home and a source of infinite abundance—becomes a wasteland to be "tamed." In return for what they wrest from the Earth, agriculturists sometimes seek ways to return fertility to the soil (through fallowing or composting), and perform seasonal ceremonies of increase and renewal.

Agriculture has been practiced in many ways by people in widely varying environments. Some farming peoples—such as the inhabitants of Ladakh in northern India—have kept their agriculture to a small scale and have a great deal in common with gardeners like the Hopi; others—like the ancient Egyptians—have made farming the basis for vast, centralized, complex civilizations. The people of Bali fall somewhere between these extremes.

Bali is a diamond-shaped island, presently part of the nation of Indonesia, and is roughly ninety miles east to west by fifty miles north to south. Temperatures on the island average 79 degrees, with little seasonal variation. Few places on Earth offer a more beautiful or fertile field for the development of human culture. The people of Bali have mixed origins, their ancestors having arrived in various migrations and invasions from India, China, Polynesia, and Melanesia. An invasion in the ninth century C.E. brought Hinduism to Bali, and the people soon adopted and absorbed this new religion into their existing social order. Today Bali is the only remaining Hindu outpost in southeast Asia.

While swidden gardening can sustain only about 70 people per square mile, the rice growers of Bali accommodate a population density of well over 1,400 in the same unit area. Rice cultivation requires a much larger and better organized labor force than does informal horticulture: planting, irrigating, maintaining terraces, and harvesting are labor intensive and require many hands doing similar work. This intensive use of land and human resources produces surpluses; at the same time, as human activity becomes more coordinated it also tends to become highly ritualized. These two incidental accompaniments to agriculture—food surpluses and the tendency toward the development of ritual—have had profound social effects for the Balinese.

Predictable surpluses of rice have enabled the Balinese gradually to increase their population over the centuries. With enough hands available to tend to basic food production, more and more people have been freed for other activities. The consequent elaboration of social roles in the society has fit nicely with the Hindu caste system. There are four castes in Bali: *Brahmins* (priests), *Ksatriyas* (rulers or warriors), *Wesya* (traders), and *Sudra* (farmers). Unlike India, Bali has no *Harijan* (untouchable) class. In modern Bali, caste means little in terms of wealth or power. Each caste—especially the *Sudra*, whose members are by far the most numerous—consists of many sub-castes, each with its unique duties and status. Anthropologist John Reader notes that in Bali all obligations, duties, organizations, temples, places, people and things are tied to a complex system of status:

"Where do you sit?", the Balinese will ask on first meeting a stranger, meaning not simply the immediate location, but location in three senses of the term—geographical, social and temporal. Each person politely places the other at mutually understood reference points in the social order. Conversation proceeds once the reference points have been established, but until then the conversants are more-or-less tongue-tied, for "where they sit" may also oblige them to use a different form of the Balinese language. There is high Balinese, low Balinese, and even middle Balinese. . . .[5]

In general, the Balinese tend to distrust anyone who is individualistic or who projects himself above the group as a whole; the collective and the maintenance of social harmony are of supreme importance.

Decision making is accomplished at the village level by the *banjar*, a social organization comprised of many families, with the authority to make and enforce laws, collect taxes, impose penalties, and organize communal work projects. All decisions require the full agreement of all married male members, a requirement ensuring that any change introduced into the society must be well considered.

The Balinese maintain two complex traditional calendars and time their frequent, elaborate festivals and ceremonies (which include offerings to the rice goddess) according to them. The people regard their many gods and goddesses as manifestations of one absolute divinity, *Sagyang Tunggul*; below the gods in their cosmic hierarchy are humans, then evil spirits, then witches, and, at the very bottom of the heap, the animals. The Balinese regard the island's principal volcano, Gunung Anung, as the mother of the world and the home of the gods.

Balinese parents lavish babies and children with love and care, regarding them as holy by virtue of having just come into the world from realms of ethereal perfection. Children are carried until they can walk, and special rites are performed in order to ensure safe passage from each stage of life to the next.

Perhaps because they inhabit an island paradise, the Balinese have managed to create an agricultural society that is relatively stable and sustainable (in this, they differ from many other farming peoples). Their social customs, by discouraging individualism, also prevent the over-concentration of power and wealth. Their rice farming, practiced in water-logged terraces where stubble and other organic matter is regularly plowed back into ground, depletes the soil far more slowly than does dryland farming of wheat or other grains.

In other times and places, agriculture has led to social and ecological results very different from those we see in Bali. For example, ancient Mesopotamia—the site of such early centers of civilization as Babylon, Nineveh, Ur, Uruk, and Persepolis—was once considered a virtual paradise. But here, as Jack Weatherford writes in *Savages and Civilization*, "the civilized way of life consumed everything around it—water, stone, metal, trees, plants, animals, and even the land itself—leaving behind a decimated landscape," the deserts of modern Iraq.[6] By encouraging population growth, agriculture has again and again led to the building first of cities, then of empires—the hallmarks of civilization. But empires typically function by the siphoning of wealth from peoples and lands on the periphery into great and growing population centers. This seems inevitably to lead not only to eventual ecological collapse (as it did in Mesopotamia, Greece, Anatolia, and the once-forested valley of Mexico), but also to social instability (such as occurred in ancient Rome during its decline).

European civilization, alone among historical empire-cultures, has so far managed to avoid the twin perils of environmental exhaustion and social collapse, and it has done so by finding new sources of land and wealth—North and South America and sub-Saharan Africa. Had the Europeans not come upon these opportunities when they did, it seems likely that their civilization would have languished. But with a tremendous infusion of gold, silver, timber, labor, and land for expansion, the opposite happened: European civilization quickly spread to cover most of the planet. In doing so, it broke through to an entirely new form of production, and a new covenant with nature.

INDUSTRIAL CIVILIZATION

Industrial society relies on agriculture for its food, but farmers grow on an even larger scale, almost entirely for market or export, using more sophisticated machines and fewer hands. Domesticated animals are likewise exploited on a far larger and more impersonal scale in industrial societies than in any others. With industrialism, machines enter into nearly every aspect of material existence. The production process is segmented and mechanized by way of the factory, and human life itself becomes increasingly mechanized and commodified as humans adapt themselves to the demands of their machines.

The transition from agriculture to industrialism began in England in the seventeenth century. Following the British Civil War in 1640, England had reverted to a feudal social order. A combination of increased population density throughout the countryside and greed on the part of nobles created a situation in which all available land (formerly a commons available to everyone) came to be enclosed—mostly for sheep pasture. Rural peasants, deprived of open land, were uprooted and inevitably gravitated to the cities. There they had no choice but to sell their labor for whatever wages were being offered. Until then, the concept of wage labor hardly existed; now, with so many people looking for work, urban employers could rely on cheap, abundant human power. This new labor pool, together with technological innovation, led to the development of the factory system.

Raw materials were beginning to flood into Europe from overseas. Given plentiful labor and material resources, all the new industrialists needed in addition were more markets and better transportation and communications systems. The demand for the latter helped encourage still more technological innovation; meanwhile, the necessity for markets intensified an already expanding race for new weapons technologies. Markets and sources of raw materials did not come willingly: they had to be seized and held. The British, for example, having conquered India, demanded that farmers there produce cotton. This was shipped to mills in England, then shipped back to India as woven cloth. The people of India—who previously had made their own cloth—were now prevented by force from doing so in order to provide a market for English textiles. Elsewhere the story was essentially the same: Industrial nations grew wealthy by forcing colonies to export raw materials and by suppressing indigenous industry and commerce. Thus "developed" and "underdeveloped" nations came into being simultaneously, the "developed" countries raising huge armies equipped with factory-made weapons to fight wars on an unprecedented scale (usually to protect sources of raw materials or overseas markets), often with heavy civilian casualties.

The social implications of industrialism have been staggering. An increasing proportion of the population live in huge cities, where they often experience intense alienation. Women—and often children—join the labor force but receive lower wages than men. Life becomes fragmented: Work is a particularized activity distinct from leisure; the home is isolated from the workplace. Children are separated from parents at an early age (at least during the day) to be educated in schools—learning factories—where they absorb knowledge that will be useful to them as they find their place in the industrial system. Both at school and at home they learn the value of adherence to a clock schedule, acceptance of arbitrary discipline, and the segmentation of tasks.

The spiritual consequences of industrialism have been no less profound than the social ones. Philosophical materialism (nurtured by society's increasing dependence on a market economy), together with a categorical, linear, analytical trend of thinking (tied to the factory system's relentless fragmentation of processes), and a swollen confidence in the ability of human beings to control nature through technology, combined to create a fundamentally new secular mode of thought. All gathering, gardening, agrarian, and pastoral societies lived in a spiritualized universe full of meaning. For the religious consciousness, there are no accidents: Everything that happens is a sign from the gods. Tragedy is always a sign of error and signifies the anger of the gods. Success or abundance are signs of favor. But the new secularized consciousness sees events as determined by impersonal laws of cause and effect, without divine participation. The working of the Cosmos is determined by the inevitable function of natural law rather than by intelligent purpose. For people rooted in the older pattern of thought, this undermining of ancient myth constitutes a cultural catastrophe. People fully conditioned to industrialism, however, see the emergence of secular consciousness as the triumph of logic over superstition.

As a covenant with nature, industrialism is one-sided. Nature gives; humans take. Nature need not give willingly; humans may use the most ingenious and torturous methods to extract what they want from soils, waters, rocks, animals, and plants. The industrial system is governed by a growth imperative: Economists believe that if it does not continue to expand, it will collapse. The owners and managers of the system publicly acknowledge no inherent limits to the increase of consumption. However, within the past few decades citizens in industrial nations have voiced concerns over ecological and environmental issues. Many environmentalists advocate soil-preserving farming practices and the protection of remaining wilderness areas. Some even counsel a reversion to nature-worship. So far, though, the environmentalists seem to be having only a marginal impact on the overall economic ethic and material momentum of industrial civilization.

ॐ

With each new covenant that humans have adopted over the past several millennia, we have seen both losses and gains. With each intensification of population density and of exploitation of resources, with each increase in the complexity of society and compounding of social alienation, has come a new level of sophistication in cultural forms—from cave art to pottery, books, symphonies, space stations, and satellite television. We are proud of these achievements, while at the same time we complain about the stress and spiritual impoverishment that our new ways of living bring with them.

But with the global human population passing 5.5 billion, topsoil vanishing, and thousands of species disappearing, it would seem that we have gone about as far as we can go in the direction of imposing our human terms on nature.

If we have come to a necessary turning point in our millennia-long march toward rulership over our environment, then it would seem vital that we understand in more detail the process that has brought us here, the tradeoffs we have made, and the opportunities and alternatives that lie ahead.

FATEFUL CHOICES, THEN AND NOW

Something obvious keeps eluding our civilization, something that involves a reciprocal relationship between nature and psyche, and that we are going to have to grasp if we are to survive as a species.

—MORRIS BERMAN

 IF WE ARRANGE HUMANITY'S primary covenants with nature—gathering, hunting, horticulture, animal herding, agriculture, and industrialism—in a chronological sequence, the resulting picture of human history can be described either as *progress* or as *degeneration*. If we see the development of ever more sophisticated technologies and ever greater concentrations of population and power as unalloyed benefits, then the path from foraging to factory farming is indeed a fruitful one. But from a perspective that emphasizes traditional spiritual values, the picture is not so simple. From the latter viewpoint, the prejudice expressed in so many ancient mythologies against technological innovation, and the nearly universal belief of archaic peoples in the perfection of beginnings and the decline of humankind through history make perfect sense.

In the present industrial era, we pride ourselves on our increased knowledge about ourselves and our world, and clearly some members of society today enjoy far greater power over their environment than did people in previous generations. Wealthy urbanites can light their homes with the flick of a switch, travel halfway around the world in a day, and have exotic foods delivered to their doors. Nevertheless, as we absorb the findings of history and anthropology, we cannot avoid the conclusion that the intensive modes of production that make these luxuries possible have exacted a terrible toll.

This toll has taken several forms. First is a general increase in social stratification and inequality: The wealthiest few percent of the population have become steadily wealthier, to the point that there are now a few people in the world who control more wealth than they could reasonably spend in a thousand lifetimes, while the poorest twenty percent of the world's people have barely enough to eat and are becoming measurably more impoverished year by year. These are people whose ancestors lived in self-sufficient village cultures, and whose subsistence farming has been made economically untenable. In country after country, rural peasants are being divested of their lands and are gravitating to shanty towns at the edges of burgeoning cities because they simply have no other choice.

Intensified modes of production also generate an increase in population density, which in turn tends to accelerate the depletion of natural resources. As cities grow, people become more dependent on primary production from the countryside. They need more trees, minerals, and food. But, since they live far away from farms, forests, and mines, they do not see the destruction and depletion that result from their expanding demands. The voice of the city is loud and strident, easily drowning the muffled moans of the soil, the rocks, and the forest. At the high end of the ramp of progress, we find ourselves living in a world where species are disappearing by the thousands, forests are decimated, and lakes, rivers, and oceans are dying.

Personal and social alienation likewise increase: Cities become so big that people engage in less and less face-to-face exchange; their interactions are typically mediated by money and by mechanized communication (telephone, fax, e-mail). Politics shifts from direct democracy (in the hunting or gathering band) to autocracy, oligarchy, or representative democracy in agricultural civilizations. In the modern democratic industrial state, few people know their representatives personally or feel that their own voice is being heard; corporate lobbyists appear to wield ultimate political power. Economics becomes entirely a matter of money: Whereas people formerly were self-sufficient, gathering or growing their food, now they merely shuffle paper and plastic, relying on various instruments of the social system to feed and clothe them. Technologies of communication and transportation connect us, but they also serve to keep the world at arm's length: As we drive our cars along paved roads and walk in factory-made shoes on cement sidewalks, we have only indirect contact with the Earth beneath our feet; we watch hours of television each day but have no time to converse with our friends or children.

Movement "up" the cultural ladder also seems to involve intensified warfare. Among the Australian Aborigines, war traditionally consisted of two groups of men standing a few yards apart, shouting insults, and lobbing spears at one another until eventually someone was injured. In the modern world, war has ceased to be personal and limited, and has become instead impersonal and total. Leaders sit in air-conditioned offices or hardened bunkers, electronically directing soldiers, planes, and computerized robots in the destruction not only of other soldiers, but also of large civilian populations. Warfare has changed not only qualitatively, but quantitatively: In his book *Civilizations, Empires and Wars: A Quantitative History of War*, historian William Eckhardt concludes that, even after population growth is taken into account, the twentieth century has been the most lethal of all.[1]

With all of these costs flowing from changes in modes of production, the question inevitably arises: *Why* did our ancestors undertake the move from food gathering and hunting to horticulture, from horticulture to agriculture? Was there some immediate payoff? Why have the more "advanced" human cultures become so violent, repressive, and alienating? This chapter explores four possible answers to these questions.

THE EVOLUTIONARY IMPERATIVE

According to the view of many anthropologists, philosophers, and historians, the progression from food gathering to horticulture to agriculture to industrial civilization has been simply a necessary and natural process of unfoldment. Human consciousness possesses an inherent evolutionary imperative which expresses itself (in part, at least) in technological innovation. People in all societies naturally search for greater power over their surroundings—for a more predictable and abundant food supply, for ways to protect themselves against the elements, and so on. Given that drive, plus the ever-increasing capacity of the human intellect, technological innovation was and is inevitable. Moreover, it is argued that human beings have always unconsciously sensed that by achieving greater concentrations of population, they could afford to diversify their efforts and thereby achieve feats impossible to small groups of nonspecialists. In a modern city, some people can devote themselves full-time to expanding the pool of knowledge available to the entire society, while others pioneer new technologies or arts. Perhaps cultures, like species, contain an inherent capacity—even a will—to evolve toward higher, more complex, forms.

Social theoretician Duane Elgin presents a humane and visionary version of this view in *Awakening Earth: Exploring the Evolution of Human Culture and Consciousness*. Like many evolution-of-culture theorists, he compares humanity's transitions in modes of production to the stages in the growth of an individual: "Just as there are recognizable stages in the movement of an individual from infancy to early adulthood, so, too, do there seem to be stages of learning that describe our maturation as a species."[2] He goes on to describe these:

> For roughly two million years our ancestors struggled in the twilight of self-recognition and self-discovery. Then, sometime during the rugged conditions of the last great ice age—roughly 35,000 years ago—physically modern humans broke free from the limited consciousness of the animal kingdom. With this initial awakening we entered an epoch of growth lasting nearly 25,000 years, during which time we developed sophisticated language, art, trading networks, musical instruments, and new tools of stone, wood, and bone. Then, roughly 10,000 years ago, we began another momentous transition by gradually shifting from the nomadic life of gathering and hunting to a settled life in small villages that relied upon a subsistence agriculture for survival. A peaceful and simple village life endured for thousands of years when, with surprising abruptness, the world's first large cities arose roughly 5,500 years ago. With the blossoming of agrarian-based civilizations, a new level of drive and dynamism entered the world. Humanity's evolutionary journey moved out of immersion within nature and began to take on a character that was uniquely human. Major civilizations emerged in Mesopotamia, India, China, and the Americas. For nearly 5,000 years these agrarian-based civilizations matured, generating the bulk of recorded history. The next momentous leap forward began roughly 300 years ago, when a revolution in science and technology propelled a portion of humanity into the urban-industrial era. The gradual pace of urbanization and material development was transformed into an explosion of technological progress—moving forward with such ferocity and speed that it now threatens to devastate the entire biosphere of the planet.[3]

Terms like "progress," "leap forward," and "development" imply that the direction of change in human societies is foreordained, inevitable, beneficial, and unidirectional. But if this is so, why should the marvelous trajectory of evolutionary unfoldment end in the threat of global extinction?

Moreover, Elgin's optimistic encapsulation of human social history does not take into account the many leaps *backward* that have occurred, when civilizations self-destructed through political repression or environmental recklessness. The cultural-evolution explanation for the origin of new modes of production assumes that whoever didn't jump on the bandwagon of progress missed out on some important boon. Yet it was the cultures who *avoided* progress, who continued to live by gathering or hunting or simple horticulture, who also avoided pitfalls that have plagued more "developed" societies.

We must ask ourselves: *By what criteria* does a more intensive mode of production constitute evolution, progress, or improvement? Does it make people happier and healthier? Does it give them more leisure time? When we say that one culture is more "advanced" than another, just what do we mean? Usually, the word merely signifies that the people use more complex technologies. But does this also mean that they are actually better off in some measurable biological or psychological way?

The widespread assumption that human beings are better off in more complex societies than in simple ones has been challenged by many anthropologists over the past twenty years on the basis both of archaeological evidence and of studies of surviving primitive societies. Anthropologists such as Stanley Diamond, Richard Lee, and Marshall Sahlins have pointed out that, compared to gathering and hunting, horticulture and agriculture require more work (the typical hunter-gatherer has to spend less than twenty hours a week securing food), and provide a diet that is less nourishing (food-gatherers may have access to scores of wild edible plants, whereas cultivators usually confine their attention to only a handful of domesticated crops). Indeed, the only immediate advantage of farming is that it feeds more people in less space.

The transition to industrialism in the eighteenth and nineteenth centuries had an even stiffer price—the destruction of rural and village life, the rapid growth of dreary manufacturing towns, and child labor in "satanic mills." Clearly, some people (the upper classes of the "developed" nations) have benefited from industrialism in certain ways (decreased infant mortality, cures for certain diseases, and vastly increased technological capability). But, as we have seen, these advances were paid for through the systematic impoverishment of people in the "underdeveloped" countries, and of exploited populations within the "developed" countries. Even the wealthy First World beneficiaries pay a tariff in the form of degenerative diseases and stress.

Why would people naturally evolve toward a way of life that is more strenuous and less rewarding, that entails more alienation, more impersonal warfare, and the dismemberment of a previously satisfying pattern of existence? Elgin tells us that transformations in culture were both necessitated by, and in turn helped nurture, the emergence of new levels and forms of human consciousness.

Now, it is true that people in different cultures think differently. Everyone who travels among non-Western peoples notices immediately this fact, which anthropologists have explored in books like *The Savage Mind* (Claude Lévi-Strauss), *The Mind of Primitive Man* (Franz Boas), *Primitive Man As Philosopher* (Paul Radin), and *The Primal Mind* (Jamake Highwater). The question is: In what sense is this change in thought patterns evolutionary? In order to answer the question objectively, we must take our own prejudices into account. Is the average city dweller really more "conscious" than the average food gatherer? It all depends on who is judging. The urbanite might feel superior in being literate, knowing some simple mathematics and a few random scientific facts, and having innumerable complex tools at hand to mediate every imaginable personal or social function. By the same token, the "primitive" person might feel superior in having the ability to survive unassisted in wild nature, in knowing the plants and animals of her environment, and in being more aware of her own internal bodily rhythms.

The idea of cultural evolution is attractive to us civilized people because we happen to be at the top of the heap in terms of the criteria we choose to emphasize—technological sophistication and the ability to accumulate wealth. Civilization does, after all, appear dynamic, inventive, and vigorous compared to traditional culture. However, those of us who live in affluent urban centers tend not to see or understand the effects that economic and technological "progress" has on the peripheral peoples who supply us with the raw materials we use to build our impressive social structure. Beneath the blaring history of civilization's triumphs can be heard the wail of self-sufficient traditional cultures being reduced, one after another, to a disenfranchised peasantry. Often when we try to get a view of what life in a noncivilized culture is like, we see only what such cultures *have become* as a result of their contacts with civilized nations. We see people who are dependent, hopeless, and desperate. Then when we compare these people's lives with those of affluent urbanites, we naturally conclude that the latter are better off, and probably smarter or more highly evolved for having achieved such status. Identifying ourselves with these fortunate ones, we conclude that the process of civilization brings great advantages. *Of course it is an evolutionary process!*—we think. But it is not hard to see why indigenous peoples often don't share this view.

The fact is, traditional peoples have *resisted* the introduction of new modes of production whenever possible. Surviving gathering or hunting peoples tend to take up farming only out of necessity; they show no sign of gradually acquiring the habit on their own. The same is true of the transition to industrialism: there has been resistance every step of the way. Right at the start of the industrial revolution, disenfranchised workers rose up and smashed the machines that were making their lives hellish; their protest ended not because they came to see the benefits of the new technology, but because British soldiers shot and hanged them for the crime of wishing to maintain their traditional work and livelihood. The story is recounted in Kirkpatrick Sale's *Rebels Against the Future: The Luddites and Their War on the Industrial Revolution*; it is a story that has largely escaped the history books precisely because it doesn't fit our view of progress.

The ideology of cultural evolution may be comforting to those who regard themselves as being at the forefront of the evolutionary wave, but in the end, it is only an article of faith. If we want to base our understanding of cultural change on evidence, we must dig deeper.

TOO MANY PEOPLE

Perhaps the rise of civilization was not so much a result of a hypothetical goal-oriented evolutionary process, but was rather a self-perpetuating, snowballing accident. Once we began to intensify our modes of production, we also began alienating ourselves from nature. We exhausted one resource base and moved on to the next, becoming ever more oblivious to our environment. The question is: What got the ball rolling?

Anthropologist Mark Cohen has suggested that *some* gathering and hunting societies turned to farming when a decline in the abundance of wild foods created population pressure (since an undersupply of food is functionally the same as an oversupply of people). Cohen does not mention an example of a contemporary gatherer or hunter society in which this transition is taking place, because there is none. He assumes that the necessary conditions existed roughly ten thousand years ago, and that the transition was once and for all. But his argument has an internal logic that can be extrapolated to explain the entire chain of transformations in modes of production.

Gatherers control their population in a variety of ways; perhaps the most effective method requires little conscious attention. Food-gathering women tend to nurse their infants for up to four years, and consume foods high in protein but very low in starch. Consequently, following their first pregnancy, it is usually several years before these women's level of body fat is high enough for ovulation to occur.

But if the people's supply of protein-rich wild game was reduced (by extinctions or by climate change, for example) then they might turn increasingly to plants; and if it became difficult for them to find enough wild plants, they might begin cultivating. This in itself requires no great burst of genius: No food-gathering society ever studied is ignorant of the role of seeds in the cycle of vegetation. But when a group took the fateful step of deciding to cultivate plants rather than merely gathering them, an inevitable series of events would have been set in motion. Because domesticated crops tend to be higher in carbohydrates and lower in proteins than wild plants and game, women in horticultural societies tend to have a higher level of body fat than food-gathering women and therefore ovulate more readily. Thus the population of the horticultural group tends to increase faster than that of the food-gathering group. In consequence, once a group adopts planting, it cannot go back to foraging because it will never be able to hunt or gather enough food to feed all the new mouths.

At a certain point, the population of the sedentary gardening community may itself overstretch its means of production, perhaps by overworking the soil. Initially, the group can overcome this problem by splitting up into smaller bands and moving to new territory. But when there are already too many groups cultivating a limited area, so that there is no new territory to which to move, then more intensive modes of production must be introduced. Tiny private garden plots can be combined into large fields and irrigated. Hoes and digging sticks can be replaced with ox-drawn plows. The new methods and tools produce enough more food that it becomes possible for part of the population to live in towns and to specialize in occupations other than food production.

More food is available, but (since the population is still increasing) there are always more mouths to feed. Eventually all of the available land has been fenced into fields, but now there are far more people living on the land than are needed to till it using the new, ever more intensive techniques. The excess people are therefore continually forced off the land into cities, where they must somehow be kept busy either in huge public-works programs or in factories that manufacture raw materials into consumer products, for which demand must be encouraged.

At every stage, overpopulation is the primary impetus for cultural change.

This process is not merely hypothetical. We see it occurring today throughout the Third World, wherever local village culture is giving way to urbanization. In thousands of localities in Asia, South and Central America, Africa, and the Pacific islands, food gatherers and traditional subsistence gardeners are being driven from their lands and conscripted into the ranks of the urban poor. And in virtually all of the cultures concerned, historically stable population levels have exploded. However, in most of these instances, the initial impetus for change has come not from within the society, but from outside it—that is, from the population pressure and resource demands of industrial civilization.

TOO MUCH STUFF: THE EFFECTS OF SURPLUS ACCUMULATION

We have not yet adequately explained what could have started this self-reinforcing process. However, before making an attempt to do so, I must digress somewhat. So far we have been focusing attention on the development of more intensified means of food production; but human life is about more than just eating. Do social problems such as inequality, oppression, and warfare automatically flow from the introduction of new food-producing techniques and population pressure? To some extent, they do. But other factors are also involved.

First, consider *stratification*—the development of social classes with unequal wealth and power. According to one widely held view, articulated in the 1960s by sociologist Gerhardt Lenski, material inequality and class stratification arise from the urge to accumulate a surplus over and above the immediate needs of the group. Gatherers and hunters tend not to accumulate a surplus; they simply share what they have among themselves until it's gone. Their societies are also highly egalitarian, few having chiefs or head men. But some food-gathering groups in unusually abundant ecological niches, rather than migrating in search of new food sources, stay in one place. In doing so, they create the opportunity to accumulate more than they can immediately consume or easily carry with them.

Surplus does not automatically result in unequal distribution: it can be allocated equally (as in the modern Israeli Kibbutzim, where profits are divided among the entire group). But some groups that produce a surplus also have an inheritance system; in these instances, the surplus tends to fall to heads of extended families, who in many cases achieve prestige by giving their wealth away at seasonal feasts. Often such groups are large enough so that gathering and hunting activities are no longer undertaken by the entire community together, but by individual families; then members of separate families have less of a tendency to share.

Meanwhile, as the group grows, population pressure creates the need for cultivation, which (for reasons outlined above) results in an even greater population increase. Families are larger, and the more successful ones gradually gain control over the sources of wealth. They may then consolidate their control by intermarriage, creating the beginnings of a class system. Members of the more powerful kinship group will avoid marriage with members of the less powerful on   over many generations, whatever surplus is available will t   trated in a single stratum of the community. Those in the "   ler to have access to land, may be forced to give up a portion   duce in order to pay rent, and they will therefore live in cons   city, while the "in" group lives in constant relative abundan   int on, as societies move from small and simple to large an   plus, scarcity, population density, and class stratification all

THE ROOTS OF VIOLENCE

Like inequality, warfare tends   ith cultural complexity. Among gathering or hunting ban   y erupt in which a man is injured or killed. Among the   istinct tribal peoples of Papua New Guinea, members of one   illage may raid another's storehouse in times of famine, or eng   arfare in which a few men are predictably hurt or sacrificed. I   icultural civilizations of Rome, China, and Central America,   nies made conquest their business. In the industrial era, killin   scientifically perfected. Whole cities can be leveled, and wh   ns wiped out in weeks, days, or a single moment.

What is the underlying cause of warfare? Most anthropologists who have examined the question have based their answers on studies of surviving nonindustrial societies. For example, Napoleon Chagnon, who has re-searched patterns of warfare among the Yanomamo Indians of the Amazon since 1964, suggests that the initial source of friction is competition for food, water, territory, or women. Confrontations that arise on this basis occasionally escalate to the point that a warrior is killed. When this happens, the victim's male relatives are bound by custom to exact blood vengeance on the offending village. If they are successful, they are rewarded with social status, the primary sign of which is new wives. Chagnon concludes that in indigenous cultures, fighting prowess is tied to reproductive success and is therefore encouraged.

Marvin Harris agrees with Chagnon that competition for food is a cause of warfare, but traces this competition back to population pressure and environmental stress. For Harris, warfare serves ultimately as nature's way of keeping a region's human population within limits.

Perhaps the largest study to date on the sources of warfare was conducted during the 1980s by Melvin Ember and Carol R. Ember of Human Relations Area Files. Their analysis of 186 nonindustrial societies does not fully confirm the theories of either Chagnon or Harris. Groups experiencing shortages of food and women did not necessarily fight more than others. The Embers found that it was the *fear* of shortages, brought on by antici-pated but unpredictable natural disasters, that was the primary indicator of violence in human societies. A secondary indicator was *fear of others*—which tends to be passed along from generation to generation in child-rearing practices that emphasize mistrust of neighbors or strangers. "War is more likely when people have a history of unpredictable disasters that destroy food supplies," they write. "People often go to war to take resources that would cushion them against future scarcity."[4]

ॐ

Let's briefly take stock of the ground covered so far. Cultural change in the direction of bigger, more stratified, centralized, populous, and techno-logically sophisticated societies is a spiraling process—though not nec-essarily an evolutionary one, if we conceive of evolution as somehow having a goal in mind or as always leading to improvement. The process seems to have gotten started ten thousand years ago with events that are still somewhat mysterious (though there is some intriguing archaeological and mythological evidence suggesting that there may have been previous civilizations that came and went even before the end of the last ice age).

We noted Mark Cohen's conclusion that it is a decline in the abundance of wild foods that creates population pressure, which in turn leads to changes in modes of food production. We also considered Melvin and Carol Ember's findings that, in the simplest societies, warfare seems most predictably to arise from food shortages created by natural disasters. One cannot help but wonder if we are looking at two effects of the same cause. Could it be that environmental circumstances started human beings down that long slope toward ever more intensified modes of production, ever greater population densities, ever greater ecological destruction, and ever more intense and widespread warfare?

But just what sort of environmental circumstances could have induced people to begin the long trek toward civilization?

3 | CATASTROPHE AND CULTURE

*O Solon, you [Greeks] are all young in your minds which hold
no store of old belief based on long tradition, no knowledge
hoary with age. The reason is this. There have been, and will be
hereafter, many divers destructions of mankind, the greatest by
fire and water . . . [these destructions being due to] a deviation
of the bodies that revolve in heaven around the Earth and a
destruction, occurring at long intervals, of things on the Earth by
a great conflagration. . . . And so you start again like children,
knowing nothing of what existed in ancient times. . . .*

—PLATO, *TIMAEUS* AND *CRITIAS*

 THE UPPER PALEOLITHIC AND NEOLITHIC ERAS, from about
20,000 to 4,000 B.C.E., were formative times for humanity. The
Aboriginal Australians remember this period as the end of the
Dreamtime—the age when the world was filled with creative
energy and giant animals roamed the land in abundance. Other
cultures have their own myths of a Golden Age of peace and plenty that
ended in catastrophe. The Egyptians spoke of the Age of Re, when there
was no suffering, and truth rained down from the heavens. The Hebrews
recalled a garden of Eden, in which God had planted every tree pleasant
to the sight and good for food. The Chinese spoke of the Age of Perfect
Virtue, when people were upright and correct without need for punishment
or reward. The *Mahabharata* of ancient India tells of the Krita Yuga—the
First Age of the world—when there was no disease and people lived as long
as they chose to live. Native American and African traditions likewise echo
the universal memory of a lost age of innocence and plenty. In virtually
every case, the myth ends with a tale of world destruction. According to

the myths, it was only after this universal catastrophe that human beings developed agriculture and writing and began to settle in towns. We, the people of today, says the universal mythic tradition, are inheritors of the legacy of these profound events that occurred when our species was young.

For decades science regarded this universal tradition as a story invented by our ancestors, having no basis in fact. The remarkable consistency of the versions of the story collected from around the world was dismissed as a problem for scholars of comparative religion. However, new discoveries in astronomy, archaeology, paleontology, and geology are forcing the recognition that both Earth history and human history have been shaped to a large degree by periodic natural disasters of extraordinary intensity and extent—events that could well have been regarded by the people who witnessed them as the end of a World Age.

We know, for example, that around 40,000 years ago, the Earth's climate changed suddenly and dramatically. Perhaps within a decade, the temperature of the entire surface of the globe fell by about 15 degrees Centigrade. Soon a sheet of ice a mile thick covered Britain, central Europe, and northern Russia. Another sheet covered North America as far south as the Great Lakes. Then 12,000 years ago—and just as suddenly—a global warming trend brought this most recent of the great ice ages to a close. Ocean levels rose by about 150 feet (300 feet total, if we begin counting from their level 17,000 years ago), and arid, semi-desert conditions came to northern Africa, Arabia, and the Near East. This climate change was so profound that geologists use it as a marker with which to define the end of the 2.5 million-year-long Pleistocene Epoch.

Toward the end of this time, a large portion of the planet's large land mammalian species perished—for reasons that are as yet unclear. The natural history museums of the world are filled with fossils that attest to the richness and variety of nature only a few thousand years ago, and paleontologists puzzle over the cause of the late-Pleistocene extinctions, which extinguished the camel, mammoth, mastodon, ground sloth, giant peccary and beaver, dire wolf, short-faced bear, mountain deer, and saber-toothed cat from America, the hippopotamus from England, and many giant mammals and birds from Australia—which, in short, removed from the world a large proportion of its most vigorous and colorful animals.

The identity of the events or mechanisms that altered Earth's climate, initiated the last Ice Age and brought it to an end, and caused the late-Pleistocene extinctions constitutes a long-standing mystery and a perennial cause for debate among experts. Increasingly, it appears that those events or mechanisms were sudden and catastrophic in nature. But the argument for recent global catastrophes has had to overcome a long-standing scientific prejudice.

THE STORY OF CATASTROPHISM

Prior to the advent of modern gradualist evolutionary geology, scientists tried to reconstruct prehistory according to the teachings of the Bible—in terms, that is, of an original Paradise that was destroyed by a universal Deluge. Catastrophism—the view that Earth history has been punctuated by at least one immense global catastrophe—was taken for granted. But the nineteenth-century debate over Darwin's theory of the evolution of species tended to subsume questions of factual evidence in arguments about theology and philosophy, as scientific discussions frequently bogged down in confrontations over the literal truth of the biblical account. By the 1870s a new generation of geologists, siding with Darwin, was rushing to bolster evolutionism by reinterpreting the geological features of the Earth in terms of slow, gradual processes occurring over vast stretches of time. Few in the scientific establishment wanted to represent a school of thought tainted by association with the Bible, and so catastrophism quietly disappeared from the intellectual arena. The geological evidence had not changed—there had been no overwhelming new discovery—but the political climate among scientists had shifted profoundly.

Both prior to and following this gradualist revision, several theorists sought to explain evidence of floods, ice ages, and mass extinctions by the collision of the Earth with giant comets and meteors. William Whiston, a pupil of Newton, contended in his *New Theory of the Earth* (1681) that the Old Testament Deluge had resulted from the impact of a comet in the third millennium B.C.E. In the nineteenth century, two other theorists—J. G. Radlof and Ignatius Donnelly—offered similar hypotheses. In the 1950s, Immanuel Velikovsky created a firestorm of debate with the assertion (published in his best-selling *Worlds in Collision*) that ancient global catastrophes had been caused by near-collisions of Earth with Venus and Mars.

These ascriptions of a cosmic source for terrestrial convulsions were either ignored or ridiculed by most geologists until the 1980s, when physicist Walter Alvarez connected the extinction of the dinosaurs—and the source of a thin layer of the rare element iridium in geological formations around the world—with a comet's impact some 65 million years ago. Suddenly catastrophism was again acceptable. Following Alvarez, several other prominent geologists, paleontologists, and astronomers have tied major events in Earth history to cosmic catastrophes. David M. Raup, in his 1991 book *Extinction: Bad Genes or Bad Luck*, attributed nearly all biological extinctions throughout geologic time to the impacts of extraterrestrial objects. And two British astronomers, Victor Clube, Dean of Astrophysics at Oxford University, and Bill Napier, astronomer at the Royal Observatory, Edinburgh, have discussed the relevance of catastrophism for our understanding of human prehistory. In *The Cosmic Winter*, they wrote:

> The standard view advocated for a century or more by experts in geology and biology, that the Earth evolves in splendid isolation from its surroundings, is proving to be wrong. What we are doing . . . is taking [recent] astronomical discoveries and applying them to timescales of historical rather than geological interest. That is, we show how the same astronomical evidence which is now leading to new insights in the earth sciences also tells us that cataracts of fire must have taken place within the last few thousand years.[1]

COMETS, GALACTIC CYCLES, AND EARTH CHANGES

But what were these "cataracts of fire"? To understand Clube's and Napier's hypothesis we must start with the galaxy. Beginning in the early part of this century, several geologists (including Arthur Holmes, R. M. MacIntyre, Steiner and Grillmair, Fischer and Arthur, Seyfert and Sirkin, and Raup and Sepkoski; as well as paleontologist D. Jablonski), noted that various Earth processes—meteoric cratering, extinctions, sea level changes, ice ages, volcanic activity, magnetic field reversals—seem to be periodic, and to be tied to either the 250 million-year cycle of Earth's passage around the galaxy or its 30 million-year cycle of up-and-down motion through the galactic disc. But none of these scientists could point to a causal link between the galactic cycles and terrestrial events.

Clube and Napier believe they have found the connection. Periodically, tidal forces from the galaxy disturb comets at the edge of the solar system (which most astronomers believe to number in the millions), stripping many from the Sun's gravitational hold altogether and sending others careening into the inner solar system.

According to Clube and Napier, "Over the few million years . . . when the Sun is deeply immersed in a spiral arm [of the Galaxy], perhaps twenty or thirty giant comets will join the inner planets," nudged from the outer reaches of the solar system toward the Sun's gravitational field by galactic forces. "Every 100,000 years or so therefore, during a high-risk period, the

Earth encounters the debris left in the inner Solar system by a disintegrating giant comet."[2]

Clube and Napier hypothesize that the encounter with the disintegrating fragments of a giant comet will most likely produce not a single giant collision, but episodes of bombardment resulting in a few cataclysmic impacts, many smaller ones, and the gravitational capture by the Earth of vast quantities of comet dust. This dust could reflect so much sunlight as to create a prolonged winter, starting a chain reaction resulting in the onset of a great ice age.

CIVILIZATION AND NATURAL DISASTERS

The most profound human implications of the British astronomers' work (implications anticipated, incidentally, by Immanuel Velikovsky in his posthumously published *Mankind in Amnesia*) may have to do with our understanding of the development of civilization. On the basis of the observed cratering rate on both the Earth and the Moon, Clube and Napier expect "a collision of several megatons energy to occur somewhere on Earth every 200 years or so." The most recent, near the Tunguska River in Siberia, took place in 1908. The missile was seen as a blinding firefall trailing a thick cloud of dust. The sound of its explosion was heard over 600 miles away; people 60 miles distant were knocked unconscious; those 150 miles away were blown off their feet; and trees were flattened for 40 miles in all directions from the epicenter. Throughout Asia and Europe for days afterward, the sky was unusually bright. Remarkably, the explosion left no crater.

The explosive energy of the Tunguska event is estimated to have been between 40 and 100 megatons. According to Clube and Napier, collision events of this magnitude are to be expected periodically: "a few dozen sporadic impacts in the tens of megatons, and a few in the 100 to 1000 megaton range, must have occurred within the past 5000 years." Perhaps an even greater impact, in the energy range of tens or hundreds of thousands of megatons, occurred at the end of the Pleistocene Epoch. This, at any rate, was the conclusion of British astronomer Fred Hoyle.

Until recently, the cause of the 100,000-year-long ice age cycle was regarded as one of the principal unsolved problems of geology. Many scientists tended to think that the glacial cycle was tied to minor irregularities in the Earth's orbit around the Sun. However, in 1981, Hoyle criticized this explanation in his book *Ice: The Ultimate Human Catastrophe*, and proposed instead that the ice ages begin with rocky meteor or comet impacts that send enough light-colored dust into the atmosphere to block sunlight for years at a time, lowering global temperatures by several degrees; and end when a *metallic* asteroid plunges to Earth, sending particles into the atmosphere that absorb rather than reflect sunlight.

If Hoyle, Clube, and Napier are right, it would mean that the fateful period of the last ice age and its conclusion, the rise of ocean levels, the drowning of coastlines, and the extinction of hundreds of species worldwide, was also a time probably punctuated by several spectacular cosmic events involving the appearance of fireballs and the envelopment of the planet in great clouds of dust obscuring the Sun for perhaps years at a time. But the catastrophes did not end with the convulsions of 12,000 and 8000 B.C.E.

"Between seven and five thousand years ago," according to Clube and Napier, "our planet was experiencing a relatively benign climate. These conditions seem to have played some part in causing communities in several different areas of Asia and North Africa to evolve the first urban economies." Perhaps this temporary environmental abundance enabled some groups to begin producing and storing surplus crops.

> Around 3000 BC however, and lasting for about two centuries, the terrestrial climate deteriorated quite markedly on a global scale. . . . During this period, too, major flooding occurred in Mesopotamia and Egypt. . . . Remarkably, the same epoch brings clear evidence of a surge in civilization; new skills, the appearance of writing and the establishment of a professional class, all coinciding essentially with the start of the historical era.[3]

In the most "advanced" cultures, the population seems to have been motivated by "a sense of urgency" (in Clube's words) toward the creation of large irrigation schemes and other public works projects, including huge pyramids.

Archaeological evidence of catastrophes in the second and third millennia B.C.E. is to be found in Mesopotamia, Egypt, Greece—indeed, the entire ancient world. Perhaps the earliest of all civilizations was that of the Indus Valley; the first of its sites to be excavated were Mohenjo Daro, some two hundred miles from the shores of the Arabian Sea, and Harappa, four hundred miles to the north. It now appears that most of the towns that comprised this cultural complex, which was already thriving over seven thousand years ago, are presently buried under mountains of sand in the

Great Indian Desert. These were not originally desert towns, however. Satellite photos reveal that the area was once the valley of a great river with fertile banks—remembered in the *Rig-Veda* as the Sarasvati—which flowed from the Tibetan Himalayas to the Arabian Sea. Geologists have proposed that the area was devastated around 1900 B.C.E. by major— and perhaps sudden—tectonic shifts, possibly accompanied by volcanic eruptions, which drastically altered both the flow of rivers and the local climate. In their book on the Sarasvati culture, *In Search of the Cradle of Civilization*, authors Georg Feuerstein, Subhash Kak, and David Frawley write:

> We . . . envision tidal waves randomly flooding large areas, and broken dams and walls of water bearing down on unsuspecting townsfolk and villagers, sweeping them miles away from their homes, together with panicky livestock, uprooted trees, boats torn loose from their anchor-points, and the debris of houses. We can also imagine the water from the Himalayas seeking new pathways, causing a similar devastation in other areas. . . . The cataclysm left behind desiccated river beds, empty canals, parched soil and, finally, abandoned towns and villages.[4]

Elsewhere we see similar catastrophic evidence. As early as the 1920s, while excavating at the city of Ur in Sumer (modern Iraq), Sir Leonard Wooley discovered a twelve-foot layer of mud separating two strata of artifacts. He calculated that the mud had been deposited by a flood at least twenty-five feet deep. The Mesopotamian empire of Akkad is now thought to have to have collapsed at the end of the second millennium B.C.E. due to a three-hundred-year-long drought brought on by volcanic eruptions. The soil was covered by ash and the people abandoned their towns. Only after the rains returned was the region of the Tigris and Euphrates reinhabited, setting the stage for the later Babylonian empire.

In about 1500 B.C.E. the Greek island of Thera (Santorini) exploded in a tremendous volcanic eruption, devastating much of the eastern Mediterranean region. A few hundred years later, the Bronze Age city of Tiryns in Anatolia (modern Turkey) appears to have been buried by flooding; this was approximately the same time the city of Troy was destroyed by an earthquake.

In 1948, archaeologist Claude Schaeffer, the excavator of Ras Shamra, noted signs of periodic, wholesale destructions of cities in Asia Minor, Armenia, the Caucasus, Iran, Syria, Cyprus, Israel, and Egypt, the most intense upheaval coinciding with the collapse of the Egyptian Middle

Kingdom. In his book *Stratigraphie comparée et chronologie de l'Asie Occidentale (IIIe and IIe millenaires)*, Schaeffer wrote:

> Our inquiry has demonstrated that these repeated crises which opened and closed the principal periods of the third and second millennia were not caused by the action of man. Far from it, because compared with the vastness of these all-embracing crises and their profound effects, the exploits of conquerers . . . would appear only insignificant.[5]

On the basis of this sort of archaeological evidence—noted by many investigators working in sites around the world—as well as the evidence from their own field of specialty, Clube and Napier identify four historical periods of widespread upheaval: 3100, 2200, 1650, and 1250 B.C.E. They suggest that the widespread destruction during each of these episodes resulted from Earth's collision with the debris from a single giant comet. Surviving remnants of that body still exist—as Encke's Comet, and as the Taurid group of meteors (which crosses Earth's orbit in late June and early November). Clube and Napier hypothesize that over a period of centuries, the great parent comet disintegrated into several smaller asteroidal bodies, some of which crashed to Earth as fireballs; and into a large mass of dust, which would have been visible as a zodiacal cloud—a pillar or hoop of light. The larger collisions would have resulted in climate change, the uprooting of civilizations, and the layering of yards-thick strata of dust over cities, causing the people's settled living to give way—at least temporarily—to nomadic existence. And this is exactly what is shown in excavations of sites dating to this period.

THE COMING OF THE SKY GODS

This neo-catastrophist interpretation of ancient history also has important implications for our understanding of the development of world religions. In the second millennium B.C.E.—during the period when, according to Clube and Napier, the principal recent comet bombardments were occurring—much of the ancient world was swept up in the worship of a new pantheon of sky gods. Previously, religious imagery had centered on the Earth Goddess and on images drawn from nature. Now, suddenly, throughout the Near East, cylinder seals, inscriptions, and mosaics depicted masculine war gods in winged chariots, celestial bulls, and star- or comet-shaped symbols. Among the Greeks, Zeus assumed authority over the celestial Mount Olympus; the Babylonians depicted the god Assur as a winged disc trailing comet symbols; and the Hebrews turned their attention toward the celestial El or Jehovah and banished the cult of the Earth-goddess Asherah. Around this time comet-shaped symbols also crop up in India, Mexico, Scandinavia, and China. In addition, Mesopotamian and Chinese rulers began to base their decisions on an elaborate omen astrology—a system fundamentally different from the later and more familiar horoscopic astrology—which sought to anticipate terrestrial catastrophes by studying signs in the sky.

This obsession with the sky was reflected as well in ancient myth and ritual—in creation myths featuring celestial giants battling one another and dominating the earthly scene, and in "fire festivals . . . involving bonfires, processions with blazing torches, tumbling burning wheels down hills, hurling lighted discs into the air and many variations on similar themes. . . ."[6] Clube and Napier suggest that it may be significant that these festivals tend to fall during early November (e.g., Halloween) and late June, the times of the Taurid meteor showers.

Of course, many historians of religion have offered other, very different explanations for the sudden appearance, during the second millennium B.C.E., of myths, rituals, and symbols connected with sky gods. Mircea Eliade, for example, wrote that "All this derives from simply contemplating the sky. . . . The transcendent quality of 'height,' or the supra-terrestrial, the infinite, is revealed to man all at once, to his intellect as to his soul as a whole. . . . The sky 'symbolizes' transcendence, power, and changelessness simply by being there."[7] But if the neo-catastrophist historians are correct in saying that the second and third millennia B.C.E. were dominated by cataclysms of celestial origin (and the archaeological, astronomical, and geological evidence to that effect is mounting), then how could the people who lived then have helped being deeply impressed by the events they witnessed—by the terrifying visions and sounds from the sky, and the consequent earthquakes, floods, and fires? Should we not *expect* to find, at this point in history, a veritable explosion of sky-based religious imagery?

The psychological effect of the catastrophes must have been devastating: whole cultures would have been traumatized. The sky gods must have appeared as terrible portents completely unlike anything on Earth, and utterly unresponsive to human control. The people's responses may be inferred from what we know of their circumstances, and about trauma victims' behavior in analogous situations in the present—which is explored in the next chapter. For the moment, suffice it to say that ancient peoples must have interpreted the horror from the skies as the anger of gods.

In many cases, they would have blamed themselves for the destruction occurring around them, internalizing a collective sense of guilt and shame. Some groups might have sought to propitiate the gods by offering elaborate sacrifices. Many people would have been so deeply traumatized that they could not help but pass their horror, guilt, and shame on to their children. Their child-rearing practices would have emphasized violence and fear. Meanwhile, the destruction of croplands would have moved some groups to raid the supplies of others more fortunate; and the latter would therefore have come to fear their neighbors and develop defensive strategies.

These are, of course, the sorts of effects that we see being played out in the development of civilization. Among the early pastoralists and agriculturists of the Near East, childhood ceased being a time of security and permissiveness (as it is among all food-gatherers); and parents began to discipline their children, to prepare them for a harsh life as members of an increasingly rigid class system. Strong leaders emerged, purporting to be representatives on Earth—even to be incarnations of—the great sky god whose wrath and vengeance could be kept in check only by the continual offering of sacrifices and tribute. Great cities arose, at whose centers were impressive pyramids and temples where a male leader could be glorified and where he could commune publicly with the celestial god. The common people were put to work farming; officials gathered, measured, and stored surpluses; and armies were sent out to conquer neighboring peoples, take captives for forced labor, and seize wealth. A pattern of existence was set in motion that has endured, with minor alterations, down to the present. While individual civilizations have come and gone— expiring in warfare, rebellion, or ecological collapse—the pattern itself has continued and intensified.

In short, all of human history may have played itself out in the shadow of celestial and terrestrial events so terrible that they have been mostly re-pressed from awareness, like the childhood traumas of many contemporary child-abuse victims; events whose unconscious imprint has continued to compel irrational behavior on a cultural scale in succeeding generations. To what degree the other factors summarized at the beginning of this chapter also contributed to the origin of civilization is unclear; yet to ignore the evidence regarding the occurrence of global catastrophes in early historical times, and the psychological reactions typical of disaster victims, would be to omit what may be crucial clues to explaining why so many myths recall a Golden Age followed by a series of world catastrophes; and to unraveling the mystery of why war, repression, and human sacrifice have so dominated the civilized institutions whose ostensible purpose was to facilitate the human search for security, meaning, peace, and progress.

Western civilization has historically exhibited a fear and hatred of nature. Francis Bacon, the founder of modern science, declared that it was the duty of humanity to "subdue," "overwhelm," and "conquer" the forces of nature, and that even a slight lapse of vigilance might permit the world to revert to "the old Chaos." This attitude of being literally at war with land, weather, "weeds," and wild animals has ironically created a condition in which another world catastrophe looms—this one humanly created. Already we appear to be entering upon what biologist Edward O. Wilson characterizes as one of the greatest mass extinction episodes in Earth history. One cannot help but wonder why any creature would be so foolish as to destroy the foundations of its own biological viability. Could it be that we act so irrationally because we are walking wounded, the children of trauma victims so devastated that they decided at some deep subliminal level that the world is an evil place?

4 | COLLECTIVE TRAUMA AND THE ORIGIN OF CIVILIZATION

If we consider mankind as a whole and substitute it for a single individual, we discover that it too has developed delusions which are inaccessible to logical criticism and which contradict reality. . . . [I]nvestigation leads us to the same explanation as in the case of the single individual. They owe their power to the element of historical truth which they have brought up from the repression of the forgotten and primeval past.

—SIGMUND FREUD

Our society is made up of vast numbers of traumatized individuals, and our culture has come into being through a universally traumatizing process. The outcome—today's technological civilization with its massive psychopathologies and unending ecological disasters—is a collective reflection of the traumatized personality.

—CHELLIS GLENDINNING

 THE IDEA THAT CIVILIZATION is fundamentally sick goes back at least to the early Greeks. Closer to our own time, Sigmund Freud once asked: "May we not be justified in reaching the diagnosis that, under the influence of cultural urges, some civilizations or some epochs of civilization—possibly the whole of mankind—have become 'neurotic'?" Unfortunately, Freud refused to follow out the implications of this question; but other psychologists have picked up where he left off. Carl Jung wrote of "politico-social delusional systems" having their roots in the collective unconscious; Wilhelm Reich believed that civilization was swept up in an "emotional plague"; and Immanuel Velikovsky theorized that humankind suffers collectively from amnesia and repetition compulsion.

Still more recently, as it has become apparent that civilization is in the process of profoundly and perhaps permanently impairing the biological viability of the entire planet, a new discipline know as "ecopsychology" has undertaken to expose the roots of civilization's omnicidal mania. Paul Shepard's *Nature and Madness*, Theodore Roszak's *The Voice of the Earth*, and Chellis Glendinning's *My Name Is Chellis and I'm in Recovery from Western Civilization* have all underscored the idea that individual psychological dysfunctions may be merely local eruptions of a collective insanity afflicting the entire civilized world. The ecopsychologists say that so-called "advanced" human societies are actually in an advanced state of a virulent cultural psychic disorder, and that in order to heal ourselves individually, and to restore our world to biological viability, we must find and treat the cause of our common derangement.

IN THE WAKE OF HORROR

Initially, as we seek to grapple with the idea of mass neurosis, we are compelled to draw analogies with individual manifestations of psychic distress. While a certain amount of caution is always required in extrapolating from the individual to the collective (and vice versa), in this case the method does yield some promising leads.

As Chellis Glendinning has pointed out, there is one disorder whose symptoms in individuals closely resemble the irrational, self-destructive attitudes and behaviors of civilized people acting together—a disorder commonly seen in war veterans and in survivors of rape, assault, abuse, or environmental disasters; psychologists call it *post-traumatic stress disorder.*

The symptoms of post-traumatic stress include:
- vigilance and scanning
- elevated startle response
- blunted affect or psychic numbing (the loss of the ability to feel)
- denial (mental reorganization of the event to reduce pain, leading sometimes even to amnesia)
- aggressive, controlling behavior
- interruption of memory and concentration
- depression

- generalized anxiety
- episodes of rage
- substance abuse
- intrusive recall and dissociative "flashback" experiences
- insomnia
- suicidal ideation
- survivor guilt

Clearly, it would be absurd to argue that all civilized people show such symptoms. Nevertheless, *some* of these symptoms do seem almost indisputably to characterize *most* members of civilized cultures. When hunter-gatherers encounter civilized people, they often remark on how the latter appear generally to be disconnected, alienated, aggressive, controlling, easily frustrated, addictive, and obsessive. But if civilization got its start as the result of mass trauma, presumably that trauma would have occurred in the distant past; why, then, would these symptoms appear in civilized people today, perhaps many millennia after the fact?

Psychiatrist Robert Jay Lifton, in his studies of the long-term psychological effects of the Hiroshima bombing in 1945 and the 1972 flood in Buffalo Creek, West Virginia, concluded that disasters affect more than the immediate victims; their impact is also transmitted to succeeding generations.[1] Because the aggressive, controlling behavior and episodes of rage exhibited by trauma victims can result in traumatic effects on others—particularly, on children and other close family members—post-traumatic stress can infect entire families and, conceivably, entire cultures.

It is not hard to catch civilized cultures in the act of passing trauma on from generation to generation. The instances are plentiful and, occasionally, brutally plain. In *For Your Own Good*, psychologist Alice Miller showed how the German people's willingness, during the first decades of the twentieth century, to submit to authoritarian domination and to participate with blind obedience in unprovoked attacks against strangers can be traced in part to violent, authoritarian pedagogical practices that were widely promulgated at the turn of the century. And these practices in turn arose from previous generations of "poisonous pedagogy." The authoritarian programming in infancy of the generation that brought Hitler to power was merely a conspicuous instance of a broader pattern: Child-rearing in Western civilization is *typically* and *systematically* abusive in comparison with that among many "primitive" peoples, particularly the food-gatherers. Miller notes that "Although parents *always* mistreat their children for psychological reasons, i.e., because of their own needs, there is a basic assumption in our society that this treatment is good for children."[2] Anthropologists Colin Turnbull and Ashley Montagu, and psychotherapist Jean Liedloff, have described and analyzed in some detail how typical Western practices surrounding childbirth, informal child-rearing, and formal education alienate the infant or child from its mother's body and its natural surroundings, suppress innate needs, implant authoritarian messages, and undermine the sense of self-worth.

In cases of severe trauma in infancy or childhood, the victim may experience extreme dissociation, culminating in multiple personality disorder. Extraordinary abuse—especially from primary caregivers—overwhelms the child's ego. To keep from being psychologically annihilated, the child hypnotizes herself into a trance, while a secondary personality emerges to take the abuse. Over time, several—even dozens—of discrete personalities may develop, each with its own ways of thinking and feeling.

Can a whole culture be dissociative? Native peoples often note that civilized people typically act at cross-purposes to their stated ideals (for example, talking about justice and mercy on Sunday morning, then practicing murderous pillage the next day). It is as though the colonial European has a divided self: "White man speaks with forked tongue." And Western civilization seems to glory in the splitting process. God is pitted against Satan, mind against body, subject against object, spirit against flesh, angelic virtue against animal instincts, and so on. Most of these distinctions appear extreme or even nonsensical to members of non-Western cultures, whose very languages usually reflect more inclusive, less categorical patterns of thought. Colin Ross, a multiple-personality researcher, says that Western culture has promoted the "executive ego self" to the exclusion of others. This executive ego is arrogant, intolerant, overly logical, and anti-intuitive. Ross writes: "A cultural dissociation barrier has been created and reinforced, the purpose of which is to keep other part selves suppressed, out of contact and communication with the executive self, and relegated to second-class status in the mind."[3]

People suffering from post-traumatic stress often develop addictions as a way to control psychic pain. Addiction is an out-of-control compulsion to fill an inner sense of emptiness with substances like alcohol or food, or with experiences like falling in love or gambling. In *The Guru Papers: Masks of Authoritarian Power*, Joel Kramer and Diana Alstad see addiction as an unconscious revolt against an inner authoritarian. If civilized people do have inner authoritarians, implanted through abusive child-rearing, it stands to reason that they might collectively exhibit addictive behaviors as a way of rebelling, as well as to distract themselves from pain and to fill inner voids. Historian Morris Berman writes: "Addiction, in one form or another, characterizes every aspect of industrial society. . . . Dependence on alcohol (food, drugs, tobacco . . .) is not formally different from dependence on prestige, career advancement, world influence, wealth, the need to build more ingenious bombs, or the need to exercise control over everything."[4] It should be noted that Berman is not merely offering a cynical commentary on our society's more egregious failures, using the word *addiction* metaphorically; he is pointing to specific addictive symptoms that are *not* shared by many traditional cultures, particularly those of gatherers and hunters, wherein the compulsive search for wealth, power, novelty, and gadgetry is, if not completely unknown, certainly comparatively rare.

Trauma victims frequently suffer from psychic numbing—the decreased ability to feel joy or sorrow, or to empathize with the feelings of others. Native peoples wonder how civilized Europeans can treat other humans, and the animals, trees, and land, with such unfeeling indifference. Of course, the relentless monetization and compartmentalization of our society are partly to blame: Trees and animals have ceased to be magical beings and have become instead "economic resources"; people have ceased to be members of a community and have become instead "workers" or "consumers," "national allies" or "enemies of the state." Nevertheless, the questions arise: Why is it that people in Western society have failed to put brakes on tendencies to turn empathic relationships into abstract, manipulative ones— even when these tendencies are clearly out of control and are acting to the detriment of people's own fundamental interests? Could it be because the population is already numbed to some extent by some ancient trauma, the destructive energy of which has been passed along from generation to generation through abusive childrearing?

Now, up to this point I have simply stated a hypothesis. Even if it is reasonable, it lacks any sort of proof. How could it be supported with evidence? One way would be to examine human societies that have been subject to horrific disasters in recent times, and see if the traumatized survivors responded *collectively* by developing the sorts of symptoms listed, and whether these symptoms led to permanent social change.

COLLECTIVE TRAUMA AND ITS EFFECTS: SOME EXAMPLES

Anthropologist Colin Turnbull's *The Mountain People* is a classic, poignant study of the Ik—a gathering and hunting people of west-central

Africa who had been driven from their former hunting grounds by the Ugandan government's creation of a new game preserve. While the Ik were not the victims of a natural disaster *per se*, they were nevertheless experiencing the equivalent of a catastrophe—slow starvation due to the loss of their means of subsistence.

Previously, the Ik (also known as the Teuso) had lived the way most gatherers and hunters do. Hunters, according to Turnbull, "frequently display those characteristics that we find so admirable in man: kindness, generosity, consideration, affection, honesty, hospitality, compassion, charity and others. This sounds like a formidable list of virtues, and so it would be if they *were* virtues, but for the hunter they are not. For the hunter in his tiny, close-knit society, these are necessities for survival; without them society would collapse."[5] As for the Ik themselves, "we have the remnants of past traditions, customs and beliefs, and something of their own oral tradition, all of which indicate that they were . . . an easy-going, loosely organized people whose fluid organization enabled them to respond with sensitivity to the ever changing demands of their environment. There is ample evidence in their language that they once held values which they no longer hold, that they understood by 'goodness' and 'happiness' something very different from what those words have come to mean now."[6]

Forced to pursue an unfamiliar agricultural life in the mountains separating Uganda, Sudan, and Kenya, on land unable to support them, the Ik had changed profoundly. In less than three generations, they had become a handful of scattered hostile bands interested only in individual survival. They had abandoned compassion, love, and kindness for the sake of mere existence. According to Turnbull: "Economic interest is centered on as many individual stomachs as there are people, and cooperation is merely a device for furthering an interest that is consciously selfish. . . . In present circumstances they are highly disputatious and given to much acrimonious fighting. . . . They have replaced human society with a mere survival system that does not take human emotion into account. . . ."[7] Children were put out of the family at age three or four; old people were sent away to die alone. "The ideal family, economically speaking and within restricted temporal limitations, is a man and his wife with no children. Children are useless appendages, like old parents. Anyone who cannot take care of himself is a burden and a hazard to the survival of others. . . . Such interaction as there is within this system is one of mutual exploitation. That is the relationship between all, old and young, parent and child, brother and sister, husband and wife, friend and friend. . . . They are brought together by self-interest alone. . . ."[8]

Turnbull sees clear parallels between what has happened to the Ik suddenly, in a matter of years, and what has happened to Western civilization
gradually, over several centuries. Today, "The very old and the very young
are separated, but we dispose of them in homes for the aged or in day schools
and summer camps instead of on the slopes of Meraniang [one of the
mountains of the Ik]." Turnbull points to "our cutthroat economics, where
almost any kind of exploitation and degradation of others, impoverishment
and ruin, is justified in terms of an expanding economy and the consequent
confinement of the world's riches in the pockets of a few."[9]

The most extensive survey of the psychological effects of mass trauma
yet published is Lewis Aptekar's *Environmental Disasters in Global Perspective*. Aptekar compares studies from traditional, "developing," and
"developed" cultures; he also explores the aftermaths of many kinds of
disasters—including chronic disasters (droughts, famines), quick onset
disasters (floods, fires, storms, earthquakes), and human-induced disasters
(wars, toxic chemical spills, nuclear plant meltdowns). The findings he
reviews are complex and varied, and researchers whose work he cites have
come to differing conclusions. There is some controversy, for example, on
a point central to the present discussion: Do the psychological effects of
disasters persist for years, perhaps generations, or are they only transitory?
After a thorough study of researchers' conflicting views, Aptekar concludes
that discrepancies in observations probably arise from differences in the
nature and severity of the disasters, the presence (or lack) of a social support
system, the degree to which the environment returns to its pre-disaster
state—as well as from differences in research methods (different studies of
victims of the same disaster sometimes produced different results).

Aptekar first dispels misconceptions about people's immediate responses to disasters. Looting and panic are rare; instead, people more
frequently display behavior that has a clear sense of purpose and is directed
toward the common good (tragically, officials who believe that social chaos
inevitably follows disasters often delay warning communities of impending
crises because they wish to avoid a panic). Nor do people flee from disaster
sites; rather, they tend to remain. In addition, outsiders usually enter the
area in order to help survivors or to search for family members, producing
what has come to be known as the "convergence phenomenon."

While Aptekar describes post-traumatic stress disorder and cites the
work of researchers who have found its symptoms among disaster victims, he cautions that "the idea that it is common for disaster victims
to develop . . . post-traumatic stress disorder . . . should be questioned."[10]
Symptoms seem to appear only after the severest disasters, and in cases

where victims are directly and personally affected. "The victims who show the greatest psychopathology are those who lose close friends and relatives."[11] Not all of the symptoms occur immediately, and reactions may appear years afterward, especially on anniversaries of the disaster. Gradually, people tend to distort their memory of the event, forgetting parts of what happened and minimizing its impact and their reactions to it.

Children appear to be particularly vulnerable after a disaster. "Galante and Foa documented the aftermath of an extremely destructive earthquake that struck the mountainous region of Lombardy, Italy on November 23, 1980. . . . Right after the earthquake the children demonstrated extreme signs of apathy and aggression."[12] Girls tended to be more affected than boys. (Aptekar notes, "Perhaps the girls were more aware of their feelings than the boys.") Boys had a greater tendency to react with aggression.[13]

Meanwhile, adverse reactions in adults can be so severe that disaster victims "pass fear and insecurity onto their children—even those yet to be born—by replacing in their child-rearing a sense of a secure world with a fearful worldview."[14]

One of the early pioneers in the study of disasters, Samuel Prince (whose work was published in the early 1920s), was convinced that disasters inevitably bring social change. Subsequent work has tended to confirm Prince's conclusions. Basing his speculations on his study of the aftermath of a large ammunition explosion aboard a ship in the harbor at Halifax, Nova Scotia, Prince hypothesized that disasters may cause changes in technology and culture in a society; and that after disasters, differences between social classes tend to increase.

Sociologist Max Weber wrote that disasters tend to produce charismatic leaders—an observation that has been confirmed in various cultural settings. In nonindustrial societies, according to Aptekar, "Before a disaster, traditional local leaders are important; but as the society adapts to the changes brought about by a disaster, new leadership skills are needed." When pastoral Somali nomads were forced by drought to assume a sedentary agricultural way of life, "their once pastoral democracy was converted to a severe hierarchy of social status; cooperative leadership changed to leadership by domination. . . ."[15]

Disasters may also bring changes in work habits, gender roles, and kinship patterns. Studies of Pacific island cultures by Firth (1959), Schneider (1957), and Spillius (1957) point out that (in Aptekar's words) "the progression of societies from traditional ways to those of the developing world is greatly speeded up by environmental disasters." Again, Aptekar:

Among the !Kung bushmen of the Kalahari desert, drought now determines where and how they live. Among the Navajo, alliances between kin and family groups changed as a result of drought. Because of drought the Tikopia of the South Pacific rescheduled their adult initiation ceremonies to occur much later, thus introducing what for them was a new developmental phase of life: adolescence. After an earthquake the Inca of Huarez, Peru, moved from a local bartering economy to an urban service economy. Typhoons on the island of Yap caused Yapians to abandon their traditional values and adopt a European lifestyle. Because of Typhoon Ophelia the people of the Micronesian island of Ulithi changed the food they ate, the style of homes they lived in, their habits of work, the way men and women related to each other, their form of government, and even their religion.[16]

In "developed" (i.e., highly civilized) cultures, patterns of reaction are somewhat different. In many instances, impacts are minimized because of the almost immediate availability of elaborate aid and support systems. Yet disaster researcher Benjamin McLuckie hypothesized (in 1977) that "the higher the society's level of technological development, the more vulnerable it would be."[17] That is because people in developed countries live in large population centers and rely on sophisticated technologies, so that there is a possibility of their being vulnerable to a large-scale collapse of interlocking systems of transportation, communication, water supply, and food distribution. It is worth remembering, in this regard, that most civilizations seem to fall because of human-made disasters.

Indeed, as Chellis Glendinning has suggested, civilization itself can be seen as a disaster-in-progress, traumatizing people as it destroys nature, relentlessly preparing the way for its own demise. The social effects noted above, quoted from Aptekar, are the same sorts of effects that vast numbers of human beings are experiencing now as a result of technological and economic change. Traditional modes of work, patterns of subsistence and nutrition, social and family relationships, religious ideas and practices, and common values are all vulnerable to the ravages of "progress."

SUMMING UP SO FAR

In history, effects become causes: Wars beget wars, which beget political, economic, and social changes that may later lead to still more wars. The search for ultimate causes is nearly always frustrating. However, natural disasters are sources of change that come from outside the human social system and that are capable of introducing influences unimaginable in a closed human system.

But then, is there any such thing as a closed human system? Clearly, there is not: All societies are dependent on soil, climate, and ecology. Civilization appears in many respects to be a pathetic and futile attempt to *create the feeling of* a closed human system. Agriculture partially unlinks humans from wild nature; the division of labor unlinks some people from the process of agriculture (leaving only their dependence on its products); and cities and technologies psychologically unlink people from their environment in manifold ways. People become ever more dependent on complex social and technological systems; their dependence on wild, natural systems persists, but is forgotten or hidden from view. Could this compulsion to escape external influences by substituting artificial systems under human control have originated as a collective strategy to elude the ravages of natural disasters?

As we have seen, in many—but not all—cases, survivors of disasters and civilized people alike

- show symptoms of post-traumatic stress disorder
- pass psychological dysfunctions onto their children, and
- tend more frequently to undertake basic changes in values, lifestyle, and social organization

than people who live in traditional societies that have not experienced a major disaster within the past few generations.

HUMANITY: WOUNDED AND PRECOCIOUS

It appears, from evidence surveyed in chapter 3, that humankind has gone through some trying times. And just as some abused children cope with adversity by plunging into intellectual or creative activities, perhaps humanity as a whole has done something similar. Neurobiologist William Calvin, in his *The Ascent of Mind: Ice Age Climates and the Evolution of Intelligence*, suggests that it was by matching wits with frequent climate changes that our early ancestors learned to develop their capacities for language, culture, technological innovation, and ethics.

For biologists, the evolution of modern *Homo sapiens* constitutes one of the greatest mysteries. We differ from the apes in a hundred ways:

language, accurate throwing ability, concealed ovulation, dramatically increased brain-to-body size ratio, different hand anatomy, lack of body hair, descended larynx, flatter face, smaller teeth, and so on. It is not so difficult to explain how one or another of these developments could have occurred in a couple of million years, but all of them taken together constitute virtually a miracle of evolutionary transformation. Calvin suggests that we look to only a few basic causes, of which each would have had multiple effects. For example, if early humans spent much of their time living in open savannas, this might account for our transition to seed eating and our upright posture. And if, as Elaine Morgan argues in *The Scars of Evolution*, we spent another phase of our development foraging for food along shorelines, living partly in water, this might explain features we share with the aquatic mammals—subcutaneous fat, salt-and-water wasting kidneys, tearing, and descended larynx, among others.

But what of brain size and intelligence? Calvin suggests that repeated, drastic climate fluctuations were the motivating factor, acting as a kind of evolutionary "pump" encouraging change in certain directions: "[W]e look at the back-and-forth ice ages and see in them not just overblown winter but a way of *amplifying* the effect of the wintertime natural selection. . . ."[18] Calvin's hypothesized winter-specialized hominid subtype—which would have relied more on hunting, and therefore would have developed better throwing skills than its more tropical cousins—would have expanded its population during warmer boom times in order to take advantage of ice-free land; when the ice returned, the hunters would simply have moved south. With each warm/cold fluctuation, the winter-specialized types would have grown to constitute a greater percentage of the overall hominid population.

Calvin suggests that these versatile hunters developed bigger brains for making, aiming, and throwing projectiles by way of a process known as *juvenilization*. If, in a given population, puberty gradually occurs earlier, somatic development will be cut short, and after many generations, the adult population will acquire juvenile characteristics. As it happens, the juveniles of most mammals have a bigger brain/body ratio than adults, as well as flatter faces and smaller teeth. Calvin argues that the alternation of harsh and hospitable climates during the past couple of million years encouraged early maturity: during boom times "there [was] a race to fill up newly available 'job slots' afforded by an environment able to feed more mouths."[19] When the ice returned, juvenile body features were retained. And once brain size had grown, new uses were quickly found for all this new gray matter—such as the invention of language and culture.

But perhaps, as Paul Shepard suggests in *Nature and Madness,* in addition to physical juvenilization we have also more recently undergone a psychological juvenilization, which amounts to a stunting of our emotional development. Civilization, according to Shepard, produces people who are incomplete and infantile—self-absorbed "adult children" who tend to be dependent on parental authority figures. This is because the initial creation of hierarchically stratified agricultural communities required the gradual reshaping of the human personality so that people would increasingly remain in an immature, dependent state even as they grew physically to maturity.

These are promising lines of thought: Drastic climate changes at unpredictable intervals led us to become intelligent tool users, and we became physically (and later psychologically) juvenilized in the process. However, neither Shepard nor Calvin was in position to appreciate the profoundly traumatizing character of the events that compelled these human adaptations. As noted in chapter 3, the astronomical, geological, and archaeological evidence of cosmic catastrophes in recent millennia is only now beginning to find its way into the scientific literature. The climate changes on which Calvin bases his theory may have been more drastic and sudden than geologists of past generations would have dreamed possible. And they may also have been accompanied by terror raining from the skies. The human survivors would have felt a profound compulsion to band together, and to watch the skies for signs and omens portending further disasters. If people repeatedly saw the world around them engulfed in flames, torn by massive earthquakes, and showered with cosmic debris, they would likely have adopted a pessimistic attitude toward life. They might well have come to believe that the gods were angry at them. What had they done wrong? Perhaps they would have concluded that we humans are flawed, sinful children who deserve the gods' (our parents') wrath; that nature is cruel and chaotic; that we must defend ourselves, propitiate the gods, and make sure we have a surplus in case disaster strikes again.

SOME PROBLEMS AND POSSIBLE SOLUTIONS

In the last chapter and in this one I am proposing an explanation for a great many cultural phenomena. The matters we have touched on are complex and raise many questions. Let us briefly consider three of the most obvious.

Problem: Why would only a few cultures react to catastrophes by developing civilizations? After all, most human cultures, historically, have maintained modest gathering, hunting, horticultural, or pastoral ways of life. Were these people not traumatized? If not, why not? If they were, why did they respond differently?

Possible solution: Even in the case of global disasters—climate change and comet impacts—effects would not have been geographically uniform. Moreover, it is entirely possible that distinct cultural groups would have been predisposed to handle trauma in varying ways. It is true that some cultures have maintained a much greater sense of harmony with nature than others; however, evidences of collective psychopathology are not unique to Western civilization: In nearly every culture it is possible to point to some institution, rite, or taboo that could have had its origin in mass psychological trauma.

Problem: Why were no other animals similarly affected? Why didn't horses, monkeys, squids, and parrots develop big brains, technology, language, and cultural neuroses?

Possible solution: Perhaps they *were* affected, but responded differently. The creation myths of many cultures speak of a time (before the catastrophes) when the animals were less aggressive or fearful and when a universal harmony prevailed throughout nature. Of course, such myths need to be regarded with healthy skepticism, but they may hold some kernel of historical truth. In most higher animals, behaviors are scripted by instinct, while in humans (for reasons William Calvin may be able to explain) culture has partly usurped instinct's role. If traumatic stress caused at least some humans to develop dysfunctional cultures, then it is possible that the same stressors caused at least some animals to develop dysfunctional instincts. The lemmings' suicidal boom-and-bust population behavior is one possible example.

Humans' unique responses to stress may be traceable partly to their unique brain structure. In *The Origin of Consciousness in the Breakdown of the Bicameral Mind*, Princeton psychologist Julian Jaynes anticipated Calvin in suggesting that "it is possible for the brain to be . . . reorganized by environmental changes."[20] With the ice ages came the development of language, and with language came the invention of an analog inner world of words, paralleling the behavioral world "even as the world of mathematics parallels the world of quantities and things."[21] Jaynes argued that, in its early stages, the use of this new linguistic ability was split between the brain's hemispheres: the right hemisphere spoke to the left, and its voice was interpreted as being that of a god. This bicamerality may have served to obviate the stress of decision-making during times of environmental change. But later, during the early historical period, as civilizations were developing, the bicameral organization of the human mind began to collapse. This, says Jaynes, was partly due to the invention of writing: Once the words of the gods were written, they became silent and could be turned to or avoided at will. But disasters also played a role: "The second millennium B.C. was heavy laden with profound and irreversible changes. Vast geological catastrophes occurred. Civilizations perished. Half the world's population became refugees. And wars, previously sporadic, came with hastening and ferocious frequency. . . ."[22] The gods fell silent, and left-brain-dominant humans were left to fend as best they could. The result was the dawn of rational self-consciousness, of alienation and anxiety, and of a condition in which "we have become our own gods."

Problem: We have suggested that the traumatic energy of ancient disasters is passed along from generation to generation via civilized child-rearing methods. If so, we might expect the post-traumatic stress symptoms evident in civilized populations to gradually dissipate over the centuries and millennia, or at worst to remain constant. Yet we now face humanly generated social and ecological problems of unprecedented scope and severity. Why would these problems be increasing, if they are the effects of some ancient trauma?

Possible solution: It may be that civilization is (or can be) a *progressive* social disease. In individuals, a progressive disease is one in which the body's natural defense systems are overwhelmed; rather than improving, the patient becomes sicker and sicker.

Civilization progressively re-traumatizes itself—not only through child-rearing practices, but through economic inequality and poverty, environmental destruction, alienation from nature, and war. Thus as civilization "advances," the effects of the original trauma are magnified. Add to this the impact of disasters that have occurred in relatively recent times—such as the Black Death in medieval Europe, in which nearly a third of the population was wiped out, and which may have helped prime the European psyche for witch hunts and bloody colonial exploits.

The idea that our psycho-social disease may be a progressive one is disturbing, of course. Even worse is the realization that we are infecting and killing our only potential therapists—the primal peoples of the world, who appear to have been less traumatized than ourselves, or at least to have found other ways of coping with their wounds. If we cannot look to them to save us from our own folly—and, realistically, we have no right to expect them to do so—then we must learn somehow to heal ourselves.

RECOVERING FROM COLLECTIVE POST-TRAUMATIC STRESS

How would one go about treating an entire culture for post-traumatic stress? The difficulties involved are considerable—especially in a chronic case, or one in which the society in question doesn't *want* to be treated. It is difficult to know even where to begin, given a "patient" so huge, powerful, and deranged as our contemporary global civilization. Such a task may actually be impossible. But perhaps we *can* heal ourselves and one another individually, at least to some degree, and thereby plant the seeds of a new sane and biologically benign culture. In order to do so, it would seem vital that we familiarize ourselves with what is presently known about individual trauma treatment and recovery.

In cases where the original trauma is long past, the most important aspect of treatment seems to be the recollection and emotional processing of the traumatic event. Whether humankind as a whole can recall events millennia ago is problematic; it seems more feasible for individuals to bring to mind and face the specific ways in which they were taught—beginning at birth—to throttle their wildness and conform to a contorted system of beliefs and behaviors. A therapist or therapeutic community is often helpful in this regard—assuming that the purpose of therapy is not seen as being merely to help the patient adjust more successfully to society as it presently is.

Another step in recovery is to learn to feel our repressed grief and rage—as well as our repressed joy. Chellis Glendinning, Buddhist scholar Joanna Macy, environmental educator Annie Prutzman, and others have suggested ways to safely uncork the vessel of our dammed-up emotions via psychodrama and storytelling.

It is also possible to benefit from techniques used in shamanic cultures for the re-integration of nature and psyche. Primal peoples resort to prayer, dancing, drumming, and purification rites in order to restore the wholeness of individual, community, and nature. While mere imitation of such rites may constitute a kind of cultural theft, non-natives may nevertheless find similar ways of working in small groups to call upon ancestors, spirits, and natural forces to assist us in our healing.

Recovery may not penetrate past the surface layers of consciousness without significant, deliberate lifestyle changes. As long as we are utterly dependent upon civilization it is difficult for us to see its influences with any objectivity, or to forge a new relationship with the natural world. But disconnecting from the civilizational system—via natural home-building, growing or gathering much of one's own food, and providing for other needs with a minimal use of money—tends to induce feelings of basic self-worth and competence.

Independence from the system need not be seen as abandonment of responsibility, however. Often a member of a dysfunctional family will stay in the abusive situation in order to try to fix it from within. In cases like this, a therapist will usually counsel the individual to leave, since it is only from a secure position outside the abusive situation that one can have a positive impact on those still within it. Perhaps something similar is true with respect to individuals awakening to the dysfunctionality of civilization: We can be of more help to other people if we are not entirely dependent on the system that is progressively reproducing its woundedness. Then our activism is grounded not just in anger and pain, but in knowledge of workable alternatives.

Regaining our autonomy and reconnecting with life require deliberate effort, but the rewards are instantaneous. New avenues for play, creativity, and love open up before us precisely to the extent that we seek them.

As we do, we provide a platform for the next generation. It may be possible to forge a path toward sustainable culture only so far in one life-time. Perhaps our greatest responsibility, therefore, is to explore whatever routes we can, go as far along them as we are able, and then pass on whatever we have learned. Children growing up in—or under—the dominant culture today are inevitably subject to nearly constant trauma, some forms of which are extremely sophisticated and seductive. Unless some young people are provided with effective tools for self-defense, self-expression, exploration, and creativity—and examples of what it is to be a relatively free and happy human—the way ahead looks bleak.

IMPLICATIONS FOR THE FUTURE

Of course, every sane person would wish to avert another disaster; everyone hopes that civilization can somehow quickly reform itself so that we don't have to face massive starvation and ecological devastation in the coming century. But it would be foolish to ignore the implications of current trends. The likelihood is that those of us who will be around in the early decades of the next century will experience a catastrophe of one sort or another first-hand—either one that is humanly caused or an "act of God" whose effects are experienced far more severely as a result of high population density and the interconnectedness and vulnerability of civilization's systems of transportation, communication, food delivery, and political control.

How will people respond? According to Lewis Aptekar, victims of humanly induced disasters often show *more* stress than victims of natural disasters because of the perceived need to find parties to blame. Whatever the eventual circumstances, it seems certain that groups in differing geographic areas, and in differing economic conditions, will react in dissimilar ways. In the case of a breakdown of communication and control, those who are more dependent on high tech will likely suffer much more than those who are still somewhat accustomed to filling their own basic needs locally. Over the short term, we are likely to see acts of extraordinary heroism alongside extreme examples of opportunism and stupidity. But what about the long-range prognosis?

If human beings are re-traumatized, will they develop even stranger and more virulent cultural neuroses than the ones they already exhibit? Or will at least some of us learn from the experience? The fact that we are now coming to understand how the human psyche typically deals with trauma is cause for hope: Perhaps a significant number of people will experience civilization's *crisis* as a *catharsis* that will reach all the way to the roots of our ancient, irrational fear of nature, and help us learn to live in peace with the world, with one another, and with ourselves.

5 | WHAT ARE OUR OPTIONS?

We need a radically different way of relating ourselves to the support systems of the planet. My experiences with aboriginal peoples have convinced me, both as a scientist and as an environmentalist, of the power and relevance of their knowledge and worldview in a time of imminent global eco-catastrophe.

—DAVID SUZUKI

 As I noted in the Introduction, my quest for an understanding of human cultures and how they change has been far from merely an academic exercise. It is motivated by an urgent desire to expand our perspective on the human situation in the present—and especially our extraordinarily destructive relationship to the natural world—so that we can get a better idea of our options for the future, and how we might best go about evaluating and implementing them.

Now, having surveyed the range of human covenants with nature that have been forged in various times and places, and having explored the roots of civilization, we now are in position to look more closely and our present state of affairs and where we seem to be headed.

THE PRESENT CROSSROADS

Today we find ourselves in a society that in many ways epitomizes basic trends that are characteristic of all civilizations—trends toward the intensification of modes of production, population increase, and economic inequality. It is also a society that is ever more obviously suffering from all of the ills that have caused previous civilizations to expire.

Throughout the world—both in the "developed" and "developing" countries—large-scale agriculture is replacing family farms, and mechanized production methods are replacing traditional, labor-intensive, subsistence techniques. It is cheaper in the short term to grow a single crop on a giant, mechanized farm and to ship the harvest to markets hundreds or thousands of miles away via subsidized transport systems than to grow diversified crops locally on small, family-owned plots. However, this economy-of-scale ignores certain hidden costs—the creation of widespread unemployment, the reduction of species diversity (which small, multicrop farms help preserve), the heightened need for public investment in new roads, and the increased requirement for pesticides and fertilizers (since monocultural crops are more vulnerable and tend to impoverish the soil more quickly). These hidden costs often come to haunt us long after we have decided to "modernize" production for the sake of "efficiency." Meanwhile, that decision continues to be made: Factories sprout up throughout the Third World to take advantage of cheap labor, and factory owners in the First World countries increasingly replace human workers with computerized robots.

The scale of social organization is also increasing dramatically worldwide. The nation state is still formally the dominant large-scale political unit, but from an economic standpoint, the power of nations has largely been usurped by transnational corporations. In many respects, our present global civilization is a modern version of medieval feudal societies, in which guilds, merchants, clergy, and nobles competed for power. While tribal and national boundaries still exist, a commercial global "culture" based on new transportation and communication technologies, driven by profit, and insinuated into the mass consciousness by brand names and advertising images, is everywhere undermining local, traditional cultural forms. But rather than creating world harmony, globalization seems instead to be exacerbating class, racial, tribal, and national rivalries by increasing competition for jobs and resources.

Demographers warn of the effects of the uncontrolled expansion of the world's population, but seldom discuss the links between population growth and industrialization. In Europe, population increase was relatively slow and steady until the advent of the industrial revolution, when suddenly birth rates began to far exceed death rates. The same phenomenon has occurred elsewhere as new modes of production have been adopted and as people have flooded to cities. For the past few generations, the global population has been doubling every forty to fifty years. This is a truly astonishing rate of growth, one that clearly cannot be sustained. Demographers disagree as to the ultimate "carrying capacity" of the planet—that is, how many people can be supported over the long term given limited global resources of fresh water, topsoil, trees, fossil fuels, and minerals. High estimates are in the range of ten to fifteen billion (about a single doubling away from the present world population of six billion); low estimates are on the order of a few hundred million.

The environmental impact of our intensified patterns of production, and of our sheer human numbers, is by now a matter of common knowledge; damage to atmosphere, ozone layer, climate, oceans, rivers, lakes, forests, and soil has been widely documented in hundreds of books and tens of thousands of newspaper and magazine articles. Perhaps the gravest statistic of all is that in a mere twenty years we will likely have lost one fifth of the world's plant and animal species forever. Clearly, these are trends that cannot continue for long.

Finally, the distinction between rich and poor, which can be traced back to the beginnings of the agriculture-based state, is increasing dramatically in our time. In the United States alone, according to the *New Republic*, "the proportion of all national income earned by the richest one percent of all families went from 8.7 percent in 1977 to 13.2 percent in 1990. For the bottom 40 percent, it dropped from 15.5 percent to 12.8 percent."[1]

Given these worrisome, unsustainable present trends, *what are our options as a society?* I see three main ones.

OPTION ONE: THE FORTIFIED TECHNOPOLIS

First, it is entirely possible that the future will look a lot like the present, only more so. This option assumes simply that present trends will continue until absolute necessity dictates change; and that change will be implemented in ways that primarily benefit the wealthy few. What if computers keep getting more powerful, rich countries (and neighborhoods) keep getting richer, poor ones keep getting poorer, shopping malls keep proliferating, and the natural environment continues to be bulldozed, uprooted, and paved over?

In that case, the next couple of centuries would be bleak for most of humankind. We shouldn't delude ourselves by thinking that technology can somehow raise the living standard of all the world's peoples to match that of middle-class Americans—at least not any time soon. The problem is that there simply aren't enough basic resources to supply the demands of even one more North America, let alone the equivalent of twenty more. And we must remember that *each year* the human population is growing by about 100 million. Could we seriously envision reproducing the totality of America's infrastructure, factories, housing, and educational and health-care facilities *every three years* just to keep up with world population growth? Sad to say, present trends suggest that within a very few decades, most people will be at or near the point of starvation.

Assuming that the wealthy minority in the "developed" nations are somehow able to maintain their relatively secure lifestyles—and even allowing for a fairly large-scale transition in those nations to renewable energy sources, conservation, and recycling—there would still be billions of undernourished worldwide who would be unable to share in the abundance; billions who would have grown up in politically unstable countries where indigenous cultural wisdom had given way first to ill-suited Western free-market values and then perhaps to fundamentalist religious movements or ultranationalist political regimes.

With increasing polarization between rich and poor, it is not hard to see how the First World's prodigious armaments could come to serve as a deadly security system to prevent the Third World from organizing Robin Hood-like raids or simply venting its frustration in meaningless violence.

For the well-off (at most, ten to twenty percent of the global population), life might have to be lived out under plastic, ultraviolet-screening domes (to filter out harmful rays from the ozone holes). For these fortunate few there would be a virtually unlimited variety of entertainment and products to consume. Tiny, ubiquitous, and powerful computers would monitor these sanitized and protected, wholly artificial settings, which might turn out to be reminiscent of Epcot Center or the West Edmonton Mall. Nature as we know it would hardly exist. Engineering would replace biology. Most wild species would become extinct (except for insects), but examples of colorful birds and cuddly mammals could be preserved in special zoos.

For the poor, life would be reduced to bare survival in shantytowns, settlement camps, or (in the industrialized countries) prisons and slums. The better-off of the poor would be given jobs in factories producing sophisticated products for wealthy consumers. However, labor and environmental standards would be virtually nonexistent, as these would interfere with profits.

We can already glimpse life under Option One in places like Mexico City and Buenos Aires, where members of the wealthy elite routinely travel in chauffeured, air conditioned Mercedes limousines past seas of human squalor created by the economically forced displacement of the peasantry from their ancestral lands.

In sum, if the world follows Option One (which means simply letting things go along as they are), it will become a place of utter desolation dotted with islands of sterile, computerized order and control.

OPTION TWO: COLLAPSE

Suppose Option One came unstuck. Unable to defend itself from Third-World nuclear terrorism (or succumbing instead perhaps to bureaucratic ineptitude, corporate greed, resource exhaustion, unemployment caused by globalization and mechanization, and the stress and dissatisfaction of the general populace), the First World falls into disarray.

Imagine, for example, the following scenario. In the early years of the new millennium, an economic depression descends over North America. Then, with the nation already in a pessimistic mood, a tremendous earthquake all but destroys Los Angeles. Because of a recently ratified balanced budget amendment, the federal government finds it impossible to offer significant aid to victims of either the depression or the 'quake. The social fabric of the country begins to unravel as each economic or ethnic group blames another for its deepening misery.

Meanwhile, GATT has disenfranchised hundreds of millions of peasant farmers throughout the Third World, who begin to organize themselves into popular resistance movements, destabilizing world trade.

In the Middle East, Islamic fundamentalists have overtaken the governments of Egypt and Saudi Arabia. Seeing the West's vulnerability, they cut off oil shipments to Europe, America, and Japan. The already beleaguered American government decides that a foreign war is the answer to its domestic problems. But widespread antiwar protests force the government's hand; with diminishing oil reserves and a recalcitrant citizenry, U.S. generals press for the use of nuclear weapons. Chaos reigns.

Each of the elements of this scenario is considered likely by at least some futurists. The combined outcome (global chaos) may seem unthinkable, but it is worth noting that there are tens of thousands of Americans—the well-armed troops of the "militia" movement—who are preparing for just such an eventuality.

Might the collapse of civilization prove to be a blessing in the long run? Perhaps. Unfortunately, however, for people forcibly stripped of their accustomed social forms and now required to eke out a subsistence, it would take many generations to achieve the cultural standard of the Aboriginal Australians or the Native Americans, whose ways of life, though materially simple, were spiritually profound and based on a detailed knowledge of the natural world. The survivors of a civilization-wide breakdown could take lessons from native peoples if only there were more of them left, and if it were not for the fact that their knowledge had been mostly suppressed and forgotten by the very process of colonization and "development" that fueled industrial civilization in the first place.

True, whoever managed to make it through the initial destruction and disorder would eventually figure out which plants are good to eat, which are poisonous, and which ones heal. Given long enough, they would learn again to respect Earth and sky, would create a stable social system, and would probably even develop a new religion centered on stories of a lost Golden Age of miracles and plenty followed by a world catastrophe.

While this scenario has a kind of mythic appeal in the abstract, the concrete reality would be horrific. It is likely that hundreds of millions or billions would perish—particularly people in the cities, who are completely dependent on sophisticated technological systems for the delivery of food, water, and power. There would be a mass exodus to the countryside, and a pathetic, violent struggle for the necessities of existence. To call such a condition of human society (which has its precedents, for example, in the German cities in the early 1920s, parts of China during much of the twentieth century, or Rome in the eighth and ninth centuries) "animalistic" would do a serious injustice to the animals.

But there is something else about this option that is less than satisfying. It would be a shame to treat the accomplishments of the last few thousand years as unmitigated error. For all the problems of civilization, surely we have learned some valuable lessons from it. A few technologies, though they have drawbacks, seem worthwhile within limits. Take writing, for example. Plato may have been correct in saying that it saps the memory, but I would never have heard of Plato had he not translated his thoughts into marks on paper. And while we could probably do very well without the automobile, television, and nuclear fission, there are surely some other recent inventions whose benefits outweigh their costs. The bicycle comes to mind and perhaps the radio, the composting toilet, and the solar water heater.

But more important, perhaps, than civilization's technologies are its growing reserves of knowledge about ourselves and our world—knowledge that could not be accumulated and passed along without writing, libraries, and scientific research. In many cases, scientific knowledge may simply duplicate the oral traditions and intuitive wisdom of ancient aboriginals, and in many respects it is partial, skewed, and unreliable. But it is a body of knowledge that is open to change and growth. Something similar could be said of the civilized arts: Bach, Mozart, and Charlie Parker may not exhaust the possibilities of human musical expression, but we would be poorer without them.

Would it not be possible for us somehow to include the past rather than repudiating it, while still making a clean break with the trends leading us toward Options One and Two?

OPTION THREE: CULTURAL RENEWAL

The third option, like the second, implies a return, though in a different sense. We would go back, not by simply abandoning civilization in one great collective spasm and throwing ourselves on the bosom of what's left of nature, but by returning to some ideals that we have lately abandoned—and doing so deliberately and systematically.

If present trends are leading to disaster, and if disaster isn't the natural goal of human existence (let's hope not), then it stands to reason that we have gotten off track somehow. How, precisely, and when? As painful as it would be, we might undertake a systematic, public critique of civilization. If it is true that an individual cannot grow morally without periodic self-examination, the same holds for a culture. Of course, the exercise could simply dissolve into an orgy of finger pointing unless at least a few leaders of economic, political, religious, and educational institutions set an example by admitting complicity in the present debacle and showing willingness to change (even if it required personal and institutional sacrifice), while refusing to blame others.

At the same time, in order for this third option to work, people everywhere would have to join in a reevaluation of the fundamental goals of human existence. If they determined (as I expect they would) that justice, peace, and sustainability are more important than profit and centralization of control, then the next step would be to decide together what technical and social means are best suited to achieving these ends.

We would, I think, come to focus our attention on finding modest ways of living in small groups in direct contact with nature. Our search for practical means of doing this would cover not just proposals from modern inventors and social scientists, but principles and strategies embodied in the whole range of human cultures, present and past.

Often in history, cultural change has been inspired by the recovery of earlier traditions. The Protestant Reformation, for example, grew from a return to reading the Bible in original texts, and from a determination to test the Church by the standards found there. In more recent times (and on a smaller scale), the Arts and Crafts movement of William Morris and Elbert Hubbard attempted to revive the values of preindustrial handcraftsmanship; it resulted in the creation of furniture, art, and buildings that are now considered the very best of their period.

We need a revitalized sense of who we are as human beings—an image of humanity that is uplifting and inclusive—and we need a new covenant with nature. Such things don't come from think tanks; they come from individuals in touch with the wilderness, the human spirit, and collective memory. Hence the healthy present public fascination with the Native Americans, Aboriginal Australians, and other primal peoples. We cannot all become like Indians and live exactly the way they lived, but we can perhaps learn from their ideals and values. The twenty-second century will probably not find us hunting wild game with bows and arrows. But we could still recover the habit of treating the natural world as sacred and reclaim our bodies, our spirit, and our creativity through new cultural forms—new songs, dances, celebrations, patterns of decision making, and biologically conservative ways of feeding, housing, and clothing ourselves.

How, concretely, might all of this come about? Consider the following scenario. Late in the present century the long-range effects of GATT become apparent: Alongside the increasing wealth of the few, the poverty of the many deepens, and with it comes social unrest. Meanwhile, resources continue to be depleted, and ecosystems ravaged, as the soaring human population flocks to the cities. Under intense pressure, the leaders of the industrialized countries admit that their problems are becoming unmanageable and declare themselves open to suggestions. Ecologists and alternative economists, suddenly finding a receptive audience, call for a mass conversion to small-scale, decentralized production and natural home-building. They offer as examples the eco-pioneers who are already enjoying self-sufficient, low-cost lifestyles using natural or recycled homebuilding materials and diversified, soil-building gardening methods.

Those on the left of the political spectrum see the movement toward self-sufficiency and localized village economies as the means to dismantle corporate empires and empower the poor. Those on the right see it as a way to expand individual freedom and limit the need for government intervention. Both sides view native peoples with renewed respect, seeking them out as consultants in the design of small-scale, sustainable systems of production and governance. Over a period of decades, people gradually desert the corporate, bureaucratic power structure.

In the Third World, the end of domination by transnational corporations via global trade and IMF (International Monetary Fund) based structural adjustment programs is seen as an opportunity to revive indigenous cultural traditions, including traditional birth control methods. A noncoercive global cultural assembly convenes to encourage the sharing of common planetary concerns and interests. Gradually, the human world makes a transition to a peaceful, self-organized village economy, enlivened by global communication networks and cultural cross-fertilization in the arts and sciences. Meanwhile, the nonhuman world regains much of its former diversity and vitality.

In essence, adopting Option Three would mean asking ourselves what is really important and meaningful in life; dispensing with all the aspects of civilization that run counter to those basic interests; and reviving cultural forms that we have perhaps discarded too hastily.

Unfortunately, this would be the most difficult of the three paths because, unlike the first two, it would require deliberate effort. It would require us, acting together, to take responsibility for our choices as we have never done before.

※

Clearly, of these three options, I advocate the third—the renewal of culture. But what would this mean, in specific, practical terms? How would we go about it? While it may be possible to outline some of the principles in a few paragraphs—as I've done here—the details are mostly unknown at this point, since they would necessarily be specific to groups of people living within unique bioregions.

Cultural renewal is not a panacea. I don't propose to fall into the same trap as nineteenth-century French visionary Charles Fourier, who foretold that in the New Age, the oceans would turn to lemonade and wild beasts would tame themselves. But we have every reason to believe that it is possible for us to achieve a stable, sustainable, and fulfilling mode of life based in enduring values—a way of life whose challenges are on a manageable, human scale—if only we are willing to make certain sacrifices and do the necessary work.

Clearly, the realization of Option Three would require not only finding different ways of doing things (growing food, building houses, making tools), but learning (or relearning) different ways of thinking and being. In order to get a deeper understanding of the nature of needed changes in our fundamental worldview, we need to take a closer look at what culture is all about, and begin to question the assumptions we unconsciously carry with us concerning the ends and means of human existence.

| # TOWARD A REBIRTH OF CULTURE

Caucasians have a more positive vision to offer humanity than European culture. I believe this. But in order to attain this vision it is necessary for the Caucasians to step outside European culture—alongside the rest of humanity—to see Europe for what it is and what it does.

—RUSSELL MEANS

 EVERY CULTURE, according to anthropologists, constitutes a way that a given group of people has adopted for finding food, resolving conflicts, caring for their young and elderly, channeling their sexuality and creativity, and dealing with strangers, novelty, and death. A healthy culture, in this sense, is a pattern of human life that connects people to one another and to their environment in such a way as to maximize survival and happiness over the long term.

As I've looked into the nature of culture in general and the history of specific societies, I've come to hold an opinion that many people seem to find shocking—that civilization is not so much a *form* of culture as a *disease* of culture. I mean this quite literally. In this chapter I intend to show why I think this is so, and to help the reader understand a little more clearly just what is being lost in the process of economic and technological "progress," as that word is ordinarily understood. For it is only by doing so that we can begin to gain perspective on what might be involved in the restoration or rebirth of healthy human cultures.

VALUING CULTURE

As we have seen, until a generation ago Western philosophers and anthropologists tended to place cultures on a scale ranging from "primitive" to "advanced," the most "advanced" ones being those that are most similar to the modern Western industrial civilization which provided these observers with their lofty vantage point. Usually this simplistic ranking was done under the pretext of *cultural evolutionism*—an explanation for cultural change discussed in chapter 2—which attempted to apply Darwinian and post-Darwinian theories about species origins to transformations in the social environment. Over the past few decades the cultural evolutionists have been challenged by anthropologists calling themselves *cultural relativists*, who argue that all cultures are equally worthy; each is a unique human creation that deserves respect in its own right. There are, after all, many examples of cultures that do not appear to be evolving toward industrialism—or even agriculture—on their own, and resist these innovations when the attempt is made to impose them.

Cultural relativism has its own critics who say that, while it is a necessary corrective to earlier blatantly Eurocentric theories, it can be difficult to uphold in all instances. True, even some of the most foreign and frightening societies (from our perspective) have found a way of life that makes sense on their terms. Still, when we come across a society built on slavery, constant predatory warfare, and human sacrifice—like that of the ancient Aztecs, for example—it is difficult to avoid the feeling that it is possible for a culture somehow to lose its way, so that it adopts ever more desperate measures in order to assert itself and to stave off collapse.

In exploring human societies we cannot deny occasional feelings of admiration or revulsion. When we read of the Khonds of Bengal selling their children to be sacrificed to the Earth goddess, we recoil; when we hear of the members of the Iroquois confederacy making their decisions with the welfare of the people seven generations into the future in mind, we cannot help but respect them for it. Of course, sometimes feelings of surprise and even disgust are based simply in our shock at encountering the unfamiliar. But do all such responses erupt merely from ethnocentric prejudice? Or are there basic, universal human ideals and values that whole cultures sometimes embody and sometimes depart from—ideals such as truth, fairness, and compassion? To the degree that such universal values and ideals exist, to suppress our sensitivity to them may be not only futile but also destructive of the original goals of anthropology—which included helping us not only to understand and tolerate other societies, but to improve our own.

But how are we to discover or agree upon these "universal" values? That is a difficult question to answer, because culture is all-pervasive in its influence. There is no way to tell just how deeply our patterns of thought have been molded by language, upbringing, and a thousand daily subliminal influences. Clearly, we cannot say much about innate or universal values if we are merely regurgitating elements of our social conditioning. The discovery of innate values, if it is to occur, must come both from outward study and inner reflection. We must ask ourselves fundamental questions like, What is it to be happy, and what leads to happiness? What are the causes of suffering, and how can those causes be mitigated?

A third school of anthropologists, sociologists, and philosophers (we might call them *culture ecologists*) believes that gradually, through living participation in the social process, meditation, reflection, and analysis, we may begin to recognize and value certain cultural characteristics wherever they appear as signs of health and well-being, while others may begin to serve as warning flags that something has gone wrong in human affairs. Culture ecologists regard cultures as human ecosystems; like natural ecosystems, they can be diverse or depleted, robust or moribund. Culture ecologists look, for instance, at how aggression and violence are dealt with in a given society. In some cultures, violence compounds itself generation after generation and is glorified at least in certain forms and instances; in others, nearly all interpersonal expressions of violence are regarded as signs of insanity. Some cultures (such as the Mongols under Ghengis Khan) are expansionist and predatory, while others (such as the Hopi) are happy to live and let live. Are certain individuals or classes privileged over others— economically, politically, religiously, or otherwise? In many societies (such as England during the age of conquest), age, gender, race, class, or wealth constitute the basis for dominance or oppression; in others (such as the Tasaday of Mindanao, prior to contact), individuals are essentially equal in power. Is the society's relationship with its natural environment ecologically sustainable? Are individuals encouraged to discover their own uniqueness and to express themselves freely?

If our hearts are engaged in the search for values as thoroughly as our minds are, say the culture ecologists, we learn ever more passionately to value autonomy over oppression; love over fear; compassion over indifference and greed; community over unbridled individualism; sustainability over power. We may debate the degree to which such values are truly innate and universal, and may be surprised to discover unfamiliar ways in which these values can be exemplified. Nevertheless, they are increasingly real and significant to us, the more we ponder and act on them.

The cultural relativist makes an important point: that every culture is really a collection of individual human beings with unique temperaments, interests, struggles, and talents, which blanket statements about "culture" tend to gloss over. This point needs continually to be borne in mind, if we choose to pursue the discovery and clarification of transcultural values. If we are to follow the culture-ecologist path, our object should not be merely to judge one culture as better or worse than another, but to search for signs of health or infirmity, and to see what specific patterns of collective action tend to lead toward further integration or disintegration. And we should not fall into the trap of viewing any culture as a monolithic entity, but always keep in mind the fact that within each society there may be individuals or sectors with interests quite different from those of the dominant group.

The judgmental attitudes that the relativist warns against tend to arise when anthropologists casts their critical gaze only at cultures other than their own. But anthropology's real payoff comes when we include our own culture in the critical process. And here—in the understanding and improvement of our own social context—is where the culture ecologists (among whom I include myself) hope to make a contribution. But in doing so, we must be prepared for the possibility that we may make some disturbing discoveries and encounter fierce resistance.

CIVILIZATION IN PERSPECTIVE

The study of patterns in anthropology quickly reveals examples of what appear to be pathologies of culture. Among gatherers or hunters, one often finds instances of ritual warfare—that is, of groups of angry men lobbing spears or shooting arrows at one another. There are also examples of shamanic sorcery, such as the bone pointing of the Australian Aboriginal "clever men" (for some reason it seems that, even in these simple societies, men are more inclined to violence than women). Many subsistence horticultural societies have instituted human sacrifice in one form or another. This seems to have been the case in the ancient Goddess-worshiping Near East (though the extent of the practice is disputed by a few feminist historians), and it was still so among the Pawnee of Nebraska until the 1830s and in New Guinea until the middle of this century. The Pawnee, for example, occasionally offered up a maiden from a neighboring tribe, killing her after months of preparatory ceremony. They did this once every few years when the Morning Star was particularly bright. While the practice was a grisly one, the actual number of victims was small.

But as we survey the historical and ethnographic scene, we come to a very few cultures that have pathological symptoms completely out of proportion to all others; ones in which the ritual sacrifice of an individual now and then becomes the impersonal slaughter of thousands or millions; ones in which the mystifying power of a local shaman expands into the totalitarian repression of the many by the few on a continent-wide or even larger scale. The cultures we are talking about have a variety of languages, geographic origins, and customs, but they have a great deal in common structurally, and there is a convenient term for the structure they share: *civilization*.

In previous chapters we have viewed civilization as a complex of social and technical innovations centering on the accumulation and unequal distribution of surpluses, the division of labor, the progressively intensified and technologically mediated exploitation of nature, and the conquest and enslavement of peripheral peoples. This, of course, is not a description of some distant and exotic social system, but of the day-to-day reality in which we find ourselves being born, living, struggling, and dying.

The point in looking at civilization critically—as if from the outside, as we're doing here—is to begin to see why it is the way it is, and to help us envision alternatives. We are accustomed to a mindset that defends and promotes civilization in countless ways. But the comparative study of cultures tends to cut through those arguments.

First, the pathologies of civilization are not (as we are so often told) temporary aberrations, quirks that further cultural "evolution" or "progress" will resolve. They are part and parcel of the phenomenon, nowhere absent, and they are never seen (except sometimes in a vaguely analogous, vestigial way) in subsistence modes of social organization. They were as characteristic of the imperial Chinese or the classical Mayan or ancient Egyptian cultures as they are of late twentieth-century America, and vice versa. In each instance we see the simultaneous creation of wealth and poverty, the deliberate destruction of peripheral tribal cultures, and the reckless abuse of the natural environment. Who can avoid the sensation of *déjà vu* when reading the words of Seneca, the Roman statesman:

> How long shall we covet and oppress, enlarge our possessions, and account that too little for one man which was formerly enough for a nation? And our luxury is as insatiable as our avarice. Where's that lake, that sea, that forest, that spot of land that is not ransacked to gratify our palate? The very earth is burdened with our buildings; not

a river nor a mountain escapes us. . . . We are at war with all living creatures. . . .[1]

Wherever and whenever civilization occurs, the story is essentially the same. As anthropologist Stanley Diamond once put it, "Civilization originates in conquest abroad and repression at home. Each is an aspect of the other."[2] Whether in Angkor Wat or Teotihuacan or Rome or Babylon or London, its achievements are always "intended for the use and pleasure of the very few at the expense of the skill and labor of the many."[3] In the present case, the obscene wealth of the First World's elites is being obtained from the labor of billions of people in the Third World, and from the systematic expropriation of their resources, with corporations serving as the instruments of pillage, and national governments legitimizing and defending the proceedings.

Second, the inequality and violence we see in the world today are not due just to universal qualities of human nature that must be restrained by law, or refined or circumvented altogether by religion and spirituality. Rather, they are conditions that are in large measure fostered by specific social arrangements.

We often tend to assume that greed and acquisitiveness are part of human nature, but people in traditional societies seem peculiarly deficient in these qualities. Property—other than a few simple tools—is unknown among food gathering peoples such as the San (Bushmen) of southern Africa and the Australian Aboriginals. The idea of an individual "owning" land is so foreign to them that in some cases it has taken generations for the idea even to be intelligible. Food is shared equally; indeed, among the San, the hunter always eats last. The San also frown upon trade: they may barter with other cultures for tobacco or trinkets, but among themselves, "when given a gift one is obliged to return the favor, but only after a reasonable time elapses, as an immediate reciprocal gift would smack of trade."[4]

While the institution of law seems to have as its goal the amelioration of injustice, as it actually develops within civilization, law effectively serves as a tool of repression. Noncivilized societies do not have written laws; they rely instead on customs for the redress of wrongs and grievances. The kin unit serves as plaintiff, judge, jury, and defendant. If an instance of violence or bad feeling disrupts the community, it is understood that the whole community shares responsibility and must ritually renew its proper relation to the cosmos at large. This communal commitment to the maintenance of social harmony, rather than undermining the individual's sense of responsibility, undergirds and nourishes it. Robert S. Rattray noted in the 1920s, with respect to the Ashanti of West Africa, "The Ashanti's idea of what we term moral responsibility for his actions must surely have been more developed than in peoples where individualism is the order of the day."[5]

Law and crime come into being simultaneously, and the earliest laws seem to have dealt with a census-tax-conscription system whereby the state asserted its authority over the individual, and with various forms of what we today call the "protection racket." In Dahomey, for example, the king formerly encouraged and licensed prostitution; prices were set by civil decree and the proceeds taxed heavily. Murder and suicide became state crimes because they deprived the state of its property—the human individual. Today, legal systems in the most advanced civilized democracies strive to ensure civil rights, which are meant to compensate for the loss of autonomy suffered by the individual in the imposition of civil law during earlier, cruder phases of civilization. "Procedure," as Stanley Diamond points out, has become "the individual's last line of defense in contemporary civilization, wherein all other associations to which he may belong [are] subordinate to the state."

Religion, in civilization, often likewise becomes a tool of repression and conquest. As I show in more detail in chapter 9, Christianity—which began as a primitivist protest against the Roman state—has been transformed into the most imperialistic religion ever known, usually (except in the case of the renegade "liberation" ministries) faithfully serving the interests of the rich over those of the poor. In primal cultures, human beings are not believed to be born in sin and to exist somehow apart from and above nature, but to be part of the natural world and inherently good. Where human nature was something to be cultivated rather than repressed, spirituality tended to be more an exploration of Mysteries than an escape from meaninglessness, which appears to be one of its main functions today.

A SOCIAL CANCER

Am I overstating the case against civilization? Should we not at least mention civilization's good side?

There are, after all, many civilized people who are seeking to cure the ills of poverty and violence. Indeed, every civilization has had its pacifists, environmentalists, and human rights activists. A few of these have even become famous as founders of world religions. But they were and are swimming against the current. One can speculate, for example, what might have happened if Mahatma Gandhi's vision of India's return to self-sufficient village culture had taken hold; but speculate one must, because India's history as a modern state has taken a very different course—one determined by foreign trade and investment, centralized state control, and the adoption of new technologies of production and transport which have had the effect of uprooting indigenous enterprise.

How about civilization's great artistic achievements? Most of us are accustomed to thinking of civilization as synonymous with high culture, and few would deny that the works of our greatest artists and musicians are worthy of admiration. However, as we come to understand better the nature of creativity, we begin to appreciate the actual human cost of artistic glory. Psychological studies show that many intensely creative people suffer from depression, dissociation, and even multiple personality disorder—conditions often linked with childhood abuse. One wonders whether the spectacular careers of some of our creative geniuses may be analogous to the beautiful but tortured growth of a bonsai tree. In traditional societies everyone is an artist and everyone has access to the songs and designs of the tradition; the creative process is fully democratized. In civilized cultures, however, art is primarily for the enjoyment of the few, who determine standards of "taste" for everyone else. Today, for example, the art world is largely controlled by a few dozen multimillionaires who are themselves often incapable of doing anything more creative than buying and selling companies or paintings. "Good art" is whatever the wealthy cognoscenti are purchasing this season. Ironically, a few of our very best artists (such as Picasso and Gauguin) have both borrowed "primitive" motifs and expressed a longing for civilized people to return to the more universal and egalitarian patterns of creativity typical of tribal society.

And what of "progress"? This is a subject taken up in more detail in chapter 11, but it fairly begs to be discussed, at least in brief, in the present context. For many people, the ideas of civilization, progress, and evolution are inextricably linked. Yet Darwinian evolution—a tenuous enough explanation for change in the biological realm—is a poor metaphor for civilization's steep trajectory. Most species are extremely stable over millions of years, showing little or no variation. Then, rather suddenly, they become extinct, or a new one appears. The mechanisms are mysterious. This is a good metaphor for traditional cultures (similar long-term stability, similar mysterious origins and disappearances), but not for civilizations. A better metaphor for civilization is cancer—a growth that consumes the resources of the body and turns healthy cells into malignant ones. Like a cancer, civilization must continually spread and grow. It must find new resources to exploit, more people to enslave (or colonize or "develop"). Evolutionary theory may be helpless to *explain* this process, but civilized people naturally find the metaphor of evolution useful in *justifying* it. In Stanley Diamond's words, "As civilization accelerates, its proponents project their historical present as the progressive destiny of the entire human race."[6]

In fact, however, some of the very phenomena we most often identify with "progress" can be interpreted as both symptoms and agents of cultural disintegration. The invention of calendars and clocks arises from a perceived need to control the flow of experience, but results in the subjective sensation of never having enough time. The invention of numbers leads to abstraction, generality, and a loss of the particularity of lived experience—which defies quantification. The invention of money leads to the proliferation of values that have little to do with real human needs, and to the accumulation of surpluses entirely out of proportion to nature's ability to renew and replenish itself. And increasingly sophisticated methods for the measurement and manipulation of time, numbers, and money combine to facilitate the expansion of commerce and the transformation of nature and human lives into mere commodities.

If civilized people are to evaluate with any objectivity the conventional view that civilization itself is humanity's greatest cultural achievement, they must surely give some thought to what this achievement looks like to native peoples. For the latter are as keen at anthropological observations as any academic. In many cases, they believe that civilization typifies *the decline of culture that occurs just before a great world renewal*. The Hopi, for example, see the proliferation of sophisticated technologies of transport and communication as signs of the approaching end of what they call the Fourth World. Native traditions also suggest that, to one degree or another, *all* cultures are traumatized as the result of catastrophic events in the distant past that put an end to a universal paradisial age of harmony. The role of culture itself, they say, is to provide a stable framework for collective human existence in accordance with the instructions of the Creator, given our post-catastrophic, traumatized status.

❧

As we have seen, a healthy culture connects people to one another and to the land so as to maximize health and happiness from generation to generation. In a word, healthy culture is *sustainable*. It is also integral: Functions that exist in civilization as disjointed subjects of study and professional practice—the collection and transmission of knowledge, healing, spiritual beliefs and practices, the making of social policy, art, music, dance—are part of a seamless whole.

Our task in creating new, life-affirming cultures must be to reintegrate all these aspects of human interest and endeavor. Somehow we must bring together what has been torn asunder.

Part II explores the arts, economics, governance, spirituality, and knowledge systems as gateways to a deeper understanding of how human culture has disintegrated, and how we may go about making it whole again.

PART II

THE ANATOMY

OF CULTURAL

RENEWAL

7 | THE ARTS: BRINGING SPIRIT DOWN TO EARTH

It don't mean a thing if it ain't got that swing.
—DUKE ELLINGTON

 A FEW YEARS AGO, three friends and I visited Pasadena's Southwest Museum, which is devoted entirely to Native American art and artifacts. One member of our party, a Cree pipe carrier, guided us through the displays with such a wealth of enthusiasm and first-hand knowledge that we were able to connect viscerally (not just visually) with the exhibited artifacts; we had the sense of knowing the people who made them. These feeling connections turned this into the most meaningful museum experience I can remember. That day I learned a great deal not only about Native American cultures, but about my own enculturation as well.

Scattered among the beaded moccasins, sacred pipes, stone *metatés*, and decorated deerskins, were a few items of European manufacture—things that had been traded to the Indians and used by them. These factory-made goods struck obviously discordant notes. Not only did they look out of place, they also *felt* different and alien. How to describe this difference? Perhaps the adjective that best describes the feeling these objects emanated is—*dead*.

Simply to say that the two groups of artifacts were from dissimilar cultures may explain why this difference of feeling arose, but it does little to convey its quality or depth. The thought cannot fully account for the feeling.

The momentary sensations I had while standing and looking at those Native American and European-American artifacts were as enlightening as any idea, but of an entirely different quality; indeed, they initiated a series of revelatory thoughts that are still unfolding as I write. These thoughts have helped me understand the feelings that gave rise to them, but they are clearly distinct from the feelings themselves.

The following, which was partly inspired by the experience I've just described, is both an exercise in what might be called sensual archaeology and a meditation on the reciprocal relationship between the arts and the rest of the elements that make up human culture.

ABORIGINAL VS. CIVILIZED ART

Both the factory goods and the Native American artifacts we saw that day in Pasadena said plenty about the people who made them. The former were mostly metal and felt cold (even though we didn't actually touch them). They had been produced in great numbers with identical, interchangeable parts, in factories, by people who worked because they needed the money. These objects—mostly guns and knives—seemed joyless.

The Native American artifacts, by contrast, still radiated the warmth of life even though their makers were long gone. They were all hand-made, and even many of the weapons were playfully decorated with animal images and geometric symbols. These objects were simple and functional, yet each— whether a cooking tool, a hunting bow, or a bit of jewelry—was fashioned with care and was one-of-a-kind. Each resonated with what can only be called a spiritual presence.

Every culture is an integrated whole, and its arts, its child-rearing practices, and its covenant with nature are merely expressions of a fundamental cultural identity. That day at the Southwest Museum, we were apprehending two cultures' identities through their artifacts in much the way a graphologist reads a personality from a sample of handwriting.

The artifacts spoke volumes about these cultures' attitudes toward art.

In civilized society, the artist is a specialist who—depending on her or his success—may be regarded as anything from a useless deadbeat or a dangerous criminal to a godlike genius. In aboriginal society, everyone is an artist. This democratization of art may result in an (apparent) absence of Leonardos, Michelangelos, and Georgia O'Keefes, but it also implies a more universal sense of participation in the processes of creation.

The purpose of art is different in aboriginal and civilized societies: in the former, art is an expression not of innovation, but of continuity; an expression not of an attempt to set oneself apart as special, but of a recognition of the interconnectedness of all life.

In civilized society, fine art, handcraft, and the design and manufacture of mass-produced consumer products constitute distinct categories of creative endeavor. A Ferrari Testarossa, a Chippendale chair, and a Goya painting are all art, but in very different senses of the term. In aboriginal society—regardless of differences in geography, language, and period—there are really only two categories of art: the everyday kind, and secret-sacred designs and objects for ceremonial purposes. Mundane creations are sacred too, in that they often incorporate religious symbols and themes (I should note, however, that few tribal societies have a word for "religion" as a category separate from the rest of human experience). But ceremonial objects are believed to carry a special power that should not be approached by the uninitiated. The degree of seriousness with which indigenous peoples regard their ceremonial art was driven home to me during a trip to Australia, where I learned that an important anthropology text had been withdrawn from publication due to Aboriginal protests about its inclusion of photographs of forbidden designs and objects. The designs, which I viewed in a rare copy of the controversial book in a private collection, have no obvious significance to Europeans. But for the Aboriginals, the publication of these symbols would have imperiled their ability to continue their traditional initiation rites, which are as central to their culture as their language and food gathering methods.

In civilized industrial society, great art goes to the highest bidder. Aboriginal art was not for sale, because in most indigenous societies there simply was no money. Everyday art could be traded, but not the secret-sacred objects. These were entrusted to caretakers—initiates of high degree who accepted their responsibility with utmost gravity.

It is possible to draw analogies between aboriginal secret-sacred art and civilized fine art; between aboriginal everyday art and civilized manufacturing and industrial or advertising design. Like the initiate in tribal society, the civilized fine artist encapsulates meanings that guide not only the aesthetic, but the spiritual and intellectual unfoldment of society. The goal of the artist is to help us *see* the world in a new way. As Henri Matisse once wrote, "To see is itself a creative operation, requiring an effort. Everything we see in our daily life is more or less distorted by acquired habits. . . . The effort needed to see things without distortion takes something very like courage."[1] On the other hand, the industrial designer and manufacturer, like the everyday artisan in tribal society, makes images and objects—machines, utensils, tools, and packaging—for practical consumption, with little regard for "higher" motives.

Up to a point, these analogies are useful. But they are intellectual exercises that in the end only tend to obscure feeling differences. While there may be some analogical connection between the making of aboriginal secret-sacred art and civilized fine art, they are often utterly alien species of creative act. The civilized artist paints or sculpts for an economic elite class capable of affording the luxury of rare paintings or sculptures. Success (which, in the modern art world, usually means *economic* success) requires innovation and originality—which often in turn require gaining notoriety by finding and breaking rules. But this iconoclastic process can only go on until there are no rules left to break; then the artist must recycle older artistic forms (hence the retro-orientation of "postmodernism"). In contrast, the aboriginal initiate works not for an economic elite, but for fellow initiates; the purpose is not to shatter tradition, but to fulfill it; and originality is subordinated to the overall imperative of ritually strengthening and articulating the connections that bind together individual, society, nature, and cosmos. For example, as anthropologist Paul Taçon has noted, Australian Aboriginal cave drawings of ancestral beings "aided the discussion of complicated matters, such as notions about life and death and reincarnation."[2]

Likewise, while one can functionally equate tribal handcraft and industrial manufacture, these products (as we have already noted) could hardly be more distinct. The tribal artisan makes one-of-a-kind objects and decorations for personal use, while the advertising artist, manufacturer, or industrial designer aims to make objects or images for a mass market. One kind of object is an extension of the self; the other often tends to be an external prop for a self that is empty and perpetually hungry. Hence the insatiable desire of consumers for ever more manufactured products—a desire that is, of course, deliberately stoked at every opportunity by the makers and advertisers of these goods. In tribal society, the act of purposefully encouraging the proliferation of wants among one's kin would be considered cruel and foolish; in civilized industrial society, it is an economic necessity.

It is these distinctions—not the rationalized analogies—that the feelings capture.

MUSIC AND THE PROFESSIONALIZATION OF THE ARTS

The same sort of transformation that has occurred in the visual arts, leading from aboriginal handcraft to the urban art gallery or industrial design studio, can be heard and felt in the world of music as well.

When we think of the word *musician*, a famous opera singer, rock star, classical instrumentalist, or jazz stylist is likely to come to mind. Only a small percentage of us tend to think of *ourselves* as musicians. But why so? It is only natural to admire the extraordinary talent and self-discipline of a great musical performer. But an increasing percentage of us tend to forego the immense pleasure of *making* music (as opposed merely to listening to it) simply because we think we're not good enough. This idea that only some of us are competent to make music likely got its start early on in the development of civilization.

One of the primary innovations of the ancient Sumerians was the full-time division of labor. In preagricultural communities, everyone was involved in the entire round of life-sustaining and celebratory activities (though, as we have seen, there was some gender-specific work, such as hunting for men and plant gathering for women). But when people began to cultivate the soil and to live in towns, some decided—or were forced—to become full-time farmers while others became soldiers, administrators, kings, cooks, scribes, artists, or musicians. By the time of the Egyptian pharaohs, professional musicians were a fixture of the royal court, providing songs for every occasion.

Down through the centuries, specialization and professionalism have permitted the development of extraordinary degrees of ability on the part of the comparatively few women and men who have chosen to make their living as performing artists. In our own century, we have seen the emergence of such stellar performers as Jascha Heifetz, Billie Holiday, and Jimi Hendrix. Millions of lives have been lit by the glow of such talents. But in most civilizations, professional or formal music has existed primarily for the enjoyment of wealthy elites (we still distinguish between "high brow" and "low brow" music), and the rigors of professionalism often discourage participation by the amateur (from the Latin *amare*, "to love," referring to one who is motivated purely by devotion to an art). When standards become so high that years of intense study are required in order to approach the performance levels to which audiences have become accustomed, few young people choose to make the investment of time and effort required in order to become musicians.

Like professionalism, the invention of musical notation has been somewhat a mixed blessing. The *writing* of music allowed composers to create longer and more complex pieces that could be reproduced by performers in remote places and in succeeding generations. Because of musical notation, we today can hear and enjoy the music of Bach, Mendelssohn, and Schubert.

But putting music on paper also tended to restrict the imaginations of performers, who increasingly were expected neither to compose nor to improvise on the spot, but simply to provide an accurate reading of a printed score.

In our century, the development of audio recording technologies has allowed us to hear spectacular musical performances at the touch of a button, any time we choose. And so we have come to *expect* this level of brilliance and convenience. As a result, recorded music is often used in situations where live performers formerly were hired, and local musicians often go begging for work.

All of these developments have led us away from patterns of music making that have always existed in simple, traditional societies, in which everyone knows the melodies, rhythms, dances, and chants of the culture and freely improvises on them; and in which music is as much a part of life as food and sleep. In Native American, African, and other tribal societies, women, men, and children have the daily opportunity to share in the joys of singing, drumming, and dancing. For example, people in West African villages drum and dance together nightly; the intricate, intense rhythms—learned through long practice and apprenticeship—induce a collective ecstasy, strengthening ties not only among individuals but between the community as a whole and the spirit world. Contrast this with the experience of a typical commuter listening to the car CD player on her way to work: in the latter instance, music becomes a consumer product to be enjoyed or appreciated not just individually, but privately. Our hypothetical commuter may even be listening to West African drum music—but even then, the experience remains voyeuristic and passive.

During the last century or so, increasing numbers of Europeans and Americans have rebelled against the exclusivity and sterility of formal, professional music by dipping back into their own hereditary tribal traditions, or by borrowing from others. In Europe, the ethnographic study of traditional music inspired composers Zoltan Kodaly and Bela Bartok to imbue their classical music with tribal vitality and intensity. In America, the imported music of Africa—an unintended byproduct of the slave trade—gave birth to several entirely new idioms ranging from gospel to ragtime, jazz, blues, and rock 'n' roll. Indeed, most of the American popular music of the twentieth century can be said to trace at least part of its ancestry to African tribal roots. Beginning in the 1950s, a folk music revival swept America, inspiring millions of amateurs to teach themselves to play the guitar and sing. In the 1960s, jazz musicians began to explore indigenous peoples' instruments, rhythms, melodies, and performance styles. And in the 1980s, "world music" became a force in the recording industry, with the traditional songs of Pacific islanders, Africans, Asians, ethnic Europeans, and Native Americans drawing ever-growing listening audiences. Even the country and western music of Nashville and Branson can be seen as a half-conscious attempt to redemocratize musical composition and performance.

ENSOULED CREATION VERSUS MANUFACTURED STUFF

The arts are about feeling. They speak to aspects of the human personality and soul that cannot be reached by any other means. They are integral to a whole cultural experience.

Thus if we wish to understand an industrial civilization's arts and artifacts, we must see them in the context of its technology, social relations, politics, economics, and all the other roots and limbs of the totality that is culture. We can explore, for example, the politics, economics, and sociology of art or music. But we can also use our artistic, or feeling sensibility to evaluate the rest of culture: How does it *feel* to live in tract housing, to pilot a car through freeway traffic to a featureless building where one works for eight hours in a fluorescent-lit office, to drive home and sit in front of an electronic entertainment machine and eat overcooked, denatured food laced with preservatives and pesticides and grown by oppressed peasants in a devastated Third-World country? Perhaps those feelings, if acknowledged and integrated, would tell us as much as any conceivable scientific study.

So: *How does* industrial civilization feel? Perhaps an enterprising sociologist will conduct a survey in order to arrive at an "objective" answer. My own response to the question would be: *It doesn't.* For the most part, we don't *want* to feel, so we numb ourselves with television and alcohol.

No wonder so many modern fine artists have produced bafflingly violent, stark, tortured images. The slick "pop" art of Andy Warhol, for example, is meant merely to emphasize to the viewer the soullessness of the advertising images we all have internalized as members of a commercial consumer society. The denatured, flat geometrical shapes of Piet Mondrian reveal an abstract, hyperintellectual internal aesthetic landscape conditioned by the numbingly relentless right angles of modern urban architecture. And Willem de Kooning's chaotic and restlessly energetic paintings of the human form suggest an image of the civilized artist as a caged animal lashing out at the canvas as though it offered some means of escape.

And it is no wonder that many people find amateur music making or handcraft a path to the deeper self. It cuts through one of the great ironies of our age—which is that while we often accuse ourselves and our culture of being too materialistic, we have in fact utterly lost touch with the rhythms, textures, and smells that are the foundation of sensate life.

If homemade art is a personal spiritual path back to authentic feeling, it is also a revolutionary protest against the factory—the centralized, automated workplace, the defining innovation of the industrial system.

We all know the benefits of factories. They make things efficiently and in abundance. Because of factories, we in the "developed" countries live like kings and queens, with the robotic equivalent of scores of slaves. Just fire up the Ford or Toyota or Mercedes, or plug in the vacuum cleaner, dishwasher, or microwave oven, and you have at your fingertips power that would humble a pharaoh.

But it is the factory, as much as any other single invention or institution, that has cut off our ability to feel. By dividing the creative act into discrete steps and stages and apportioning these to separate workers and machines, factory production robs us of the direct experience of creation—which is a process with a beginning, middle, and end. On an assembly line, making cars or toasters or computers, we participate in only a fragment of the creative process. The factory worker—who may spend the entirety of her workday, year in and year out, soldering electronic components in a factory that makes, let us say, television sets—therefore naturally tends to feel little responsibility for that process as a whole. After all, it is not she who decides what chemicals to use to wash the circuit boards she is assembling. And so she can hardly be held responsible for the pollution generated by the factory in which she is employed; nor can she feel an undiluted sense of pride in the completed TV sets, which she had no part in designing and whose internal operation she only vaguely understands. (In a nation of factories the soldier or laborer can often be excused for crimes if he was "only following orders." Such an excuse is inconceivable in aboriginal society.)

The factory also alienates us from materials. Find a pharmacopaeia from the 1920s: Nearly all of the medicines it lists are made from plants, most of which were familiar to the average person at the time. Today drugs are made from synthesized chemicals; only a few specialized chemists and the workers at drug laboratories know what goes into them. When we become accustomed to manufactured products made not by ourselves but by people we don't know, and in ways we don't understand, we can no longer *feel* the materials of our environment in their raw state, nor can we understand and take responsibility for the transformations they have undergone. The finished product (with its dollar price to the consumer, and its profit or loss—the "bottom line"—to the manufacturer) looms larger than the actual process of creation, and so ends tend to justify means. We therefore find it perfectly acceptable to incorporate noxious materials into everyday products, to discard mountains of waste, and to pollute water, air, and soil—acceptable precisely to the degree that we are willing to numb our feelings.

The factory can make so many things so quickly that we find ourselves surrounded with piles of consumer products that we ourselves would never have had the time or resources to make. This seems like a good thing until it's time to move house, when we realize just how much stuff we've accumulated—boxes and crates and truckloads of stuff, most of it rarely used. We have gradually become convinced that we need all this stuff: A dozen or so electrical gadgets for the kitchen. Entertainment machines. Furniture. Storage bins to put stuff in. And of course we also need more money to pay for our stuff; but it takes time to make all that money, so we seldom have enough time left over to really enjoy or even properly maintain the stuff we have. Meanwhile, we hear on the news (via one of our entertainment machines) that we are running out of raw materials and places to bury worn-out stuff.

But what does all our stuff really mean to us? What joy can we take in an object produced in a factory by people (or robots) we've never met, bought with intrinsically valueless monetary symbols? Does any of this stuff make us better parents, friends, or neighbors? Does it make us happier in the long run? Does it help us know our own soul?

THE POWER OF HANDCRAFT

To make something from basic materials and with basic tools, to sing and dance, to heal oneself and others with song, touch, and herbs, and to grow and prepare the simplest foods (or better, to find and gather wild, edible plants) are ways to reclaim both the bodily world of feeling and the inner world of the soul. They are also sure paths to personal responsibility and self-esteem—which is not to be confused with the inflated self-image of the general, the politician, or the industrialist.

A lifestyle devoid of direct, manual creativity is spiritual poison. Yet more and more of us spend our days shuffling papers, accounting, computing, speculating, managing, soldiering—or, worst of all perhaps, growing up in poverty without even these skills.

True, working manually with factory-made objects can offer some of the satisfaction of handcraft. Some people get satisfaction from tinkering with sewing machines or refurbishing old Studebakers. But the simpler and more natural the materials, the more potentially enriching the experience. Back in the 1950s—long before the dawn of the compact disc—it was common for hobbyists to build their own hi-fi systems from kits, assembling the miscellaneous vacuum tubes, resistors, capacitors, knobs, and speakers on tables in their basements, learning the basic principles of electronics as they went. Now, with modern printed circuit boards, even the talented hobbyist can do little more than plug together automated factory-assembled modules.

I get a certain amount of satisfaction from writing on my computer (as I am doing now), and yet I've taken to doing my correspondence with an old fountain pen. The computer speeds the process, but sometimes the process itself is the thing—the means and end are identical—in which case speed and efficiency can only diminish the quality of the experience. I'm more present in my handwritten letters, even when they look a little messy or take longer to write.

THE SPIRITUALITY OF LIMITS

To work with one's hands is to accept the limitations of materials. It is also to accept the limitations of our environments and of our own humanness—of our own bodies.

When we stop working with our hands, we get into our heads. If we do this too much, then feeling atrophies and thought becomes unbalanced.

The mind is a powerful faculty: it can imagine things that are only potential or even physically impossible. It can generalize. Through our minds, we can contact the infinite. And our desire and ability to escape material restraints and to overleap the particular is part of what makes us human. Indeed, we usually associate spirituality with the infinite, with transcendence, and with general principles such as truth, light, and love.

And yet life as we actually live it from day to day is neither infinite nor general; it is limited and specific. Without denying the value of transcendence, I would nevertheless argue that there is a side to spirituality that aboriginal peoples knew but that we in the civilized world studiously ignore: the spirituality of limits, and of particularity as opposed to generality.

Abstraction and generality seem to flourish alongside civilization; primal peoples prefer to remain rooted in existential reality. Anthropologist Franz Boas wrote: "Discourses on qualities without connection with the object to which the qualities belong, or of activities or states disconnected from the idea of the actor or the subject being in a certain state, will hardly occur in primitive speech. Thus the Indian will not speak of goodness as such, although he may very well speak of the goodness of a person."[3] Stanley Diamond likewise notes that the Anaguta of the High Nigerian Plateau "never count in the abstract but count only with reference to concrete things or people. . . . Yet the Anaguta are fully capable of grasping number unrelated to particular objects. But they do not deify or reify number; there is no occasion for doing so in their society, and the idea seems meaningless to them."[4]

By overleaping the particular, the civilized mathematician, philosopher, or scientist gains power—and at the same time creates signs without referents. And so we talk about "the environment" without reference to *particular* trees, streams, and animals. We talk about "the labor market" without reference to the actual work experience of specific people. We use our categories and generalities to deal with vast numbers of people, places, and things; we combine, divide, and conquer. We succeed thereby in producing immense wealth and administering giant bureaucracies. But for whose benefit?

As an example of how the general sometimes betrays the particular, consider our increasing reliance on the Gross Domestic Product—an aggregate statistic summarizing the total economic activity in the country. Political leaders routinely make decisions so as to optimize the GDP, and these decisions eventually affect individual people and specific places. In order to arrive at a simple number (let us say, a GDP growth of three percentage points per year), a universe of detail must be sacrificed. Data must be gathered according to certain rules (e.g., the rule that monetary expenditures count, but other kinds of economic activity don't), and evaluated according certain assumptions (e.g., the assumption that economic growth is inherently good and can or should continue indefinitely). But in the real world, these rules and assumptions can generate absurdities. For example, because natural disasters result in increased monetary expenditures (for cleanup and the replacement of damaged property), they are good for the GDP. The same is true of wars. And so wars sometimes become as much a matter of economic expediency as of political strategy. (In 1914 the United States was in a serious recession, but by the next year war orders from England had stimulated the economy and, in the words of Richard Hofstadter, "America became bound up with the Allies in a fateful union of war and prosperity.") Ultimately, the horrible deaths of millions of people may be rationalized as being "good for business."[5]

The particularities and limits of our environment, of our materials, and of our own humanness establish a frame within which moral action and authentic creation are possible. When we pursue transcendence without acknowledging our limits, we lose touch with reality. We convince ourselves that somehow we can always have more—immortality in the flesh, perhaps, or unlimited growth. We act as though we had infinite resources and infinite time, or as though the world could support an infinitely large human population. We strain at the gates of heaven and fall into a pit. We reach for infinity and attain zero.

Now, it could be objected that we as a species have already transcended many apparent limits. We can fly, we've gone to the Moon, we've conquered diseases. Isn't the transcendence of limitation the very essence of the human project? I would answer: Not quite. It is half of it; my point is that we've missed the other half, which is the ability to make the most of what we already have—our bodies, our personal relationships, the plants, animals, and soil of our immediate environment. If transcendence is the height of our experience, the ability to work within limits is its depth.

The real essence of wisdom is neither transcendence nor limitation *per se*; it is balance—knowing when to challenge and when to honor boundaries. Our problem is that we have gotten out of balance and lost the knowledge of how to maintain our equilibrium. One of the symptoms of this loss of balance, it seems to me, is the generation by a society of a class of people who are "above" working with their hands. This is how bureaucracy kills spirit.

At their best, the arts help us relearn the importance of simplicity and of limits, and aid us to regain the ability to feel. The arts thus have a central role to play in the renewal of culture. But conversely it is also true that it is only by bringing the rest of culture—our economics, patterns of governance, and technologies—back to a human scale that we can restore the arts to their former life-giving functions. Then, perhaps, we may once again know the joy of singing and dancing together as communities, and of using tools full of soul.

8 | ECONOMICS: IS MONEY EVIL?

It seems that the other cultures don't see trees. They see money.

—GWAGANAD, A HAIDA WOMAN OF HAADA GWAII (THE QUEEN CHARLOTTE ISLANDS), TESTIFYING IN 1985 BEFORE THE SUPREME COURT OF BRITISH COLUMBIA IN THE MATTER OF THE APPLICATION BY FRANK BEBAN LOGGING AND WESTERN FOREST PRODUCTS LTD. FOR AN INJUNCTION TO PROHIBIT THE HAIDA FROM PICKETING LOGGING ROADS ON LYELL ISLAND, SOUTH MORESBY.

 ON THE FACE OF IT, the question seems absurd. We in the modern world need money in order to survive. It is almost as necessary as food, water, or air. When I ask my friends whether money might be evil, many look at me with a mixture of surprise and pity. They tell me that money is either good (in the sense that the more you have of it, the better) or neutral (in that its effects depend on the purposes for which it is used). It would be crazy, they tell me, to think differently.

From the perspective of people living in an industrialized country in the late twentieth century, this attitude is logical, obvious, even necessary. Maybe it *is* crazy to think differently. However, I'm not asking the question as a test of personal morality, but as a matter of cultural inquiry. Money, after all, is a cultural phenomenon, not a biologically innate feature of human existence.

Not all societies have used money—far from it. In *The Story of Money*, Norman Angell wrote:

> There have been prosperous and orderly forms of society into which money practically did not enter, into which indeed neither barter nor exchange entered. The feudal chieftainship, the medieval manor, the monastery, the pueblo, and other vaster and more complex elaborations . . . are outstanding types of a form of social organization which might be described as an enlargement of the household, operating by what some writers have called the "natural" economy as distinct from the money economy; societies often highly complex in their division of labor, in which neither money nor exchange nor barter entered any more than it need into the relationships between members of a family.[1]

Moneyless societies include all gathering or hunting cultures and nearly all gardening-based cultures. Even at their height, the Egyptian, Incan, and early Chinese civilizations were virtually moneyless. While a medium of exchange and even a simple form of banking may have existed in Egypt, for example, these were for the exclusive use of a small privileged class; they rarely entered into the lives of the vast majority of people.

In most cultures that *have* had money, historically speaking, it has been used primarily for luxuries; the basic necessities—food and shelter—were freely available to everyone. The horticultural societies of the Pacific islands once used porpoise teeth, whale teeth, feathers, stones, and shells as money, but it was good only for certain purposes—fines, penalties, contributions to feasts, fees in secret societies, and payment for wives. It is only in certain urban centers like ancient Athens and Rome, in later Imperial China, and in the modern industrialized world that the basic necessities of life, and human labor (in many cases including human beings themselves), have come to be evaluated, bought, and sold.

It is in this broad cultural sense and context that I ask whether money is good, neutral, or evil.

IT'S ONLY A TOOL

In order to arrive at an answer, we first need to decide whether we believe that it is even *possible* for money to be evil. Money is essentially a kind of tool for the facilitation of trade, and according to some social philosophers, *all* tools are morally neutral; if this is so, my question makes no sense. Others say that each technology embodies certain values, and that one cannot use a tool without being changed by it. If that is true, then we can inquire whether this particular tool embodies values that somehow undermine the ultimate human good. Admittedly this line of thinking is problematic, because it requires that we define the nature of the ultimate human good so as to see whether it is being undermined. (I personally believe that whatever is *good* leads ultimately to life, happiness, and health; while *evil* leads ultimately to sickness, unhappiness, and death. But there are other valid definitions.) Still, even though it forces us to forge a path into the nebulous realm of values and ideals, it seems to me that the latter proposition—that technologies are *not* morally neutral—is closer to the truth. And while this view is hardly universally held, more and more people seem to be coming around to it.

Consider, for example, the tools known as guns. Currently, many Americans favor increased legal controls on the sale of guns, apparently because they believe that guns are inherently destructive. The National Rifle Association has for years argued that "guns don't kill people; people kill people"—in other words, that this (and presumably every) technology is good or neutral; only its misuse creates problems. But both logic and evidence contradict the NRA stance. Logically, since guns are designed to kill either people or animals (and handguns and assault rifles make questionable hunting weapons), then the more guns there are, the more people will likely be killed by them. Experience bears this out: America, which has far more guns in circulation than other countries, has far more deaths and injuries from them than do nations with stiffer controls. And it almost goes without saying that most of us tend to agree that the specter of multitudes of annual injuries and deaths from gunshot wounds does not jibe with our idea of the ultimate human good.

So with regard to guns, most people are beginning to take the view that it is possible for a technology to be inherently destructive; and that if it is shown to be so, then its use should be discouraged. But with regard to other technologies, many people still tend toward NRA logic. This is true for newer technologies like television, nuclear energy, and genetic engineering, and also for older and more basic ones like money. Most people apparently believe that the problems that seem to worsen as a society uses money increasingly (resource depletion, centralization of power, crime, and social disintegration) are the fault not of money itself, but of people.

People are naturally self-centered and greedy, but money is a neutral tool. If people can be educated to use money more wisely, then it can be a tool for great good.

Maybe. But what does the evidence say? Is it possible to explore the issue scientifically?

LET'S TRY AN EXPERIMENT...

Some scientists seem to believe that the only way to obtain truly objective data is to perform an animal study. I disagree. But despite my moral objections to animal experiments, I shall cite one. In *The Biology of Art*, zoologist Desmond Morris tells of introducing the "profit motive" to a group of apes. First he taught them to draw and paint. The apes enjoyed this; and some of their productions, according to Morris, were quite appealing. Once they had become established as artists, Morris began to "pay" the apes, rewarding their efforts with peanuts. Under this new reward system their artwork quickly deteriorated and they began making hasty scrawls just to trade for peanuts. "Money" in the form of peanuts didn't seem to make the apes happier; it made them more compulsive and servile.

Granted, Morris's experiment is hardly conclusive. After all, not everyone who works for a paycheck does shoddy work, and it isn't always possible to draw parallels between animal and human behavior. So, what happens to a human society when it adopts money?

Let us consider a contemporary example. Helena Norberg-Hodge, a linguist who has for nearly twenty years closely observed the process of economic development in the traditional society of Ladakh in northern India, is in as good a position as anybody to comment. In her eloquent book *Ancient Futures: Learning from Ladakh*, Norberg-Hodge describes the transformation of a Tibetan Buddhist agrarian village culture—from moneyless to mercantile—in a single generation.

What was Ladakh like in the old days? "In the traditional society," writes Norberg-Hodge, "villagers provided for their basic needs without money. They had developed skills that enabled them to grow barley at 12,000 feet and to manage yaks and other animals at even higher elevations. People knew how to build houses with their own hands from the materials in their immediate surroundings. The only thing they actually needed from outside the region was salt, for which they traded. They used money in only a limited way, mainly for luxuries."[2] And they seemed happy. "I have never met people who seem so healthy emotionally, so secure, as the Ladakhis."[3]

But by the mid-1970s Ladakh was beginning to change. The biggest town in the region, Leh, had been linked by road with the rest of India and trucks were beginning to carry in manufactured goods. Tourists were arriving. Money was changing hands. And the close-knit social fabric of the Ladakhis was starting to unravel. "For centuries, people worked as equals and friends—helping one another by turn. Now that there is paid labor during the harvest, the person paying the money wants to pay as little as possible, while the person receiving wants to have as much as possible. The money becomes a wedge between people, pushing them further and further apart."[4] The increasing use of money also increases the gap between rich and poor. "In the traditional economy there were differences in wealth, but its accumulation had natural limits. You could only care for so many yaks or store so many kilos of barley. Money, on the other hand, is easily stored in the bank. . . ."[5]

Norberg-Hodge quotes the Development Commissioner in Ladakh in 1981 as saying: "If Ladakh is ever going to be developed we have to figure out how to make these people greedy. You just can't motivate them otherwise."[6] This was still in the early years of "development." Norberg-Hodge writes: "When I first arrived in Ladakh the absence of greed was striking . . . people were not particularly interested in sacrificing their leisure or pleasure simply for material gain. In those years, tourists were perplexed when people refused to sell them things, no matter how much money they offered. Now, after several years of development, making money has become a major preoccupation. New needs have been created."[7]

Before, people were self-sufficient; now they feel the need for money, and young men go to the city to look for jobs. At the same time, traditional controls on population growth have broken down and the population is rising quickly. "In traditional Ladakh there was no such thing as unemployment. But in the modern sector there is now intense competition for a very limited number of paying jobs, principally in the government. As a result, unemployment is already a serious problem."[8]

Norberg-Hodge acknowledges that many things about old Ladakh were far from ideal: Communication with the outside world was limited, literacy rates were negligible, and infant mortality was higher and life expectancy lower than in the industrialized West. But, in the context of the traditional society, these were not serious problems.

If economic "development" has such disastrous consequences, why do people go along with it? Partly because they cannot see the long-term consequences. (A Kashmiri trader told Norberg-Hodge proudly, "Our vegetables are much better than the local ones. We have at least seven different chemicals on ours."⁹) They want to be like the rich American tourists who seem to have an endless supply of money and who never seem to work. They have no idea that America is polluted and crime-ridden and that Americans suffer from stress and degenerative diseases brought on by their fast-paced lifestyle. They have been told that their traditional way of life is inferior, that they are *poor*.

Norberg-Hodge believes that, on the whole, the new money economy is a disaster for the people of Ladakh because "the emphasis is not on human welfare but on commercial gain." And in her book she makes a powerful case that Ladakh is a microcosm of the world: The process of development is essentially similar throughout the Third World. Her statements regarding the impact of the money economy on the Ladakhis are widely confirmed by observers elsewhere. Anthropologist John Bodley writes that

> Careful examination of the acculturation data which compares . . . the former condition of self-sufficient tribal peoples with their condition following their incorporation into the world market economy, leads almost invariably to the conclusion that their standard of living is *lowered*, not raised, by economic progress—and often to a dramatic degree.[10]

Moreover, Norberg-Hodge points out that what is called "development" when it occurs in the Third World is the same as what Westerners call "economic growth" or "progress" at home, and as the result of it our culture is degenerating as surely as is the Ladakhis', and in similar ways.

WHAT'S MONEY FOR, ANYWAY?

If the purpose of guns is to kill, then what is money's purpose? And is it a purpose that serves the ultimate human good?

Money is a medium of exchange. It allows us to quantify value (an hour of your life is worth how many dollars?) and thereby to equate the value of fundamentally dissimilar things (such as an owl, a gram of plutonium, and an idea). It facilitates the trade—and therefore indirectly the extraction, production, or movement—of resources and manufactured goods. The more abstract the medium of exchange, the more these processes can be expanded and speeded up. If trade is based on the exchange of yaks, it can go only so far and so fast. Gold and silver offer somewhat more fluidity, but still imply a certain discipline. If trade is based on electronic impulses that can be flashed around the world in nanoseconds, its limits are virtually nonexistent.

This much is beyond argument. Now, is this a good purpose? Many people (principally those involved in trade) would say that it is. But others argue that we already extract far too many resources far too recklessly, and that many of our manufactured products are superfluous, polluting, or shoddy. As the Haida woman quoted at the beginning of this chapter put it: We don't see trees; we see dollars. In other words, some values resist quantification and therefore tend to be progressively discounted as a society becomes increasingly monetized. And these are often the most important values from the standpoint of what many people might define as the ultimate human good: values like truth, community, mutual understanding, and a sense of responsibility to future generations and to the rest of life.

SOME OBJECTIONS

When I've discussed among friends this way of looking at money, they repeatedly posed the same questions and objections, which have in turn prompted me to deepen my inquiry.

Does money have *to undermine "higher" human values? After all, many people use their money to help good causes.*

Assuming a society with money, it is true that some of its uses will be more beneficial than others. For example, it may be morally more ennobling to spend one's dollars protecting an old-growth forest from being logged than to invest them in shares of Louisiana-Pacific Corporation. Similarly, one can use a gun either to defend oneself against a burglar or to murder a cashier while one is robbing a convenience store. But that doesn't tell us whether, on the whole, our society would be better off with more or fewer guns. My question is whether, in sum, a culture is better off when more or less money changes hands. As the example of Ladakh demonstrates, a society with little money can get along quite well.

Isn't this whole discussion pointlessly unrealistic? What do you expect people to do—give all their money away and live on acorns? Besides, the purchase of this very book requires money: Aren't you a hypocrite?

Maybe. But as members of this society, our ability to refuse participation in its economic system is limited. Even self-sufficient food gatherers from the Amazon rainforest who, for one reason or another, find themselves in a modern city are forced to find ways to obtain money in order to survive. It *is* possible, as a homeless person, to live almost entirely on handouts. But that only shifts the economic responsibility for one's existence onto others' shoulders. Again, my purpose in this discussion is not to question personal morality so much as cultural conventions and tools.

We can, of course, individually lead our lives according to values *somewhat* different from those of the society as a whole and thereby push the envelope of possibility in certain directions. We can, for example, choose to build our own houses out of natural or recycled materials and feed ourselves as much as possible by way of organic, sustainable horticulture.

Meanwhile, I'm thankful for the money I receive: I treat it as a symbol of life energy and use it carefully. For those interested in transforming their relationship with money, I would recommend *Your Money Or Your Life*, by Joe Dominguez and Vicki Robin, which guides the reader through a process of self-evaluation regarding goals, priorities, and expenditures. The first step in escaping from addiction to an inherently destructive technology is to use it more consciously and deliberately.

But isn't it ridiculous even to think of eliminating money from the modern world? Wouldn't we all have to go back to living in the woods and wearing animal skins? Not many people are voluntarily going to do that, and those few who try invariably fail.

This is not necessarily a discussion of absolutes. Ladakh got along very well using money on a small scale, so long as the people kept to their self-sufficient, land-based traditions. It is only when money invades all departments of a culture that it tends to cause widespread and progressive social disintegration.

It is indeed difficult to swim against the current of our society, which flows so powerfully in the direction of economic growth and increased global trade. Sadly, some of the most vulnerable people in the present situation are culturally some of the most valuable—small-scale farmers who know and care for their land, and indigenous peoples with rich cultural traditions. Still, there are millions of others who are quietly withdrawing from participation in the mainstream of civilization and who together constitute an alternative stream flowing toward a life of Earth-centered values and simple pleasures. It is easy to underestimate the true significance of this movement of what Helena Norberg-Hodge calls "counter-development," which is occurring both in the industrialized countries and the Third

World. Norberg-Hodge's own Ladakh Project and International Society for Ecology and Culture (ISEC) are important sources of information, examples, and opportunities in this regard. ISEC study groups explore the economic, social, and historical roots of today's environmental crises, as well as practical, local, human-scale solutions.[11]

Frankly, I'm uncomfortable thinking of money as evil, no matter what you say. For one thing, by doing so, I may somehow be psychically repelling needed funds from my life and attracting poverty. Also, it makes me feel guilty for all the thousands of dollars I've made and spent. Why should I feel guilty for doing what I must in order to survive? Also, I've seen the entrenched habit of fighting evil turn good people into bitter, frustrated, and angry partisans.

Excellent points. Rather than hating the evil of money, which pits us against social trends far too vast for any one of us personally to reverse, perhaps we should concentrate instead on loving the good of a life lived close to our basic means of sustenance, a life of conscious mutual inter-dependence. Rather than spending our time weeping over our losses, we might better invest our energy in sowing fresh seed. We could, for example, join with friends to create a local currency that keeps wealth within the community and helps people have more direct control over their economic lives. I have more to say about this suggestion in a later chapter.

Meanwhile, it seems to me that it is essential to have a realistic view of the society in which we are living. I freely admit to using the word *evil* primarily for shock value. My aim in the present discussion has been to dissipate a particularly virulent form of cultural trance. To inquire whether money is a destructive force in our collective affairs is to raise the possibility of fundamental and deliberate cultural change. Until that possibility is considered, we are simply being swept along by forces we neither control nor understand. We must learn to ask the real costs of economic growth—in individual peace of mind, in cultural integrity, in our own health and that of the biosphere—and also to ask ourselves what we value most. For it is only when our values rest on firm biological and spiritual footings that we can know the true meaning of wealth. And it is only when the direction of social change is determined by reaffirmed innate values that the whole world can begin once again to share in the abundance that is our wild biotic birthright.

GOVERNANCE: FREEDOM, NECESSITY, AND POWER

[T]here is . . . little prospect of overcoming the defects of the power system by any attack that employs mass organization and mass efforts of persuasion; for these mass methods support the very system they attack. The changes that have so far been effective, and that give promise of further success, are those that have been initiated by animated individual minds, small groups, and local communities nibbling at the edges of the power structure by breaking routines and defying regulations. Such an attack seeks, not to capture the citadel of power, but to withdraw from it and quietly paralyze it. Once such initiatives become widespread, as they at last show signs of becoming, it will restore power and confident authority to its proper source: the human personality and the small face-to-face community.

—LEWIS MUMFORD

 JUST AS WE CIVILIZED PEOPLE take money for granted, we do the same with government. We equate lack of organized government with anarchy, and anarchy with destruction and chaos. Yet at the same time we distrust government and wish to retain as much individual freedom as possible. This deep tension between the apparently irreconcilable necessity of order and the longing for freedom is at the very heart of civilization.

In *Disinherited,* Dale Van Every wrote of the Native Americans that

The foundation principle of [their] government had always been the rejection of government. The freedom of the individual was regarded by practically all Indians north of Mexico as a canon infinitely more precious than the individual's duty to his community or nation. This anarchistic attitude ruled all behavior, beginning with the smallest social unit, the family. The Indian parent was constitutionally reluctant to discipline his children. Their every exhibition of self-will was accepted as a favorable indication of the development of maturing character.... [1]

It is perhaps an oversimplification to say that primitive government consisted of no government at all. But, as Van Every makes clear, the food gatherers, hunters, and simple horticulturists of pre-Columbian America (excepting the people of the Aztec, Mayan, and Incan empires) were relatively unaccustomed to coercion. And the same could be said of peoples living in similar conditions on other continents. It is only with the development of centralized and technologically sophisticated societies that the state's power over the individual comes to be seen as valid and necessary.

Among some groups, such as the Masai of Kenya and Tanzania, the functions of government were traditionally diffused among the adult male population. In other cases, certain positions of authority existed, but the privileges attached to them were very slight. Indeed, in some cases leadership was regarded more as a burden than an advantage. Regarding the Native American tribes, for example, Francis Huxley once wrote, "It is the business of a chief to be generous and to give what is asked of him. In some Indian tribes you can always tell the chief because he has the fewest possessions and wears the shabbiest ornaments. He has had to give away everything else."[2]

The transition from this sort of limited, provisional chieftainship to a more powerful and coercive system of kingship and the increasing centralization and stratification of the society as a whole appear to be closely related. If a king wishes to have greater authority, he must offer his followers some material advantage. If his followers are few, he may be able to provide this advantage from his own resources. But as the governed territory grows, the king must resort to tribute or (in monied societies) taxation, and the plunder of neighboring societies, to obtain the wealth needed to purchase the loyalty of followers. For example, the Alur chiefs of East Africa claimed the right hind leg of every animal caught, the tusks of elephants, and the skins of leopards and lions. Craftsmen were expected to contribute ironwork and woven baskets. In addition, according to Lucy Mair in *Primitive Government*,

Alur subjects worked for their chiefs. They hoed the chief's fields and built his houses and grain bins. Sometimes the people at a distance from the chief's place cultivated fields at their own villages, the produce of which was brought to him at the harvest. All this was done on such a small scale that there was no need for special officials to organize it.[3]

How are the king's subjects persuaded to participate in such an arrangement? Primarily by appeal to their desire for security. Not only is some of the collected tribute available for distribution should famine arise, but the king also promises to protect the people from external enemies in time of war or to expand the wealth of the kingdom through conquest. Moreover, where a chief or king enjoys considerable authority and privilege, these benefits are nearly always justified by myth. Very often local folk traditions say that the people originally lived in misery and squalor; it was the first king who taught the people agriculture, house building, writing, or whatever skills happen to exist in the society. This was supposedly the case with the first Chinese emperors, who were said to have imparted the arts of civilization to the people, who lived at the time like wild animals; and also with the Chwezi, a legendary dynasty of superhuman kings remembered by the Nyoro, Toro, and Nkole of western Uganda. These legendary monarchs are said to have taught the people even how to hunt.

The journey from voluntary to forced tribute is a short one, and eventually the state assumes the function of a protection racket. Rulers employ a special class of followers to inflict punishments on subjects who dare to withhold tribute. It is said, for example, that the Anuak nobles of East Africa once kept pet birds or animals in the hope that some child would injure one; the noble could then punish the offense by seizing the goods of the child's father. As Jeremy Bentham once put it, "Property and law are born together and die together."

Eventually the power of the king, and therefore of the state, becomes nearly absolute. Especially brutal examples seem to crop up in the early stages of state formation, where former ties of custom and mutual aid among individuals and families are severed so that economically or politically formalized relations can take their place. William Seagle, in *The History of Law*, quotes an early chronicler of the Slave Coast of Northwest Africa, describing the former customs of the Dahomey:

> Children are taken from their mothers at an early age, and distributed to places remote from their village of nativity, where they remain with

little chance of ever being seen, or at least recognized, by their parents afterwards. The motive for this is that there may be no family connections or combinations, no associations that might prove injurious to the King's unlimited power.[4]

From this point on, the evolution of the state consists largely in the elaboration and sophistication of methods of control. The state may, for example, dispense with the institution of kingship; yet it retains the authority to coerce and punish, and to seize tribute.

Since governments generally act to restrict the freedom of people who are not in positions of power, virtually all of the libertarian social advances of Western civilization (democracy and constitutional government are prime examples) are best understood as merely partial correctives for past excesses of authoritarian control.

But tragically, today even these gains are increasingly imperiled. As civilizations begin to disintegrate because of overpopulation and the exhaustion of soils, the entire social fabric tends to fray. Opportunism and suspicion increase; basic human goodwill evaporates. The people, who have been conditioned not to trust themselves and who feel an increasing need for protection against the specter of chaos, then may be easily persuaded to cede to authorities whatever freedoms they have retained or regained. Personal liberty—especially for the members of the exploited classes—comes to be seen as an unaffordable luxury, given the harsh necessities of the times.

Historical examples of this kind of civilizational distress include Rome in the early centuries of the current era, China and Russia on several occasions in their histories, and the Mayan cities immediately prior to their abandonment. In China, for instance, the Ch'in emperors succeeded in unifying the country only by outlawing philosophical discussion of any kind, as well as praise of the past or criticism of the present. These rulers, known as Legalists, believed that talent, wisdom, and virtue count for little in government; what matters is power. A ruler must therefore do everything possible to guard and expand his authority over others. To ensure that the intellectuals of the realm got the message, the Emperor in 212 B.C.E. had 460 scholars executed and buried in a common grave as a warning against any future defiance of his orders. Predictably, the Ch'in empire was undone in 206 B.C.E. by the harshness of its laws. A certain peasant named Ch'en She, who had been put in charge of a group of draftees being mustered for service on the frontier, was delayed by heavy rains. Knowing that his contingent would miss its rendezvous and that the penalty for all of the soldiers would be severe, he persuaded his small following that they might as well be outlaws as convicts. Soon thousands of malcontents rallied around him and hundreds of similar rebellions erupted throughout the empire, leading to its collapse.

These days we are witnessing similar, though for the most part less dramatic, conflicts between freedom, necessity, and power throughout society. These contradictions are likely to intensify dramatically in the years ahead. As more and harsher ecological and social crises erupt, arguments for greater control will likely gain credibility. It will seem to most people that the remedy for the ills of civilization (ills that, as we have seen, arise from centralized authoritarian control and the exploitation of nature and people) is *more civilization*.

The only hope for an escape from this infernal double bind—and for the freeing of the human spirit—will come from an increased understanding of the basic dynamics of civilizational control systems, and of the more stable and life-enhancing patterns of existence that at least some noncivilized human societies have pursued for millennia.

FOR THE GOOD OF THE WHOLE

As a way of illustrating the conflict between freedom and necessity in concrete terms, it may be helpful to review two current instances in which protective government regulation is having the effect of extinguishing personal liberty.

Recently in the United States, the Supreme Court rendered a decision against a member of the Native American Church who had been fired from his counseling job for using peyote—a traditional sacrament of the Church. While lower courts had ruled that his firing constituted a violation of his constitutionally protected freedom of religion, the Supreme Court declared that in this instance—because it involves the use of an otherwise prohibited psychoactive plant—freedom of religion is "a luxury that this country can no longer afford."

In an apparently unrelated instance, another branch of the U.S. Government—the Food and Drug Administration—has sought to regulate the sale of virtually all herbal and nutritional supplement products. It seems that for years several unscrupulous companies made unproved claims for a few such products; also, in one highly publicized case, a woman was injured by her excessive ingestion of comfrey. According to a professional herbalist of my acquaintance, the herb and supplement industries generally agree that more regulation of product labeling is needed. But, since the FDA recruits many of its employees from pharmaceutical corporations and from law enforcement agencies, it tends to see every situation that falls under its jurisdiction in terms of drugs and guns. The FDA therefore intends to treat herbs (which in most cases have been used safely and effectively for thousands of years), as well as vitamins and amino acids, as if they were truly dangerous substances. But restricting their sale could, by simple regulatory decree, turn thousands of peaceful, health-conscious herbalists into criminals—in much the same way that marijuana laws have turned tens of thousands of innocuous pot smokers into convicts. In anticipation of the new rules, gun-wielding FDA agents invaded the office of a doctor who was giving his patients "forbidden" nutritional supplements and seized his files. However, the incident backfired, generating so much negative publicity for the FDA (through a health-food store public relations campaign) that its spokespeople later bent over backwards to assure consumers that vitamins and herbs would remain on the shelves.

In both of these cases, the objective was public safety; the means were authoritarian; and the result—or potential result—was an erosion of freedom.

THE CONFLICTS AHEAD

Peyote and mislabeled herbs may appear to be minor threats to society, ones that hardly justify harsh repressive measures. But there are other problems that are genuinely menacing to the welfare of the general public, and as they intensify in the years ahead, it may become difficult even for reasonable people to discount authoritarian solutions.

Perhaps the greatest threat to our global environment and to social stability is overpopulation. Unless this problem is dealt with, all efforts toward the salvaging of ecosystems and human cultures are doomed. Some say that the most just and humane way to reduce population growth is somehow to grant increased economic and social power to women in Third World countries. However, this solution is unlikely to be realized. In fact, the poor are getting poorer as the economic reins of the multinational corporations—via globalization and GATT—strangle indigenous subsistence cultures. Meanwhile, official Islamic and Roman Catholic religious policies are discouraging poor women's access to birth control. The only other imaginable way to induce people to have fewer children involves legal restrictions of some kind—such as ones that have been in effect in China for several years. Yet such restrictions are unimaginably intrusive and are almost inevitably applied with greater force against the powerless poor; thus one could hardly withhold sympathy from anyone who resisted them.

Crime, drug abuse, child abuse, pollution, the proliferation of handguns and assault weapons, and the wanton destruction of ecosystems are all desperate crises crying out for solutions. How are we to solve them other than through the application of state power? Yet in many situations where state power is exercised, abuse and injustice only multiply.

Take the case of crime: As the social fabric disintegrates, and as more regulations are imposed in order to deal with the resulting chaos, more citizens are criminalized. The interests of the accused are in obvious conflict with the apparent civic necessity for law and order, and so the rights of poor and indigent prisoners tend to be restricted or ignored. It may be a truism that two wrongs don't make a right, but the criminal justice system often strives to prove otherwise.

Recently, in refusing to hear the case of Jesse Dwayne Jacobs, a manifestly innocent indigent prisoner on Texas's Death Row, the U.S. Supreme Court ruled that the issue of guilt or innocence is essentially irrelevant in terms of its jurisdiction; only questions of procedural correctness constitute proper grounds for the Court's review of cases. The State of Texas had convicted Jacobs fair and square, so it really didn't matter that another person was later tried and convicted of the same crime, and that the State acknowledged during this second trial that Jacobs was completely innocent. Shortly before retiring, Justice Harry Blackmun commented that "the execution of a person who can show that he is innocent comes perilously close to murder"; Jacobs himself believed that it comes more than "close": His last words before being put to death were, "I have news for you. There is not going to be an execution. This is premeditated murder."

Meanwhile, in California, courts have ruled that if an accused person in county jail exercises his right to self-representation, he does not have the right of personal access to the jail law library, a telephone, or a typewriter. And the U.S. Congress, in its enthusiasm to pass anti-crime legislation (who, after all, is *for* crime?) has now severely limited the protections in the U.S. Constitution against unlawful search and seizure.

The contradictions inherent in our desires for both freedom and security within a complex society tend to obliterate distinctions between "liberal" and "conservative" social agendas. The conservative's concern for the rights of handgun owners, crime victims, and fetuses is as sincere as the liberal's concern for the poor, women, and racial minorities. One group's freedom implies another's restriction; all seek to influence the power structure to their own benefit. Is it ever possible to make the power structure completely fair? Or does the concentration of power in and of itself necessitate injustice?

IRONIES OF POWER

In stratified societies, rules tend to be made by the powerful for the benefit of the powerful. Even when the problems that the rules address are ones created by the abuse of power, implementation tends to favor those with prior advantage. For example, there are many regulations aimed at minimizing industrial pollution—which is a byproduct of the exercise of technological and economic power. However, corporations are often able to resist or defuse such regulations, as by shipping industrial wastes to Third World countries. But even in the worst case, when a corporation is held to be in violation of the law, the fine is likely to be negligible and company officials are not held personally accountable. Increasingly, corporations have been able to have the regulations removed entirely merely by making campaign contributions to congressional candidates. Indeed, in the U.S., an antiregulatory fever has swept the Congress, leading to the wholesale imperilment of environmental protection, worker safety, and civil rights laws.

It is only when the simple relationship between rules and power (i.e., those with power make the rules, and they tend to do so to benefit themselves) is thoroughly understood that we can begin to make sense of the ironies that arise when individual freedom is pitted against the necessities of the "greater good." One such irony is that it is often "conservative," pro-corporate politicians who appear to be standing up for personal liberty, while "liberals" tend to favor more regulation and restriction. In the FDA case cited above, for example, it was the arch-"conservative" Senator Orrin Hatch who introduced a bill to protect herbs and vitamins from regulation, while the "liberal" Senator Ted Kennedy favored giving the FDA free rein. For some "conservatives" (those who, ironically, don't have much interest in conserving nature or culture), personal liberty generally translates as freedom for the rich to exploit people and nature without limit. But sometimes the cup of freedom overflows a bit so that the less powerful are granted a taste as well, thus helping to promote the popularity of the cause. "Liberals," meanwhile, are more concerned to restrict the excesses of exploiters and to safeguard the public against every sort of danger and abuse; but in most instances they are far from being immune to economic and political pressures, and so the regulations they impose are easily subverted to serve the interests of those who are apparently being regulated. Meanwhile, the bureaucracy created by their seemingly well-intended efforts takes on a life of its own, and often fails miserably to meet the actual needs of people in their inevitably unique situations.

The engine of civilization is driven by people with power, or those seeking power. However, when things start to fall apart, it is the poor and disadvantaged who are the preferred scapegoats. Currently in the U.S., illegal immigrants are convenient scapegoats, with anti-immigrant hysteria serving to deflect public attention from the corporate free-trade agenda of lowering labor costs and undermining pollution restrictions. In this instance, it is worth noting that many government leaders have favored the issuing of national identity cards—which could serve as a means for the eventual restriction of all kinds of personal freedoms—as a way of deterring illegal immigration. In the Pacific Northwest, environmentalists are scapegoated to deflect attention from the disastrous forestry practices of the timber companies. And internationally, Third-World "terrorists" (who in many cases are merely acting from within their own countries to resist foreign domination) are frequently scapegoated by the U.S., a nation whose "intelligence" agency has practiced or supported large-scale international terrorism as a standard policy for decades (in Vietnam, Cambodia, Cuba, Chile, Nicaragua, El Salvador, Grenada, Panama, East Timor, Angola, etc.).

POWER AND PROPORTION

Civilization is about power. The division of labor, the expansion of markets, and the creation of new technologies (from the plow to the computer) are ways of leveraging and concentrating power. As a society becomes more "advanced," the amount of power available to people in positions of influence increases, and the society as a whole becomes more formidable. Thus "developed" nations always overcome "underdeveloped" ones when they compete economically or militarily.

Ultimately, the problem of social justice is insoluble in the terms in which it is customarily posed. It is usually seen as a problem of the abuse of power, or of the reins of power being in the wrong hands. Most people tacitly assume that power itself—economic, technological, and political—is either good or neutral. Many social critics say that our historical development of more sophisticated means of concentrating power has outpaced our moral growth, and that to survive as a society or a species, we must mature to the point of being able to use our power responsibly.

The idea of questioning power itself seldom occurs to anyone. But is it not possible that power is "good" only when it exists in proportion to its context, and that disproportionate power is destructive regardless of who is wielding it or with what intent?

Consider a modern military force equipped with nuclear weapons: It represents an extraordinary achievement in the leveraging of social and technological power. But in what conceivable instance could such power be used "responsibly," when to unleash it fully under any circumstances might mean the end of all higher life on this planet? What solace would it be, following a nuclear war, to know that it had been fought for a "good cause"? Might it not be preferable for the warring politicians simply to settle their differences personally with stones and clubs?

Essentially the same argument can be advanced with respect to all technological and hierarchical power that is capable of overwhelming the biological context of human bodies, of families and face-to-face communities, of ecosystems, plants, animals, soil, air, and water. That context is a given, and no amount of "progress" can erase our utter dependence upon it; nor would we likely be better off, in any real sense, if we could somehow escape from it, whether into outer space, virtual reality, or a disembodied spiritual realm of some kind. When power is disproportionate to that fundamental context, it becomes difficult or impossible to use such power responsibly.

At what point does power become disproportionate? Is fire a disproportionate form of power? If uncontrolled, it is capable of overwhelming a local habitat; yet fires occur naturally as the result of lightning. Clearly, some means of power are entirely natural and necessary: The human body is itself a marvelous instrument for leveraging power, and the primitive foraging band offers a certain amount of social leveraging in relation to survival activities. At these levels of power, prudence, goodwill, and reciprocity are decisive in determining the effects of power's use. But as increasingly intensive means of concentrating power come into play, motives seem to become irrelevant. The effects of power's use tend to be destructive no matter what the intent. Then more rules are needed, and freedom slips away.

Perhaps, if we were to attempt to define a certain stage of power concentration beyond which even well-motivated use is destructive, it would be the stage characterized by the lifetime division of labor and the implementation of technologies whose use results in the permanent degradation of the natural world. Every civilization has passed that stage—it is virtually a definition of civilization—and ours to the greatest degree of any in history.

THE PATH TO FREEDOM

Here is perhaps the greatest irony of all. From the very beginnings of civilization, we have assumed that by concentrating power, we can gain freedom. After all, in some sense, power *is* freedom. By concentrating technological and economic power in an airline ticket, I gain the freedom to travel quickly from place to place. By concentrating military power, an entire country may gain the freedoms that great wealth brings. But it is also true that as we increase power, we create new restrictions. Whatever social group gains power tends to do so at the expense of another; meanwhile the cumulative effect of our "freeing" and "labor-saving" technologies is that the Earth itself is being drained of life so that future generations will be denied the freedom ever to see an intact ecosystem, or perhaps even to live in a habitable world.

When a civilization is in its early stages, the tradeoffs of freedom and sustainability for security and power may seem worthwhile, at least from the perspective of the dominant social group. But as a civilization reaches its climax phase, solutions to burgeoning social and ecological crises can no longer be found in the exercise of accumulated military, economic, or technological power, however vast. Then, the only hope lies in dismantling the centralized power structures themselves—even though that may mean an increase of chaos in the short run.

For us today, the path to freedom and sanity is one of finding ways to gain independence from institutional power structures and of forging personal bonds of mutual aid with others who are likewise awakening to the necessity of operating within the design of our biological context.

But, even assuming that the global imperial power structure implodes over the next few decades (a safe bet) and that we are able to plant seeds of new, stable and sustainable cultures, what's to keep the same thing from happening all over again? If the more powerful people, social groups, and nations always win, then how are we to resist the accumulation of power once it gets started? Only by learning the nature of the tradeoffs clearly, so that we refuse to make them again. The events of the next century may provide stark object lessons in that regard.

Meanwhile, we have everything to learn from the world's surviving primal peoples, who are living demonstrations of the fact that it is possible to live within the biological context indefinitely, and to do so with dignity, autonomy, and responsibility. As I have said, the new cultures we create in the centuries ahead will likely not be ones based entirely on gathering or hunting, and they may benefit from many of civilization's discoveries. But the world cannot endure yet another parasitic empire culture that survives only by draining the energy systems of the biosphere. Like the primal peoples, we who are the children of industrial civilization must learn to integrate ourselves into the fabric of the wilderness, for it is only within that fabric that life can persist and unfold in all its riotous creativity. And it is only in such a context that we can know the freedom we all long for.

The new prophets were men of a modest human disposition: they brought life back to the village scale and the normal human dimensions; and out of this weakness they made a new kind of strength, not recognized in the palace or the marketplace. These meek, withdrawn, low-keyed, outwardly humble men appeared alone, or with a handful of equally humble followers, unarmed, unprotected. They did not look for institutional support: on the contrary, they dared to condemn and defy those in established positions. . . .

—LEWIS MUMFORD

 SPIRITUALITY MEANS DIFFERENT THINGS to different people—humility before a higher power or powers; compassion for the suffering of others; the perpetuation of a lineage or tradition; a felt connection with particular places, plants, or animals; evolution toward "higher" states of consciousness; or a mystical experience of oneness with all living things or with God.

It seems that at some point in life nearly everyone feels the need for contact with the spiritual dimension, however defined. This may involve formal association with a religious community, or may instead consist of a personal search for meaning and values. Sometimes a dramatic inner experience—such as a near-death experience—triggers this search. However approached, the spiritual dimension is a source of inspiration, and moments of direct contact with it are invariably understood to be an awakening from the slumber of our routinely narrowed perceptions. They are openings into an expanded awareness of the eternal *now*.

But if spirituality is by nature expansive, why are so many religious people narrowminded, even bigoted? Why, during the course of the development of religious movements, does spontaneous spirituality so often become progressively regimented, dogmatized, even militarized? How can the universal spiritual impulse be responsible—apparently—for both enlightenment and cultic mind control; for the dream of universal brotherhood and sisterhood and for genocidal religious wars; for selfless generosity and for arrogant intolerance?

The answer, it seems to me, has to do not only with individual human strengths and weaknesses, but also with the relationship between spirituality and the cultural context in which it appears. Simply put: With the growth of civilization, humanity's natural capacities for forming connections and meanings have been systematically subverted. The result is a disease of the spirit describable by the word *religiosity*. Dogmatic materialism—the flight from traditional spirituality—is understandable as a reaction to that disease and, in at least some instances, as a form of it.

In this chapter I propose briefly to outline the role of spirituality in various societal contexts, and how the subversion process works. As a classic and highly relevant example, we will recall the origin of Christianity and how spirituality turned to religiosity in first-century Judaea. Then we will explore some implications of this study for spirituality in our present historical-cultural situation.

SPIRITUALITY FROM CAVE TO PYRAMID TO SKYSCRAPER

Food gathering societies tend to make no distinction between sacred and secular aspects of life. Theirs is a completely magical view of the world— everything is sacred, and all aspects of nature and society are tied together by myth and ritual. Language, arts, social relations, and economy are all integrated. The only specialist in the realms of the sacred is the shaman, who comes to her or his calling through the resolution of a personal crisis and offers healing or guidance to others primarily on a one-to-one basis. Superstition and taboo exist, but often in forms that are immediately practical and functional (as in the taboo of the Aranada Aborigines of central Australia against the killing of red kangaroos in their best habitat). Spirituality centers on the relationship between the individual and the powers of nature and cosmos, and on kinship ties and obligations.

With the beginnings of horticulture and agriculture, new social pressures produced new characteristic religious forms. While the foraging or hunting group was small and mobile, and while the individual in it was self-sufficient and free to develop and express his or her own unique personality, the planting community was larger, more sedentary, and more anxious about its boundaries. Individuals had to stay in one place and work harder, and had to renounce a certain degree of freedom and autonomy for the sake of the group. The major themes of myth and ritual in early horticultural or agricultural societies had to do with group identification and with sacrifice—the sacrifice both of the seed (which dies that the plant may live) and of a representative member of the group (who dies so that the tribe may live). The ancient Babylonians' Tammuz myth, in which the hero dies in the winter and returns to life in the spring, and their practice of ritually slaying the king in Tammuz' place, are well-attested examples of this kind of religious thought and practice.

With early civilization—that is, with the appearance of cities, armies, slavery, and kingship—these communal pressures reached a new intensity. The complete regimentation of the individual within a hierarchical social power structure was validated through reference to a *cosmic* power structure. The king was considered the human symbol or incarnation of the chief of the gods, usually the Sun, and the social pyramid operated as a giant machine responding to his sacred wishes—often (as in Egypt, China, and Central America) building stone pyramids to concretize the chain of command from Sun god to slave. Religion becomes bureaucratized and mediated.

As civilization evolves past kingship into industrial democracy, the state itself becomes an object of religious devotion (via patriotism) and wage labor replaces slavery, casting money in the role of secondary deity. Science and technology, as sources of knowledge and power, take the place of myth and ritual. Nevertheless, residues of older religious beliefs and practices persist, and to the extent that consumerism, science, and patriotism fail to meet people's spiritual needs, traditional religions may mutate into "fundamentalist" forms as a reaction against the perceived threat of modernism.

This is, of course, merely a schematic outline of the relationship between spirituality and its social context. It must be supplemented with an understanding of the role of environmental catastrophe in social change and the role of collective post-traumatic stress syndrome in the introduction of obviously pathological ritual practices such as human sacrifice (see chapter 3). There is, in addition, one other important phenomenon that has played a primary part in shaping the history of religious ideas— the periodic eruptions of religious reforms that run against the current of "progress" by reinvoking the spiritual values humanity knew in its most direct relationship with nature. One of the earliest of these reforms was persuasive and pervasive enough to challenge the very existence of civilization.

RAW SPIRITUALITY CONFRONTS CIVILIZATION

Around 600 B.C.E.—many centuries after civilization had appeared in Egypt and Mesopotamia, but as it was just beginning to take hold elsewhere —a revolt began brewing. Lewis Mumford writes:

> This revolt began in the mind, and it proceeded to deny the materialistic assumptions that equated human welfare and the will of the gods with centralized political power, military dominance, and increasing economic exploitation—symbolized as these were in the walls, towers, palaces, temples of the great urban centers. All over Europe, the Middle East and Asia—and notably out of the villages rather than the cities—new voices arose, those of an Amos, a Hesiod, a Lao Tze, deriding the cult of power, pronouncing it iniquitous, futile, and anti-human, and proclaiming a new set of values, the antithesis of those upon which the myth of the megamachine had been built. Not power but righteousness, these prophets said, was the basis of human society: not snatching, seizing and fighting, but sharing, cooperating, even loving: not pride, but humility: not limitless wealth, but a noble self-restricting poverty and chastity.[1]

The Buddha and (later) Jesus were exponents of this new philosophy that advocated voluntary simplicity, a "golden mean" of living in which material pursuits are secondary. For the yogi, monk, prophet, hermit, or disciple, an outer return to nature was the necessary accompaniment to an inner return to spiritual origins. Excessive involvement with the world of money and possessions was a hindrance to the pursuit of this loftier goal, which could be described as a direct, unmediated relationship with the sacred.

After this great reform, spiritual teachers of all faiths tended to agree that the true purpose of life has little or nothing to do with conveniences and inventions, or with coercive authority and wealth; it centers, rather, on the development and expression of innate qualities of being—compassion, wisdom, and love. They described the natural world as either the embodiment or the expression of an *interior* dimension of sacred power and truth. They advised their followers to "consider the lilies of the field" (Jesus), to "dwell free from greed" (the Buddha), and to "renounce selfish attachments" (Krishna). They claimed that "poverty is my pride" (Muhammad), and that "he who embraces Nature's way as his own will not easily go astray" (Lao Tze). While none of these spiritual teachers was an anthropologist, all were to one degree or another preaching the adoption of an existence similar to that of the food gatherers—a free, autonomous, generous, trusting way of life.

But this mode of being was incompatible with the basic methods and goals of civilization. How to resolve the resulting tension?

SPIRITUALITY GETS COOKED

The word *co-opt* describes the process whereby a power system undermines groups it considers threatening by infiltrating and assimilating them, perhaps even elevating them to positions of apparent authority, while marginalizing their criticisms and demands. The term came into wide use during the student rebellions of the 1960s, but the tactic it names is ancient.

In China, Confucius (Kung Fu Tze) reformulated early Taoist teachings —which were profoundly primitivist in spirit—in terms more acceptable to the reigning bureaucracy. Gradually, the authorities came to discourage and even suppress Taoism while elevating Confucianism to the status of official state religion. The spontaneous way of the hermit, as described in the sayings of the possibly apocryphal Lao Tze, came to be seen as impractical and self-indulgent; scores of generations of young Chinese were instructed instead in the subtleties of maintaining a correct deportment for one's station in life.

In India, Aryan tradition had crystallized society into a rigid, hierarchical caste system. Gautama the Buddha decried caste and material privilege. Rather than challenging secular powers, however, his followers set up their own parallel hierarchy of philosophers and monks. For a millennium Buddhism was ascendant in India, and even the great Emperor Ashoka converted to the Eightfold Path. His change of heart was deep and genuine, it would appear: Ashoka issued an edict saying that henceforth he would practice gentleness and would bear all wrongs done to himself with meekness and patience. He also forbade the slaughter of animals in the court and granted official privileges to Buddhist monks and missionaries. Gradually, small, local monasteries were abandoned in favor of great monastic centers where philosophical and secular learning could be pursued for their own sake. The general population of India lost interest in supporting a priesthood that no longer participated much in the day-to-day struggles and pleasures of village life, and left the few remaining monasteries undefended against invading Huns and Muslims. Buddhism virtually disappeared from India by 1200 C.E., but the caste system survived and even thrived.

Without doubt the clearest and most dramatic example of spiritual co-optation occurred among the early Christians. Since it is such a clear instance of the phenomenon, and since Christianity is currently by far the most popular religion in the world, we might profitably explore at some length just what happened in the Near East two millennia ago.

DECODING THE GOSPELS

The search for the origins of Christianity and for the historical Jesus has been going on for more than a century now. Scholars (including historians, archaeologists, anthropologists, linguists, and literary experts) have approached the New Testament the same way they would any other piece of ancient writing, directing their efforts simultaneously along two lines: first, the *literary analysis* of the gospels and of related texts, including the Dead Sea Scrolls and the Nag Hammadi scrolls (What do they have in common? In what ways are they different? When were they written and by whom? What sources did the authors draw upon?); and second, *historical studies* of events and characters, and anthropological research into their cultural context (What religious ideas, philosophies, and myths were current in the Near East during the first century? What was the political and social situation in Palestine? What were the cultural backgrounds of the people mentioned in the narratives?).

Today most textual analysts agree that the earliest stratum in the Jesus literature is comprised of the genuine sayings of the master. The Jesus Seminar—an ongoing collaboration of eminent New Testament scholars seeking to determine the most probably authentic teachings of Jesus—has helped somewhat to clarify the conclusion that most independent investigators had already reached: that the authors of the canonical gospels (which were written several decades after the events they describe, and almost certainly *not* by the individuals to whom they are attributed) each drew upon a lost so-called sayings gospel. Known by the scholars as "Q" (for *Quelle*, German for "source"), this text was recently reconstructed and published by Burton Mack of Claremont College in his popular book *The Lost Gospel: The Book of Q and Christian Origins*. Scholars may still dispute the authenticity of individual sayings, but the gist of Jesus' original message, which we will explore later, seems clear enough.

The narrative biography of Jesus contained in the gospels is another matter, however. Clearly, some elements were derived from mythical sources. We know, for instance, that Mithras (a Syrian hero-god whose cult was popular throughout the Roman Empire during the first century) was believed to have been born in the company of shepherds and to have shared a last supper with his followers, later commemorated by them in a communion of bread and wine. Mithraism also taught the immortality of the soul and a future judgment and resurrection of the dead. The idea of a god who dies in order to save, redeem, or give life to the world had antecedents not only in the mythic biography of Mithras, but those of Osiris, Attis, Adonis, and Tammuz as well. Even the ascension story easily fits a mythic type well known during this period: All admired Roman emperors were said to have ascended to heaven after their deaths; as Morton Smith (author of *The Secret Gospel* and *Jesus the Magician*) tells us, "By the early second century there was a regular ritual to assure the ascension. Augustus's ascension was attested to the senate by the sworn witness of a Roman Praetorian."[2]

But there is disagreement over just how much of the biography is history and how much is myth. Burton Mack argues that we must assume that *everything* but the sayings is myth; he writes: "The first followers of Jesus did not know about or imagine any of the dramatic events upon which the narrative gospels hinge. These include the baptism of Jesus; his conflict with the Jewish authorities and their plot to kill him; Jesus' instruction to the disciples; Jesus' transfiguration, march to Jerusalem, last supper, trial, and crucifixion as king of the Jews; and finally, his resurrection from the dead and the stories of an empty tomb. All of these events must and can be accounted for as mythmaking in the [early] Jesus movements. . . ."[3] On the other hand, Morton Smith and John Dominick Crossan (author of *The Historical Jesus* and *Jesus: A Revolutionary Biography*) accept at least some of the narrative material as factual; Smith contends, for instance, that the miracle stories resemble reports of the works of itinerant magicians who flourished throughout the Near East during the time in question, and proposes that Jesus was merely an example of the type.

WHO WAS JESUS?

Which brings us to the question, *Who was the utterer of the sayings on which so great a religion was built?*

To grasp, to any significant degree, how Jesus' contemporaries viewed him, we must first try to understand the context of the place and times in which he lived. During the first few decades of the first century, Palestine was a center of religious and political ferment. The Hellenistic culture that had come to dominate the eastern Mediterranean region during the previous three hundred years had also profoundly affected Jewish society, and many myths, cults, and philosophies were current in the land. Politically, Palestine was under Roman domination, and the Jews were a repressed and exploited people whose aspirations for independence would erupt in the war of 66–73 C.E.

Anthropologists and historians agree that revelatory worldviews tend predictably to spring from situations of intense social conflict and crisis. Such revelations take forms appropriate to the unique circumstances of time and place. In the case in point, according to Mack, "One important phenomenon of the Greco-Roman age was the appearance of the religious and philosophical entrepreneur, sometimes called the divine man, sometimes the sophist or sage. The entrepreneur stepped into the void left vacant by the demise of traditional priestly functions at the ancient temple sites and addressed the confusion, concern, and curiosity of people confronted with a complex world that was felt to be at the mercy of the fates." In addition to freelance visionaries and prophets, the eastern Mediterranean during the first century was also home to magicians, protesters, bandits, messiahs, and revolutionaries. Jesus seems to have fit well into this milieu.

As we have already noted, Morton Smith sees Jesus primarily as a magician or miracle worker. Smith cites magical texts of the period, in which not only the major elements but even many minor details in the gospel stories find parallels. For example, he sees the eucharist as "a variant form of an attested magical rite for binding the celebrant and the recipient together in love; a number of other forms are found in magical papyri; the verbal parallels are unmistakable."[4]

Burton Mack, who puts more weight on Jesus' sayings and less on the details of his biographies, tends to view him as a wandering wisdom teacher in the tradition of Diogenes the Cynic. The Cynics taught the renunciation of desires and appetites imposed by civilization, equality among people, and the virtue of a natural life free from social conventions and possessions. They were critics and rejecters of civilization. In modern parlance, the term *cynical* is fraught with negative connotations; these, however, can be traced to a somewhat unfair caricature of a school of scruffy but courageous philosophers known, in Mack's words, for "voluntary poverty, renunciation of needs, severance of family ties, fearless and carefree attitudes, and troublesome public behavior."[5] Cynicism, according to Crossan, "involved practice and not just theory, life-style and not just mind-set in opposition to the cultural heart of Mediterranean civilization, a way of looking and dressing, of eating, living, and relating that announced its contempt for honor and shame, for patronage and clientage."[6] Jesus' sayings closely parallel Cynic teachings; and, in the Hellenistic era, the philosophy of Diogenes would likely have been well known in Galilee. But Jesus, as a Jewish peasant Cynic, seems to have added a unique and significant twist to the established tradition: Unlike urban Greek Cynics, he advocated the formation of a rural social movement.

So, whence comes the image of Jesus as the only Son of God, the second Person of the Trinity, forgiver of sins, hearer of prayers? Was this how Jesus thought of himself? Was it how his first followers viewed him? The historical and textual evidence gives us little reason for thinking that it was, and offers instead an account of how and why these ideas came into currency decades or centuries after the period in question.

But what of millions of people's dreams, visions, and near-death encounters with Jesus; what of miraculous conversions and healings, of prayers answered and lives changed? Perhaps these should be accorded precisely as much legitimacy and significance as, for example, an Australian native shaman's experience of totemic ancestral spirit-beings; an early Egyptian's experience of Osiris; or a West African peasant's experience of being possessed by Legba. Which is to say: The experience is no doubt real, and in many cases the healings and miracles may also be real—all products of the human mind's extraordinary need for symbols of transcendence, and of its ability both to generate meaningful and internally consistent worldviews, and to alter its own perceptions and the physical body's abilities and state of health and vigor in order to fit those views.

THE TEACHINGS OF JESUS

If Jesus was an itinerant teacher somewhat in the tradition of Diogenes, what was the message he sought to convey? Burton Mack summarizes some of the significant themes in the reconstructed sayings gospel:

- Voluntary poverty
- Lending without expectation of return
- Critique of riches
- Etiquette for begging
- Etiquette for troublesome encounters in public
- Nonretaliation

- Rejoicing in the face of reproach
- Severance of family ties
- Renunciation of needs
- Call for authenticity
- Critique of hypocrisy
- Fearless and carefree attitude
- Confidence in God's care
- Single-mindedness in the pursuit of God's kingdom

Again and again, Jesus exhorts his followers to seek the kingdom of God—a metaphor for an alternative social order in which people live according to nature, free and equal, in a direct relationship with the divine. The idea of God in the earliest core of sayings is of a universal power—or "father"—who "makes his sun rise on the evil and the good," that "sends rain on the just and on the unjust." "Be merciful even as your Father is merciful"; "If God puts beautiful clothes on the grass . . . won't he put clothes on you? Your father knows that you need these things." Jesus was, according to Crossan, "neither broker nor mediator but, somewhat paradoxically, the announcer that neither should exist between humanity and divinity or between humanity and itself. Miracle and parable, healing and eating were calculated to force individuals into unmediated physical and spiritual contact with God and unmediated physical and spiritual contact with one another. He announced, in other words, the brokerless kingdom of God."[7]

Many scholars agree that some of the sayings attributed to Jesus are later additions; these include apocalyptic warnings about the Final Judgment, pronouncements against the Pharisees, pronouncements against towns that reject the movement, congratulations to those that accept the movement, the lament over Jerusalem, and the story of the temptations in the wilderness.

It is possible to trace, via shifts in discourse in the added material, just how the early Jesus community developed. At the earliest layer, according to Mack, "the discourse . . . was playful and the behavior public. Individuals were challenging one another to behave with integrity despite the social consequences. . . . If we ask about the character of the speaker of this king of material, it has its nearest analogy in contemporary profiles of the Cynic-sage."[8] Then, in the next layer of sayings, "selected imperatives were elaborated as community rules . . . Jesus' voice was now that of a founder-teacher giving instructions for the manner of life that should characterize his school."[9] We see the beginnings of social conflict surrounding the movement. By degrees, the voice of Jesus is made to utter things that only the wisdom of God could have known. The last layer of sayings dates from immediately after the Roman-Jewish war. According to Mack, "A retreat took place from the vigor with which these people had engaged their social environment to a kind of resignation, an acceptance of the fact that the rule of God was a matter of personal and ethical integrity. An amazing accommodation seems to have been made with a Jewish piety against which earlier battles had been fought. And Jesus was now imagined as the son of God whose kingdom would only be revealed at the end of time."[10]

In the earliest level of sayings we hear Jesus preaching, "How fortunate are the poor; they have the kingdom"; "Everyone who glorifies himself will be humiliated, and the one who humbles himself will be praised." He is proposing a social experiment—a classless society in which all are equal in the sight of God. It is a society governed not by power and wealth, nor by rigid laws, but by charity and kindness.

AN UNHOLY ALLIANCE

Jesus' egalitarian social philosophy has special relevance for us now, living as we do in one of the most polarized and stratified societies in history. Indeed, today's multinational, corporate-dominated, industrial system owes much to institutions and practices pioneered by the Roman empire. Like twentieth-century America and Europe, first-century Rome was at a pinnacle of economic and technological "progress." It was a colonial power, the center of a far-flung trade network. It was also an urban center in which extremes of wealth and poverty coexisted. Like the European colonists of the past five centuries, the Romans were destroyers of indigenous cultures and voracious consumers of "raw materials" (such as forests); and like us, they relied upon unsustainable, soil-killing farming practices.

While the earliest reconstructed collection of Jesus' sayings does not mention Satan, it does suggest (e.g., in the rejection of "all the kingdoms of the world") the idea that the pursuit of power and glory is at the heart of social evils. And in later additions to the sayings gospel, in which the devil (literally, "the accuser") makes his first appearance, he clearly serves as a personification of institutionalized social dominance.

The new scholarship portrays the historical Jesus as an anti-authoritarian and a primitivist. According to Crossan, the earliest Jesus people were the equivalent of "hippies among the Augustinian yuppies." Jesus' message was a challenge to social power in all its manifestations. Yet within only a few generations, that message had been twisted and co-opted almost beyond recognition. Through a gradual process of subversion, Christian teachings were first mythologized and then appropriated by the ruling elite of the Empire. First, Paul (a Roman who had never met Jesus) sought to popularize Jesus' teachings by "Romanizing" them with elements of popular mythology; later, Constantine would make Christianity the state religion, but only in return for certain doctrinal concessions that made it less threatening to the ruling class. Instead of enjoying an unmediated relationship with the sacred, Christians now would have to approach the divine through a complex hierarchy eventually consisting of priest, bishop, archbishop, cardinal, and pope. As a result of all this tinkering, Christianity became a kind of time capsule in which were preserved fragments of Greek, Roman, and Near Eastern myths and philosophies, the theologies of Paul, Constantine, and Augustine, and the imperialist social program of ancient Rome. It is surely fair to say that most of this is far from what Jesus originally had in mind.

Of course, through it all, the words of the Galilean sage have continued to shine: "Do not worry about your life, what you will eat, or about your body, what you will wear. Isn't life more than food, and the body more than clothing?" And, where individuals or groups have drawn inspiration from this earliest layer of teachings, a St. Francis or a St. Clair has come forward to propose the sort of "liberation" or "creation" theology that Jesus himself might have embraced.

But as an institution, Christianity eventually became the handmaiden of the capitalist industrial state, supplying the theological justification for colonialism and a work ethic for the factory system. Today, some "fundamentalists" claiming to represent the true teachings of the Galilean promote an anti-environmental, anti-feminist, anti-gay, pro-corporate, pro-technology agenda utterly opposed to the message of modern-day prophets of social justice and voluntary simplicity. Surely this constitutes one of the bitterest ironies in all of history.

A NEW REVELATION?

At the end of the twentieth century we stand on the brink of a global civilization whose might and sophistication would have delighted a Roman emperor to no end. The wealthiest one percent of the world's population live in unimaginable opulence, while hundreds of millions exist near the point of starvation. If we are to understand the devil as Jesus apparently did—not as an otherworldly malevolent being, but as the tendency toward the accumulation and centralization of political and economic power—then it appears that in our generation virtually the whole world is coming to be possessed by the devil.

In such circumstances, one cannot help but yearn for a new revelation, a new Cynic philosopher to stir things up. Where is the Jesus, the Buddha, or the Lao Tze who will come to remind us of the timeless and essential values of life, of the sponetaneous way of nature, of the freedom of desirelessness? Perhaps, if we look, we will see that there are many such prophets about. Our century has not lacked courageous individuals who criticized power while announcing the immanence of the divine. Gandhi was one; others include Lewis Mumford, the deep ecologists (such as Arne Naess, Gary Snyder, Dolores La Chapelle, and Paul Shepard), and the proponents of eco-spirituality (Joanna Macy, John Seed, Charlene Spretnak, Starhawk, and John Cobb).

If our present global crisis is a crisis of civilization itself—the horrific fruition of longstanding trends toward increasing population density, urbanization, mechanization, alienation, and centralization of control—then, to be helpful in this context, spirituality must resume the work it began over two thousand years ago—that of offering an effective brake to civilization. Now the stakes are higher, but the work is essentially the same. And with the benefit of hindsight, it may be possible to avoid the pitfalls that weakened and distorted that earlier revolt.

In order to learn and succeed, would-be prophets of a new spirituality must take two lessons to heart.

First, they must take care to focus their attention on essence above form. A new spirituality will inevitably draw some of its inspiration from ancient and surviving tribal societies. But it is easier merely to appropriate isolated religious forms from those cultures than it is to perceive and internalize the spirit that created and animated those forms. Simply put: Rediscovering "raw" spirituality is not just a matter of taking up African drumming or building Indian sweat lodges. The appropriation of tribal customs by civilized European-Americans amounts merely to a kind of cultural looting. These forms can be useful in evoking the essence of a new spirituality *only* if one takes the trouble to meet and interact with the people for whom they are part of a living tradition; if one uses the forms as gateways into these people's complete cultural experience—their way of thinking and feeling, of perceiving time, and of being in nature; and then takes on indigenous peoples' struggles as one's own.

Second, the new spirituality cannot emerge apart from a deepening critique of civilization, and those who seek to embody it must have a clear understanding of the process by which raw spirituality gets "cooked" by established interests. There is certainly a place for "New Age" schools of psychology and spirituality that address the problem of how to feel good about oneself while existing within a denatured and dehumanizing system. As a first step, we must heal ourselves and find our footing. But such an approach is inherently limited and easily co-opted. A raw and radical spirituality must constitute an *alternative* to civilization, and awakening to it must involve a defection from the system.

Of course, defection from our hydra-headed civilization requires courage and the ability to think and feel for oneself—not only about religious beliefs, but about the ways money, technology, and history shape our most private thoughts and our most mundane daily choices and acts. There are potentially as many ways of defecting as there are people.

As one finds personally meaningful ways to defect, it gets easier to distinguish raw from cooked spirituality. Cooked spirituality often has sat on the shelf for a long time before it gets to you. Its preparation requires following a recipe closely. Moreover, the cooking process has usually destroyed the emotional and psychic enzymes and vitamins that the human personality requires for its full nourishment. You can exist almost indefinitely on cooked spirituality, but only at the risk of the eventual development of degenerative diseases like shrinkage of the neurons or terminal boredom. Raw spirituality is best plucked straight from the soil or from the trees. It is juicy and fresh—not afraid to be exuberant, spontaneous, idiosyncratic, tribal, playful, and even subversive. It is wary of co-optation and institutionalization. It gets your organs working properly and keeps you healthy and flexible.

The rediscovery of raw spirituality will require that we get in touch with our own deepest needs and learn to fill them personally and communally; that we find our own internal source of meaning and learn to express it authentically. That would seem like a tall order if it weren't the most natural thing in the world.

II | SCIENCE: MORSELS OF KNOWLEDGE, BANQUETS OF IGNORANCE

A state of thoroughly conscious ignorance is the prelude to every real advance of knowledge.

—JAMES CLERK MAXWELL

 CULTURE CONSISTS, IN LARGE measure, of commonly shared sets of assumptions and expectations about reality. It is a kind of lens through which we look at the world, one that is implanted in us in infancy and childhood and that we continually readjust throughout life. Given the curvature and distortion of our lens, some things appear substantive that are actually only phantoms, while other things that are indeed quite solid and real are, to us, invisible.

We take this cultural astigmatism for granted in religion and politics. For example, few people would seriously expect Christianity to fold up shop if it were shown that Jesus did not in fact rise from the dead, that he was an itinerant wisdom teacher of a kind fairly common in the Middle East during his historical era, and that most of the New Testament was written long after the events described, by people who did not witness them, in order to advance a certain politico-religious cause. Scholars can talk about such matters at great length, but it makes little difference to those who dutifully flock to church each Sunday morning. After all, many derive deep comfort from their faith.

Similarly in politics, facts are widely understood to be merely incidental to worldviews constructed to serve ideological and economic purposes. For example, recently most Americans have been convinced by politicians that crime is the result of too few people being in prisons—this despite the well-known fact that their nation already incarcerates a greater percentage of its citizens than does any other, with little observed effect on the crime rate. They are likewise convinced that the poverty of the Third World is due to the sad circumstance that people in certain "backward" countries are "not yet ready for democracy," are inherently unindustrious, or are overburdened by irrational tradition. Meanwhile nearly everyone (in the U.S., though this is not so much the case elsewhere) studiously ignores the clear fact that the Third World has been—and continues to be—systematically plundered by corporations using the power of the CIA, the World Bank and International Monetary Fund, and (if necessary) the U.S. military to dominate or undermine indigenous enterprise. While this fact *is* frequently pointed out by certain "radical" political scientists and by the alternative press, it is rarely mentioned by career politicians or by the mainstream media because its widespread acknowledgment would be inimical to the purposes of power. But no one is surprised by this state of affairs, because most people have come to understand that *this is how politics works:* In complex societies, political worldviews are *always* shaped more by the self-interest of powerful individuals and groups than by mere facts.

Science is supposed to be different, and to a certain extent it is. The goal of the founders of Western science was to create a system of inquiry based on evidence, one in which theories would be continually tested, discarded, and replaced according to the impersonal dictates of fact and reason. Science is meant to *stand above* culture.

But science's quest for objectivity has always had to contend with two unalterable obstacles: scientists themselves are human beings with prejudices, fears, and ambitions; and the practice of science takes place within a cultural context wherein the economic goals of elites, class power relations, and a host of shared unconscious assumptions exert an unavoidable and mostly invisible influence on the proceedings. Science does not stand above culture; it swims in it. In science, as in religion and politics, there are power bases to protect, careers to maintain, masses to convert, empires to build. And so the history of science is full of examples of dogmas constructed and defended, evidence suppressed or twisted, and alternative theories ignored.

Such historical examples as the disbelief of early nineteenth-century scientists in the existence of meteors, Lord Kelvin's denunciation of X-rays as a hoax, and the unwillingness of eighteenth-century chemists to abandon the phlogiston theory (which regarded fire as a fundamental material substance), make for interesting reading. But we seldom look at contemporary science with the degree of skepticism that such past failings would seem to warrant. Yet when a lengthy series of theoretical presuppositions is necessary to form the concepts which lead to experimental and equipment design in a typical research project, which then yields data that must be processed according to the same theoretical presuppositions in order to make sense, then it should be clear to us that even many of the "observed facts" of modern science are largely hypothetical.

That is not the impression one gets when reading science articles in news magazines, or when watching television science documentaries, in which we are told repeatedly that scientists "know" that the Universe began fifteen billion years ago in a Big Bang; that life on this planet evolved first from terrestrial chemical processes and then by way of competition and natural selection; that atoms are made up of tiny charged particles; and so on.

My purpose in this chapter is not to denigrate science and scientists, but rather to view science in perspective—as our civilization's version of an activity that is pursued in one form or another in every society. While our science has many impressive accomplishments to its credit, it has also created or reinforced some of our culture's blind spots. Moreover, as I show toward the end of this chapter, the "sciences" of many traditional societies have produced accomplishments of their own that are well worth preserving.

First, however, let us briefly reconnoiter the boundaries of our collective ignorance in a few selected fields.

PHYSICS

In the sixteenth and seventeenth centuries, the Copernican and Newtonian revolutions shattered the geocentric, dogmatically religious, Aristotelian world picture of medieval times. In our own century, thanks to Einstein, Rutherford, Bohr, and Heisenberg, we have taken a great step beyond Newton. Instead of a dead, clockwork universe, we now live in a spacetime continuum that is relative and uncertain. In exchanging Aristotle for Newton, and Newton for Einstein, we have replaced one conceptual model of reality with another that is (we assume) somewhat more complete. However, one seldom reads a statement by one of the New Physics proponents suggesting that, just as Einstein and Bohr supplanted Newton, they will be followed by yet other great paradigm shifters. One gets the impression not that relativity and quantum mechanics are mortal, limited *theories*, but that they are *discoveries* that are beyond argument—like a new comet that has appeared in the sky for everyone to see. But is this a realistic view?

Unfortunately, the quantum theory of Bohr and the relativity theories of Einstein are incompatible. Over the past few decades, various physicists have tried to come up with a Grand Unified Theory that would overcome the contradictions, but so far none has fully succeeded. No less a physicist than David Bohm once admitted that "Physics is now faced with a crisis in which . . . further changes will have to take place, which will probably be as revolutionary compared to relativity and the quantum theory as these theories are compared to classical physics."

ASTRONOMY

One of the greatest difficulties faced by astronomers is that in most cases they cannot directly probe the objects of their study; rather, they must analyze infinitesimal traces of radiation that have presumably traveled thousands or millions of years to arrive here from stars, galaxies, quasars, and even more exotic objects lying at unimaginable distances. With so little to go on, their analyses of these traces must inevitably incorporate some of the very hypotheses they seek to validate. This can lead to problems.

Lying at the foundation of modern cosmology is the observed spectrographic "red shift" of light from distant objects, which has been interpreted to mean that these objects are moving away from us. According to current views, the objects with the greatest red shifts are furthest distant and are receding fastest, which means that the universe is expanding in every direction. Hence it must have originated in a huge explosion—the famous Big Bang.

But not everyone subscribes to this interpretation. H. Arp was listed as one of the top twenty astronomers in the world, until he began cataloging celestial objects that appear to be close enough to one another to be interacting gravitationally, but that have widely differing red shifts. He openly suggested that at least some red shifts are not a measure of recessional velocity and distance. His reputation plummeted. H. Alfven, a Nobel Prize winner in physics, posits a Universe shaped more by electromagnetic than gravitational forces; his theory rules out the possibility that the Universe could ever have had a diameter less than one-tenth its present one—hence no Big Bang.

The upshot of all of this is that we really do not know when or how—or if!—the Universe began; nor do we know what forces are primarily responsible for shaping it; nor do we know for certain how far away distant objects are or whether they are moving toward or away from us.

Closer to home, serious questions have been raised about how the Sun generates its energy, where comets come from, and how Mars lost its former atmosphere and lakes of water. Astronomer Tom Van Flandern has pointed out that current theories of the history of the solar system are incapable of adequately explaining the current arrangement and appearance of the planets, their moons, and the asteroids.[1]

GEOLOGY

The geological record is formed from layers of rock that geologists liken to pages in a book. Unfortunately, that book is far from complete. In fact, of the ten major geological periods, only five or fewer are represented on two-thirds of the Earth's land surface. In some places the "periods" occur in the wrong order. And most fossils used for dating rock layers overlap from a few to all ten layers. This means that the "geological column" by which we construct Earth history is largely hypothetical.

Most geologists interpret this "column" on the basis of the theory of uniformity, according to which the origin of major land features is to be attributed to mechanisms similar to those we see acting today, with small effects accumulating over vast stretches of time. However, as we saw in chapter 3, there is growing evidence to suggest that the planet's surface may have been shaped to a large extent by ancient global cataclysms, some of extraterrestrial origin—that is, by collisions with comets and other interplanetary or interstellar debris. With the dinosaur extinctions now widely attributed to a comet impact, the theory of cosmic catastrophism as it applies to the geologic past is gaining popularity. But despite the pioneering work of astronomers Victor Clube, Bill Napier, and Fred Hoyle, the idea that similar bombardments could have occurred during the past few thousand years is still officially unthinkable.

Geologists believe that the age of rocks can be found by the precise measurement of the radioactive minerals and decay products embedded within them. A similar analysis of a radioactive isotope of carbon is used by archaeologists to tell the age of less ancient organic materials. Critics of radiometric dating have questioned the assumptions on which these methods rest. (For example, does the radioactive decay rate remain constant despite changes in temperature, cosmic ray influx, and pressure? Evidence suggests that it may not.) Critics also cite instances in which objects of known age, such as freshly cooled volcanic rocks or just-felled trees, have yielded wildly inaccurate radiometric dates. But if the radiometric techniques are essentially useless, then how seriously are we to take the interminably repeated assertion that scientists "know" that the Earth is four-and-a-half billion years old?

The Earth's magnetic field is collapsing. At the present rate it will fall to zero in about 1200 years. No one knows why.

BIOLOGY

The problems in biology are so numerous and basic that it is hard to know where to begin, and I cannot hope to do more than name a few of the most glaring ones. Biology is, of course, the science of life; but biologists are generally averse to telling us just what life *is*. The currently popular strategy is to try to erase the conceptual boundary between life and non-life, though even the simplest living cell has characteristics profoundly different from those of any non-living entity. The difficulty comes because many scientists *assume* that biology should be reducible to chemistry and physics; they abhor the idea that living things might possess some fundamental principle not present in non-living matter. And yet all attempts to generate life out of chemicals—that is, to reproduce the processes that *must* (according to theory) have brought about the beginnings of life on Earth—have fallen far short of their goal.

A host of difficulties surround Darwinian and neo-Darwinian theories of evolution. In its essence, the word *evolution* simply means "directional change over time." There is little question that evolution in this sense has taken place. But what kind of evolution, and what has driven it? The idea that chance genetic mutations could add up constructively seems far-fetched, since so few beneficial mutations are likely to occur amid so many harmful ones. And then there are structures, like the vertebrate eye, that simply would not have functioned until an entire complex of individual features was in place, though none of these features by itself would have conferred any advantage to the organism.

Neo-Darwinian theorists treat the idea of natural selection with a kind of religious awe, but critics point out that it is essentially tautological: we say that the fittest survive, but how are we to *define* "the fittest," except as "those who survive?" Moreover, natural selection implies fierce, unending competition. Yet, as entomologist P. S. Messenger puts it, "Actual competition is difficult to see in nature." Nature instead produces unending examples of cooperation. Differing species, and members of the same species, go well out of their way to *avoid* competition wherever possible.

The science of genetics has gone a long way toward explaining how the physical characteristics of organisms are passed along through generations. But genetics is still unable to explain cell differentiation in embryos, the ability of simple organisms to regenerate lost limbs and organs, and the transmission of instinct.

The battle of evolutionary biologists with the Bible-based creationists has unfortunately served mostly to harden the ranks of the former against admissions that serious problems such as these exist. Our overwhelming ignorance is masked by sweeping declarations about the creative powers of natural selection, and we are deprived of the insights that might come from an honest assessment of the limits of our knowledge of life's origin and development. Meanwhile, unorthodox but promising ideas—such as Fred Hoyle's cosmic evolutionism (the proposal that life was seeded on Earth from comets), Ludwig von Bertalanffy's theory of living systems, and Rupert Sheldrake's theory of formative causation—are typically given short shrift.

ANTHROPOLOGY

Human origins are no less mysterious than those of other living things. In the past few decades, new techniques—such as the tracing of mutations in mitochondrial DNA—have offered intriguing clues as to the timing of our early ancestors' significant migrations. But these techniques are not without difficulties.

In addition, we humans exhibit a host of biological features and be-havioral characteristics shared by none of our primate relatives, and these beg for explanations. Why our bipedal stance, limb proportions, smooth skin, large brain size, tendency to perspire, and ability to breathe volun-tarily? Why are humans uniquely prone to lower back pain, varicose veins, hemorrhoids, sunburn, acne, dandruff, obesity, and swollen adenoids?

British science writer Elaine Morgan, in her books *The Aquatic Ape: A Theory of Human Evolution* and *The Scars of Evolution: What Our Bodies Tell Us About Human Origins*, has offered a promising proposal—that during our early evolution we humans passed through a long phase of adaptation to the shallow water of lakes, rivers, and sea coasts. Morgan points out that the features that separate us from other primates are precisely ones that appear in aquatic mammals such as manatees, dolphins, sea lions, and whales. Lower back pain, varicose veins, and hemorrhoids may derive from our shift from walking in shallow water to walking on land; acne and dandruff from our continuing to secrete fur-waterproofing sebum in an aquatic environment in which we became furless; and swollen adenoids from our descended larynx, characteristic of an aquatic mouth-breather.

Morgan's hypothesis also goes a long way toward explaining the dearth of early human fossil remains. During past Ice Ages the level of the oceans was up to three hundred feet lower than at present. If human beings were shore-dwellers, most of their remains were likely buried under water.

Yet Morgan's proposals are still considered eccentric by the establishment.

ARCHAEOLOGY

For decades archaeologists have maintained that the first people to set foot in the Americas crossed a land bridge over the Bering Sea roughly 12,000 years ago. But in several instances, human artifacts or remains have turned up in deposits that are much older. While most experts continue to discount these anomalies, others are quietly beginning to concede that human beings may have been living in the Americas for twenty to fifty thousand years—or more.

According to standard history, Native American cultures evolved in isolation from the rest of the world. For over a century, renegade archaeologists have theorized that the Mayas and Aztecs were contacted by Egyptian, Phoenician, or Chinese explorers. Most such theories perished for lack of incontrovertible evidence. During the past two decades, however, Barry Fell of Harvard, and others, have published descriptions of coins, petroglyphs, and other artifacts that seem to prove that Celts, Basques, Libyans, Arabians, Romans, Egyptians, Hebrews, and Chinese all visited North America at one time or another. The scientific establishment remains unconvinced.

In recent years amateur Egyptologist John Anthony West has called attention to the remarkable weathering patterns on the Sphinx on the Giza plateau. A geologist he has consulted (Robert Schoch of Boston University) agrees that the weathering was caused by water and indicates an age for the Sphinx of seven to ten thousand years. Since virtually no other Egyptian monument shows similar weathering (despite similarity of materials), this would seem to indicate that the Sphinx was built in an era long predating the pharaohs. Professional Egyptologists are adamant that the Sphinx is less than five thousand years old and was constructed by the pharaoh Khephren, and ask: If the Sphinx is an artifact of an earlier civilization, where is the corroborating evidence for that civilization's existence? Good question. But the archaeologists offer no reasonable alternative explanation for the Sphinx's deep water channels.

PSYCHOLOGY

Just as biology deals with life by explaining it away, psychology often treats consciousness (the natural object of its study) as an epiphenomenon, or even—in the case of behaviorism—as something to be ignored altogether. Despite some progress in the past decade, we still have no generally accepted theory of consciousness and we still do not know how memories are stored and accessed.

Because psychology is forced to exist within the mechanistic framework of the rest of science (excepting quantum physics), most psychologists avoid consideration of "paranormal" phenomena such as precognition, telepathy, and clairvoyance, which resist materialist explanations. Nevertheless, both anecdotal and experimental evidence for such psychic phenomena persists, albeit in maddeningly elusive forms.

These days the idea that the mind can influence the body via the immune system is becoming widely accepted. But extraordinary mind-body phenomena are difficult to understand in terms of known biophysical processes. How is it that, in a single individual with multiple-personality disorder, one personality may suffer from severe food allergies to which another personality is immune?

According to conventional views in psychology, higher mental phenomena are supposed to take place in the cerebral cortex, a late evolutionary development. How, then, is one to explain cases of hydrocephalus in which the cortex is only a millimeter or so thick, but the affected individual shows no obvious mental impairment? British Neurologist John Lorber, in research published during the 1980s, cited the case of a Sheffield University student with an IQ of 126 who had virtually no brain. What does this do to our beliefs about the relationship between the brain and consciousness?

The notion that human consciousness is affected by geomagnetic fields is still at the fringe of scientific acceptability. Two surveys (one by Stevenson, published in 1970; the other by Braud and Dennis in 1989) suggest that paranormal experiences coincide with days of minimal geomagnetic activity; another (by Raps, Avi, *et al.*, published in 1992) shows a high correlation between solar activity (which seems to influence the geomagnetic field) and the outbreak of psychiatric illnesses. Given that the Earth's magnetic field is diminishing, should we prepare ourselves for the widespread occurrence of psychic—and psychopathic—phenomena?

THE RECOVERY OF PRIMAL KNOWLEDGE

Readers already familiar with the study of scientific anomalies will know that we have hardly scratched the surface. In virtually every field, widely accepted views are plagued by internal contradictions; and in many cases these problems are hardly peripheral, but pertain to bedrock issues. Moreover, they tend to compound one another: A scientist in one discipline (such as astronomy), in order to clear up a problem, will often rely on "facts" from another discipline (such as physics), believing that the conclusions he or she reaches thereby are solidly supported—when in reality they may be resting upon the flimsiest of foundations. This process snowballs from discipline to discipline, specialist relying upon specialist.

When one begins to see the same pattern of anomaly, dogma, and denial cropping up in field after field, the overall picture of science one gets is of *a worldview that is virtually a house of cards.* We have created a system of knowledge consisting of millions of observed facts arranged in such a way as to give an essentially uncertain and probably false view of the nature of reality. My point is not that science has made no valuable contributions— it has—but that we always need to see those contributions in context and to appreciate their limits and the tradeoffs we have made for their sake. Lao Tze reputedly wrote, "To know how little one knows is to have genuine knowledge." Ironically, we in the industrialized world—who pride ourselves on living in an "information age"—are perhaps further from having genuine knowledge than were people in most "primitive" cultures throughout history.

The only sane course of action in this circumstance would be to take an attitude of extreme skepticism with regard to all scientific explanations, admit our ignorance, and adopt a stance of great caution with regard to actions we might take with respect to nature and society based on scientific theories. At the same time, we should begin to pay more attention to the knowledge systems of primal peoples as a way of counterbalancing some of the excesses of our accustomed ways of thinking.

The study of native peoples' systems of knowledge is known academically as *ethnoscience*. Most of ethnoscience's specialties—which include ethnoastronomy, ethnobotany, ethnopharmacology, ethnopsychology, and ethnozoology—have emerged as legitimate fields of inquiry only within the last half of the twentieth century. Even prior to 1970, most scientists still assumed that the empirical knowledge of nonindustrial peoples was rudimentary or vestigial. Evidence to the contrary was usually greeted with disbelief. Gradually, a few pioneering ethnologists have managed to shift the established view.

Today, some branches of ethnoscience are rising stars in the academic community. Ethnopharmacologists routinely visit rainforest villages to gather information about local healing techniques and herbs. Seed companies send ethnobotanists to recover specimens of cultivars from indigenous subsistence gardeners. And archaeo- and ethnoastronomers debate in journals and international congresses the nature and extent of tribal cultures' knowledge of the sky.

But the practical knowledge common to members of traditional cultures does not represent merely an accumulation of isolated facts and observations; it is part of a comprehensive worldview. Without some understanding of the quality of that worldview, the information gathered from a tribal shaman here or a village elder there is just so much looted intellectual property.

All human thought is a striving for order, and the forms that order may take are endless. As we grow up in any given culture, we become accustomed to organizing our perceptions in certain ways that seem to us to be so self-evidently correct and necessary that we hardly ever bother to wonder if there might be alternatives. When we come into contact with a radically different culture, its ways of thinking seem strange and challenging.

Nevertheless, the more we learn about unfamiliar peoples, the more perspective we tend to gain not only on the general range of our society's beliefs and practices, but on *the very attitudes that motivate the project of investigating other cultures*. These attitudes, beliefs, and practices are part and parcel of what we call science. And so one of the potential results of cross-cultural research is an increased understanding of the nature of the basic form of thought that pervades modern science, and how it differs from the form of thought used by traditional peoples in their pursuit of knowledge.

The French anthropologist Claude Lévi-Strauss explored this fundamental difference in his 1962 book *The Savage Mind*. While previous researchers had theorized that science and primal thought are expressions of different stages in the evolution of human intelligence, Lévi-Strauss emphatically disagreed, concluding instead that Western science and traditional wisdom constitute two equally valid forms of knowledge. "These are certainly not a function of different stages of development of the human mind," wrote Lévi-Strauss, "but rather of two strategic levels at which nature is accessible to scientific enquiry: one roughly adapted to that of perception and the imagination: the other at a remove from it. It is as if the necessary connections which are the object of all science . . . could be arrived at by two different routes, one very close to, and the other more remote from, sensible intuition."[2]

Native wisdom is, in Lévi-Strauss's phrase, "supremely concrete": It deals in the sensible qualities of things. It is primary, existential, multisensory, holistic, and visceral. It deals in *signs*, which are midway between percepts (raw sensory data) and concepts (purely intellectual ideas and principles abstracted from experience). For the tribal shaman, the Sun and Moon *signify* spiritual principles at work in the world; their appearance in the sky carries meaning in relation to both natural and human affairs. For the scientist, the Sun and Moon are distant bodies with certain material properties. Our scientific conceptions of the Sun and Moon are abstracted from experience; these concepts allow us to stand apart from the immediate reports of our senses and to discover causal relations that may not be intuitively obvious—such as the fact that the apparent daily motion of the Sun actually results from the rotation of the Earth.

Primal knowledge relies on exhaustive observation and the systematic cataloging of relations and connections between things. It arises from concrete encounters with game animals, wild plants, storms and droughts, and the shape, color, and feel of specific local landforms that have been studied in the minutest detail throughout the seasons. These elements of daily experience are also the subject of dreams and visions, which for the primal person are additional sources of knowledge. Thus the actions of observing and cataloging do not separate the primal observer from the world, but rather include her or him in it. The shaman participates in nature *just as it is*, in its totality. Biologist R. B. Fox writes that the Pinatubo Negrito of the Philippines "is an intrinsic part of his environment, and what is still more important, continually studies his surroundings. Many times I have seen a Negrito, who, when not being certain of the identification of a particular plant, will taste the fruit, smell the leaves, break and examine the stem, comment upon its habitat, and only after all of this, pronounce whether he did or did not know the plant."[3] And, as Lévi-Strauss notes, this participative, holistic mode of observation often leads to scientifically valid results.

The scientist likewise relies on observation, but in a different way. His method is to isolate the component parts of a phenomenon so as to deduce the nature of their relations. This requires that he formalize his own participation in events. He regards what is observed as something distant and separate from himself that can be broken down into constituent elements and forces and reassembled by way of universal laws deduced from observation. His ultimate goal is a complete theoretical picture of the universe. This approach clearly leads to the ability to understand, predict, and control a vast range of phenomena. But the scientist's "objective" aloofness has its pitfalls: Whatever phenomena cannot be reduced to concrete, well-understood components tend to be ignored and discounted. Meanwhile, nature ceases to be an extension of the self and becomes instead a laboratory or a storehouse of resources. And the intensified application of the scientific method in more and more areas requires increasing specialization, so that the scientific specialist—whose task is to learn more and more about less and less—ultimately ends up knowing everything about nothing and nothing about everything.

Again, Lévi-Strauss warns us that " . . . it is important not to make the mistake of thinking that these are two stages or phases in the evolution of knowledge. Both approaches are equally valid"; "the difference lies, not in the quality of the intellectual process, but in the nature of the things to which it is applied."[4] Indeed, it is useful to see the approach of the scientist and the shaman not as competing or as mutually exclusive, but as complementary: the strengths of one tend to balance the weaknesses of the other.

The premises of primal knowledge can perhaps be summarized in the following five points:

🞂 *Everything is interrelated.* For the primal individual, it is impossible to separate "religion" from "science," "nature" from "society," or to conceive of dozens of other distinctions that we in industrial societies take for granted. Moreover, primal peoples often draw connections that appear baffling or groundless to us. The Pima of Arizona, for example, attribute throat diseases to the badger; swellings, headaches, and fever to the bear; and diseases of the lungs to the deer. These correspondences derive from myths of primordial conflicts between animals, plants, and humans, in which animals responded to human treachery by sending diseases. While they make little sense from the standpoint of modern medical theory, within the Pima's social and ecological context these reputed relationships serve the practical purpose of providing a system of disease classification that ties the human and animal worlds together in an overarching ethical system.

❧ *Humans are not superior to, but part of and responsible to, the rest of nature.* Primal peoples do not think of nature as a *kingdom* in which humans are the divinely (or intellectually) ordained regents, but as a *kindom* in which family members have mutual obligations. People in nearly all traditional cultures perform periodic world renewal ceremonies because they believe that it is humankind's duty to help maintain the balance of nature. This duty extends also to daily acts of gratitude and reciprocity, such as asking and thanking the spirit of an animal that is to be killed for food. Each species is seen as having its own unique gifts and powers. Far from seeing human beings as lords and masters of the world, some native peoples go so far as to regard people as inherently inferior to the animals.

❧ *The world is alive.* Primal peoples assume that the universe is aware, conscious, and responsive to human thoughts and feelings, and they therefore call upon the spirits of the wind, clouds, water, animals, and plants and in return listen for their blessings, advice, warnings, and protests. All of nature is regarded as being pervaded by vital energy.

❧ *The world is sacred.* In primal society no object or being is purely physical, and no circumstance arises by chance. Each species, each land form, has *meaning.*

❧ *Time is cyclical.* We tend to view time as a linear progression of events. We see natural history in terms of evolution and human history in terms of progress. Primal peoples experience time as a circle or spiral. The daily round of light and darkness, the seasonal round of growth and decay, and the lifetime round of birth, childhood, adulthood, old age, and death, serve as models for a view of time as a mesh of interlinked cycles (in nature), and as recurrent periods of inspiration and moral crisis (in human society).

Many writers have noted that the first premise of primal knowledge—the interrelatedness of all things—agrees closely with the relatively recent findings of the science of ecology, which highlights the interconnectivity of processes within ecosystems and even leads (via the Gaia hypothesis of James Lovelock and Lynn Margulis) to the idea that the Earth itself is, at very least in a metaphorical sense, alive. That science and primal thought sometimes arrive at the same conclusions may be heartening, but this should not be taken to mean that one or the other path by which those conclusions were arrived at is thereby rendered superfluous. In both science and primal thought, the means for the attainment of knowledge (the scientific method on one hand, the existential involvement with the natural world on the other) are in some respects ends in themselves.

So far we have contrasted modern science and primal knowledge as though each were a uniform pattern of thought. It is true that the knowledge systems of primal peoples in all parts of the world have much in common. But it is also important to remember that there are important differences among the worldviews of native cultures.

This variety of perspectives constitutes a final difference between science and primal knowledge. Western science assumes that it will eventually arrive at a single composite theoretical view of reality that is universally true—a completely objective and accurate understanding of nature. But this may be an unrealistic goal because, as Lévi-Strauss points out, "The scientist never carries on a dialogue with nature pure and simple but rather with a particular relationship between nature and culture definable in terms of his particular period and civilization and the material means at his disposal."[5] Every scientific theory is based upon cultural assumptions that are at least in part unconscious and unexamined. This suggests that there are potentially as many valid paths by which science *could* develop as there are cultures. In the study of primal knowledge we have the opportunity to glimpse not merely new sets of information, but alternative ways of constructing reality. To ignore these alternatives is to cut ourselves off from the wellspring of possibility at the core of human existence.

WHOSE INTELLECTUAL PROPERTY?

Current academic and commercial interest in indigenous knowledge may help preserve and spread some of that knowledge, but the way this interest is being expressed often works to the detriment of primal peoples themselves. When ethnobotanists transfer knowledge from traditional healers to pharmaceutical firms, and when genetic resource conservationists transfer knowledge from indigenous farmers to seed corporations, the intellectual property rights go to the corporations, not to the farmers and healers. Over time, this appropriation of knowledge tends to destroy the ecological and cultural context in which the knowledge was generated and preserved.

Corporations are collecting primal knowledge for profit, medical researchers are sifting it for new healing techniques and pharmaceuticals, and universities are establishing programs in the various subdisciplines of ethnoscience. Meanwhile, primal peoples are being forced into the cash economy, driven from their ancestral lands, propelled into urban slums, coerced into adopting new religions, and in all too many cases simply gunned down in the forests. In the sixteenth century, European explorers wanted land and gold. Today, corporations want information. From the perspective of the indigenous peoples, very little has changed. Only now, the very survival of the world's last primal cultures—and their vast and immeasurably valuable storehouse of tribal wisdom—is at stake.

Meanwhile, the practical wisdom of the world's primal peoples acquires ever-increasing importance as we seek to restore ecological balances that have lately been overwhelmed by the economic activities of civilization. These days, we in the industrialized world are beginning to appreciate the importance of genetic diversity and of cultural sustainability. We are coming to see how vital it is that we find a way to live in balance with nature. The knowledge of how to maintain biodiversity and to live sustainably already exists, but tragically we are still trying to force our own fragmented, commercialized, and speeded-up way of life on the few remaining people who maintain that knowledge.

The recovery and preservation of primal knowledge won't eliminate all the world's problems. But its loss will make many of the worst of those problems far harder to solve in the future. This is knowledge that, once forfeited, may require generations—in some cases tens or hundreds of generations—to regain. Our future may therefore hinge on our willingness to stop imposing our economic, educational, and social agenda on the traditional land-based peasants and the wandering savages of the world and to learn instead to listen to what they have to say. As we do, we may find their message deeply challenging not only to our reigning scientific paradigms but to our entire way of life. Yet it is a message we cannot afford to ignore.

As Karl Polanyi has noted, the industrial revolution was marked by "an almost miraculous improvement in the tools of production" and by "a catastrophic dislocation of the lives of the common people." Gradually, and often without reflection or recognition, the vacuum began to be filled by the very aims and activities that had begun undermining security in the first place. Deprived of roots, traditions, and secure ties to a community in which a place was guaranteed, people began to try to reduce their anxiety by identifying with their increasing power over nature. The accumulation of wealth and material comforts, rather than secure rooting in a frame and context, began to form the primary basis for quelling the feelings of vulnerability that inevitably afflict us.

—PAUL WACHTEL

 DURING THE 1950S AND '60s, when I was growing up in the American Midwest, the evidence of progress was everywhere. Each year the cars grew lower, longer, and sleeker. Television was still a relative novelty, and virtually all of the consumer products it advertised were "new" and "improved." On Sunday evenings the family gathered to watch The Walt Disney Hour, which featured scenes from Tomorrowland, with rocket-shaped cars guided along elevated highways. I especially relished occasions when Dr. Wernher von Braun appeared on the show to explain the principles of rocketry and space travel. I also remember when the first shopping mall was built on the outskirts of my home city; and when, over the next few years, the downtown area, with its stately old brick buildings, slowly began to die. One Christmas my parents fed my fascination with science by buying me a Calculo Analog Computer—which turned out to be a useless toy (it was basically an electronic slide rule); still, I was intrigued by the idea that an ordinary person could own a computer.

Those were also years when everyone was dogged by a smoldering fear of the possibility of nuclear war: The same miraculous technology that was brightening our vision of the future was threatening also to obliterate that future instantaneously, at any moment, without warning. But for the most part, we envisioned the future as a world in which space travel would be commonplace and in which everyone would lead a life of leisure and sophistication. All human problems, it seemed, would soon give way to progress.

Sadly, the future isn't all it was cracked up to be. In the past thirty years, we've gone to the Moon and we've sent probes to other planets. Today the cars are sleeker and more sophisticated (and more expensive) than ever. Now I have a computer that is *not* a useless toy, but an amazingly versatile publishing tool. Still, I think most people would agree that progress has brought as many dilemmas as delights. The world of 1996 is, on the whole, a much scarier place than was the world of, say, 1959—with the notable exception of an apparent reduction in the likelihood of all-out nuclear conflagration. Then we were already well on our way toward overpopulation, species extinctions, air and water pollution, deforestation, loss of topsoil, the destruction of traditional cultures, the spread of poverty, and all the other problems that hound us today. Yet in those days most people could still afford to ignore whatever warning signs were appearing. Then we had an easy answer: No matter what the difficulty, progress would solve it. Now we're not so sure.

Has progress failed? Or is it just getting warmed up? Perhaps the time has come to examine more closely just what it is that we have put so much faith in.

THE ORIGIN AND PROGRESS OF THE IDEA OF PROGRESS

While the earliest Greek mythology is suffused with the idea of a past Golden Age and the subsequent degeneration of humanity, by the fifth century B.C.E. this rather pessimistic worldview was being widely replaced by a belief in the gradual betterment of life. Increasingly, philosophers described the original condition of human beings as "brutish," "animal-like," and "disorderly," and described history as a process whereby, "little by little," life was becoming more secure and refined for everyone.

The idea of progress didn't catch on immediately. It has always had to contend—as it did in the case of the Greeks—with the contrary doctrine of a primordial paradise whose tragic loss has led to humanity's moral decline. These two philosophies seem to serve different purposes and to condition people toward different kinds of social experiences. The ideology of progress serves the purposes of civilization by systematically downgrading the worth of the past, of "unimproved" nature, and of uncivilized life; by extolling the present, the future, and all that has been "improved" by human action; and by exhorting people to have faith that all of the problems created by our divorce from nature will be solved by more invention and sophistication. The paradisal worldview, in contrast, because of its idealization of an age when people lived without artifice, is inherently more appropriate to traditional, humble, stable, and sustainable cultures.

A couple of thousand years ago, the philosophers and theologians of the Roman Empire began to explore ways to co-opt the paradisal doctrine so that it too could further the interests of civilization. One strategy consisted of positing a future restored paradise that would take the form of a perfected city with golden streets littered with gems. The present age may be "fallen," but the trajectory of history reaches toward a grand goal nevertheless. If people will sacrifice and work hard, this future paradise (or at least an otherworldly facsimile) can be brought within reach.

In the nineteenth century, the progressive impulse got another boost through its marriage with the theory of evolution. Over millions of years, said the proponents of this union, nature has inexorably transformed itself, with simple creatures giving way to more complex ones; perhaps human society is destined to undergo a similar process. Of course, this was really only a rough analogy at best: The actual mechanics of evolution were poorly understood then (and still are), and progress was a social rather than a purely biological phenomenon. But the commingling of the two ideas lent progress a quasi-scientific aura of inevitability and gave evolution a new human relevance. Moreover, it resulted in an offspring: social Darwinism, the proposal that since (as it was then believed) evolution proceeds by natural selection—the strongest and fittest surviving to pass their characteristics along to the next generation—therefore progress must likewise depend upon the subordination of the "unfit," i.e., the poor and the politically powerless, to the socially "fit," epitomized by the leaders of finance and industry.

Despite social Darwinism's justification of the triumph of the strong over the weak, many people in the late nineteenth and early twentieth centuries envisioned progress as promoting not only the accumulation of wealth and power and the invention of new means of production, but "higher" human values as well—knowledge, holiness, compassion, and justice. In the future, everyone would be fed; war would become obsolete; knowledge and understanding would proliferate; perhaps all humankind would even become spiritually unified in an ontological "omega point."

These days faith in this humanitarian version of the idea of progress is still alive, though badly shaken. We have abolished slavery by law, but it still exists in many parts of the world; we are more keenly aware of the need for governments to respect human rights, but abuses of those rights persist on a vast scale. Meanwhile, anthropologists have shown fairly conclusively that people in many primitive societies enjoyed freedoms and rights in degrees that put even the most enlightened modern industrial democracies to shame. While scientific knowledge continues to accumulate, it seems to benefit fewer and fewer people. And though there is no way to gauge whether the population as a whole is more spiritually enlightened today than in the past, one cannot help but be struck by the mean-spiritedness of the current political climate throughout the West.

At the end of the twentieth century, the realization of our vision of the gold and crystal city of the future seems more elusive than ever, as does the goal of the universal moral upliftment of humanity. Progress is undeniable. But when we get down to cases, we see that it has come about primarily in terms of technological innovation and economic growth. *These* form the real core of what progress has actually meant to us. But are economic growth and technological innovation, in themselves, necessarily good things? Perhaps we can find out by looking a little more closely at the history not just of the *idea*, but of the actual *process* of progress.

HOW PROGRESS HAS WORKED SO FAR

While the course of economic and technological innovation and growth can be traced in many societies and eras, the most dramatic and relevant example of progress is surely to be seen in the industrial revolution in Europe.

According to most historians, the economic foundation for the industrial revolution was laid by the enclosure movement, which began in England in the sixteenth century. "Enclosure" meant to surround pieces of open land with barriers to free travel, placing it under private control. This was done through acts of Parliament, license from the king, and (occasionally) by common agreement of the members of the village commune.

Until the enclosure movement, the common people of Europe held much land communally. The village commons was administered democratically through peasant councils, which decided when to plant, harvest, and rotate crops; how many animals could graze; how water should be allocated; and how many trees could be cut. For centuries the system of the village commons provided a stable base for European society.

However, beginning in the 1500s, increased urban demand for food created inflation, which meant reduced income to landlords whose rents had been fixed at pre-inflationary rates. Simultaneously, the textile industry was expanding, requiring more wool. Landlords borrowed money from the new bourgeois class of merchants and bankers, bought up common lands, and turned them into pasture for sheep. This resulted in millions of peasants being forced off the land and into the cities, where they formed a huge and expanding pool of cheap labor. On many occasions the peasants rebelled, but the law was against them and enclosure proceeded until the village commons finally became extinct in the early nineteenth century.

Enclosure has been described as "the revolution of the rich against the poor." Especially during the second wave of enclosure in the 1700s, English society underwent a catastrophic transformation. Increasingly, a few individuals were freed—indeed, encouraged by laissez-faire economic philosophers—to pursue their self-interest without being held accountable to a larger community. Meanwhile, the majority of people became economically and culturally disenfranchised and were forced to sell their labor to the highest bidder. Complex social units—the village, the neighborhood, the extended family—disintegrated into simpler ones—the nuclear family, the married couple, the individual.

With human labor available in surplus, and with seemingly boundless new sources of raw materials being discovered in (and expropriated from) overseas colonies, investors found plentiful opportunities for profit. Markets were expanding, transportation systems were being improved, and inventors were finding new ways to intensify the means of production. The factory was born, and with it an entirely new pattern of life for the average person.

Today enclosure continues both in the Third World, where tribal common lands are being privatized at a furious pace, and in the older industrial nation-states, where the process is being extended to genetic materials in plants and animals, information, and technical knowledge.

By detaching people from land and land-based customs, enclosure has led to ever greater reliance on the market for the satisfaction of all human needs. Markets, in order to operate successfully, require profits. And profits can come in only three ways: by the growth of the market, so that incomes expand for most or all people within the system; by one firm winning orders previously filled by another firm (so that someone's profit comes at the expense of someone else); and by raising prices, which leads to inflation. Since the second and third alternatives are clearly of limited use, economists have put overwhelming emphasis on the first—economic growth. Today, with all industries relying on borrowing, for which interest must be paid, economic growth is not merely desirable; it is a necessity. Without it, the economy does not merely continue at a steady rate; it collapses.

Economic growth is progress. But it is also a form of collective addiction that, in the long run, intensifies the problems (unemployment and inflation) that it is meant to solve. As economist Herman Daly and others have pointed out, our world is finite, and in a finite world unlimited economic growth must eventually lead to disaster. And as Donnella Meadows has shown in her books *The Limits to Growth* and *Beyond the Limits*, we have already followed the path of economic growth further than it may prudently be trod.

But progress is not a matter of economics alone. Over the past three centuries we have witnessed revolution after revolution in the technologies of transportation, communication, manufacture, warfare, and entertainment. The world has seen the birth of the automobile, telephone, computer, robot, radio, television, microwave oven, fax machine, and nuclear missile. When most people think of progress, this is what they mean.

When we use a new technology to satisfy a basic human need, are we thereby enhancing life? A few decades ago virtually everyone would have answered unquestioningly in the affirmative. Today there is a growing chorus of doubters. Many new technologies claim to save time and labor. In individual cases they indisputably do. But when we add in all of the extra costs that a new technology entails, these sometimes more than cancel out any short-term benefit. Today the typical American is surrounded by labor-saving devices, and yet the European pre-enclosure peasant actually worked fewer hours per week on average than a modern American with a full-time job.

The dilemmas of technology are perhaps best illustrated in the fields of human health and health care. The people with the simplest technologies— the food gatherers—are also generally quite healthy, with no cancer or heart disease, typically perfect teeth, vision, and hearing, and few infectious or degenerative diseases. The domestication of animals several millennia ago introduced smallpox, measles, typhus, salmonella, influenza, and parasites into the human population, and agricultural life brought poorer nutrition and dentition and increased stress. Modern industrial living entails a raft of still more new ailments resulting from air and water pollution, chemicals in food, nuclear radiation, and computer- and job-related stress. The miracles of modern drugs and surgery are only partly able to keep up with these burgeoning diseases of civilization and have produced a wide range of damaging side effects of their own. Today the average human life span is longer than ever before, mostly because of a dramatic reduction in infant mortality, but the resulting overpopulation introduces the threat of famine and pestilence on an unimaginable scale. Modern medicine continues to make impressive strides; meanwhile, compared to our gatherer or hunter ancestors, the typical civilized human is overweight yet poorly nourished, lacking in muscular development, overstressed, and unhappy.

Each new technology changes society, and not all of these changes are desirable or foreseeable. But once a technology has been adopted, society tends to remold itself around the new tool so that it becomes an essential part of life. Therefore people find it nearly impossible to reject a technology, once adopted, even if its effects are later found to be mostly negative. While some chemical pesticides have been banned in America, their makers have merely opened markets to the south and overseas; and while nearly everyone would likely agree that nuclear weapons are the worst invention in history, governments continue to manufacture, test, and "improve" them.

The true role of technology in society becomes clearer when we see beyond its magical aura and view it in functional, historical terms as *a means of economic change*. When, because of enclosure, people are separated from their lands and cultures and thrust into cities, they can no longer satisfy their needs directly and communally. They therefore tend to find ways to fill them indirectly and artificially through technology. New technologies create new opportunities for economic growth, and are therefore encouraged regardless of tradeoffs and long-term costs. Novelty comes to be valued for its own sake.

MUST PROGRESS ALWAYS WORK THIS WAY?

All of this suggests that the "progress" of the industrial revolution reflected certain unique historical developments. Enclosure, colonialism, capitalism, and an intensified interest in analytical science all converged to create an economic and technological transformation of unprecedented scope and intensity with horrendous unanticipated costs. But must all progress follow this same pattern?

Perhaps not. There are two important reasons why European progress turned out the way it did.

First: Because of the availability of cheap labor and raw materials, economic and technological change came so readily and produced such successes (from the standpoint of those in positions of power) that it became tempting to see the whole of human life purely in economic and mechanical terms and to ignore the entire range of human interests that do not reduce to money and machines. It is said that to a person whose only tool is a hammer, all problems look like nails. A person whose primary social tools are money and technology is likely to see life mostly in terms of personal gain, short-term profit, growth, speed, and novelty for its own sake. Health, community, the sense of belonging, the appreciation for human and natural diversity, the feeling of connection with the land where one lives, the satisfaction of meaningful work, play, the sense of self-worth, self-determination, and of sympathy and solidarity across generational lines simply do not register on the scale of monetary values (or do so at best only indirectly), and are therefore of little concern to *Homo economicus*.

Second: Because economics and technology have been cut off from these deeper and broader priorities, they have themselves developed along skewed lines. As Herman Daly and John Cobb point out in their book *For the Common Good*, the word *economics* derives from the Greek *oikonomia*, which referred to the management of the household so as to increase its use value to all members over the long run. Implicit in this original meaning were a sense of community and a mutual responsibility to future generations. Aristotle carefully distinguished economics, in this sense, from *chrematistics*, which is the branch of political economy relating to the manipulation of property and wealth so as to maximize short-term monetary exchange value to the owner. In the early industrial period, wealthy elites pursued chrematistics so successfully (again, from their standpoint) that they tended to confuse it with economics, and this confusion has only grown with the passage of decades and centuries.

But things need not have gone this way. It should not be difficult to imagine an economics that is not utterly subservient to chrematistics; after all, every stable traditional society on Earth has had one. And there is every reason to think that, within such a reconstituted economics, progress (in the sense of gradual refinement or improvement) would be possible.

The same applies to technology. Many people assume that technology is somehow value- and context-free; that when people anywhere become smart enough, they will inevitably invent the same technologies we have. But this assumption flies in the face of data from history and anthropology. In fact, every technology reflects and embodies specific, nonarbitrary social values. For example, a decentralized, egalitarian, nature-loving society—no matter how advanced or sophisticated—would never invent the atomic reactor, because nuclear technology requires a centralized managerial bureaucracy, uranium mines, and toxic waste storage facilities, which such a society would never tolerate. But what technologies *would* such a society eventually create? Perhaps technological progress, in such a context, might take a form quite different from what we have come to know and expect. It might, for example, concentrate on the refinement of the simplest, most versatile, and most easily obtainable tools, so that every member of the society could participate in their manufacture, use, and improvement. This is, in fact, the trend of technological development that we see in the traditional egalitarian societies that have been studied.

To put the matter as succinctly as possible: Western civilization has developed in the way it has because it has allowed its collective values and goals to be artificially narrowed for the sake of the short-term gain of a relative few at the expense of the many. The ecological and social problems that have resulted are not attributable directly to human nature, nor to evolutionary necessity. The course of Western civilization may be described as progress, but it is progress of a very peculiar kind.

REINVENTING PROGRESS

The idea of progress has been—and is being—used to justify all manner of mischief. One is therefore tempted to reject it altogether in favor of the older paradisal worldview. After all, from the standpoint of native peoples and other species, civilization has proven itself to be the scourge of the Earth. Perhaps we would all be better off in noncivilized cultures that look to ancestral tradition—rather than new theories and gadgets—for answers to life's challenges.

And yet it is difficult to give up the anticipation that somehow we can together learn, change, and improve our society. Granted, our criteria for what constitutes "improvement" have become grotesquely twisted by our addiction to certain dangerous brands of economic and technological development. But if we were to base those criteria on deeper and more universal values, then might we not still enjoy a certain cultural dynamism? The alternative to progress-as-we-know-it need neither be cultural nostalgia nor permanent stasis.

The first step toward this new kind of progress would be to sort out our collective interests, values, goals, and priorities. This sorting process is not likely to be accomplished once-and-for-all in a single stroke. It will itself provide an arena for ongoing refinement.

Once we have made some headway in getting back in touch with our real needs and innate values, we may find that the actions required to fulfill and further them will be ones that appear, from our present perspective, to be *regressive*. That is, we may find it necessary to undo some of our old economic and technological "progress." We may, for example, find it necessary to restore the commons and to rediscover the participatory, communal attitudes that once enabled us to live in a world without borders. We may wish to do away with our sophisticated systems for monetary speculation and manipulation. We may also find ourselves giving up cars, fossil fuels, and factories—and breathing a sigh of relief as we do so.

All the while, we will not be moving toward some idealized image of the past, but will instead be using our freshly clarified priorities as a foundation on which to build anew. The economies and technologies of the Middle Ages or of tribal societies may offer encouraging examples along the way, but they need not serve as our goals. *When values that were implicit and instinctive in those societies become conscious and explicit in ours, then we may see progress of a kind that is altogether unprecedented.*

Perhaps vistas of opportunity await us that are far grander than those advertised by even the most eloquent of our twentieth-century social engineers. Perhaps evolution and progress *can* converge in a single process as we reenter the free community of sovereign species as equal (not dominant) members, and devote our attention to the welfare of that entire community. Perhaps we may eventually even realize our Promethean dream of being space explorers . . . though not as Star-Trek colonists and cosmocrats, but as children waking from sleep, ready to go outside and play. Given different criteria of progress, we could find healthy feelings of cultural pride and loyalty being rekindled within and among us. We might find ourselves simultaneously savoring the present in a way that most civilized people have forgotten how to do, and regarding the future with optimism and confidence. We might come to enjoy a future in which the principal economic currency is human caring; a future in which each new generation is concerned to be *kinder* than the last, rather than *richer*; a future where the only technologies that matter are those that make the world a healthier, happier, and more beautiful place for all creatures.

That, I suggest, would be *progress*.

❧

In Part I, we saw how humanity's covenants with nature, leading from gathering to hunting, horticulture, agriculture, and industrialism come to a dead end with the development of a global hyperindustrial electronic civilization. Civilization survives only by predation and growth, and it is presently running out of new territory, new sources of "raw materials," and peripheral peoples to enslave. In the past, geographically limited civilizations have collapsed for environmental or political reasons. Now civilization *per se* is facing an existential crisis. We therefore stand at the brink of a cultural transition as profound and fateful as any that our kind has ever undertaken.

In Part II, we have explored the nuts and bolts of cultural change—both as it has occurred in past revolutions in means of production, and as it must occur now if we are to create a new, biologically sound and sustainable pattern of life. Then and now, the creation of culture is both an integrative and an elaborative process that encompasses the arts, patterns of governance, economics, technologies, knowledge systems, and spirituality. In each of these fields of human action, we have seen how civilization has undermined our innate biological wisdom; and in each field we see the direction in which sustainability lies.

We are not, however, observing this process of cultural transformation from some distant, disembodied, "objective" position. We are all embroiled in it. And we deal with the reality of it daily in our work and family life, in our eating, shopping, driving, recreation, and entertainment.

Traditional peoples such as the Hopi have somehow understood that the inherent contradictions of civilization would eventually lead to a crisis. In 1970, the "Hopi Traditional Village Elders" (consisting of Dan Katchongva of Hotevila, Mina Lansa of Oraibi, Claude Kawangyawma of Shongopovi, Starlie Lomayaktewa of Mishongnovi, and an interpreter) wrote a letter to President Richard Nixon, in which they expressed the essence of their people's prophecy for our age. They noted that

> Today, almost all of the prophecies have come to pass. Great roads
> like rivers pass along the landscape; man talks to man through the
> cobwebs of his telephone lines; man travels along the roads in the sky

in his airplanes; two great wars have been waged by those bearing the swastika or the rising Sun; man is tampering with the Moon and the stars. Most men have strayed from the path shown to us by the Great Spirit. . . .[1]

The Hopi call this time of transition the Great Purification. It is a period in which civilization as we have known it will face the gravest of challenges. According to Dan Katchongva:

> There will be earthquakes and floods causing great disasters, changes in the seasons, and in the weather, disappearance of wildlife and famine in different forms. There will be gradual corruption and confusion among the leaders and the people all over the world, and wars will come about like powerful winds.[2]

> Those gifted with the knowledge of sacred instructions will then live very cautiously, for they will remember and have faith in these instructions, and it will be on their shoulders that the fate of the world shall rest.[3]

Much of the Hopi prophecy is yet to be fulfilled. Yet enough has been by now that, in reading the words of Dan Katchongva and other elders, one cannot escape the sense that we are living in the time these people have long foreseen.

But what does it actually mean, in concrete human terms, to be living in the time of the Great Purification? How do we personally deal with the stress of accelerating change in a world seemingly gone mad? Is it possible, in the face of overwhelming social and ecological disintegration, to plant seeds of a new, sustainable, peaceful culture?

PART III

THE GREAT

PURIFICATION

13 | LESSONS IN HUMILITY

To speak of wilderness is to speak of wholeness. Human beings came out of that wholeness, and to consider the possibility of reactivating membership in the Assembly of All Beings is in no way regressive.

—GARY SNYDER

 THE IMAGE IS AS GROTESQUE as it is inescapable: virtually the entire arable land surface of the planet drafted and regimented to one purpose, and one purpose only—the feeding of hungry humans.

Already, "somewhere between 20 and 40 percent of the earth's primary productivity, from plant photosynthesis on land and in the sea, is . . . appropriated for human use," according to Royal Society research professor Robert M. May, writing in the March, 1993, *Scientific American*. With our population inexorably growing (UNESCO conservatively estimates that there will be about twice as many of us by the year 2050 as there are presently), in only a couple of generations the planet will have little room for anything but people, food for people, and whatever bugs, microbes, fish, and small land animals that can manage to escape us.

Meanwhile, we or our immediate successors will be living through what biologist Edward O. Wilson, in *The Diversity of Life*, describes as one of the greatest mass extinctions in Earth's history. Previous comparable extinction episodes of which we find traces in the fossil record apparently required between 10 million and 100 million years to be compensated for through new speciation. Even the shorter of these durations is much greater than the total age of the species *Homo sapiens* (according to prevailing views), let alone the total length of recorded history, and is therefore a period of time we cannot really comprehend.

For humanitarians, however, this wholesale disappearance of basic kinds of living things is of infinitely less concern than the problem of finding ways to feed the one species whose proliferation is necessitating the deaths of so many others. This response strikes me as more than a little strange; to others, it is so natural as to be beyond comment. The contest between the worldviews that underpin these two attitudes is still barely detectable in public debate, but in the decades ahead it may decide the fate not only of thousands of plant and animal species, but of human civilization as well.

THE CROWN OF CREATION

The mass extinction of the twenty-first century will be no accident. Neither will it be entirely the consequence of evil intent, greed, stupidity, and poor planning (though these will have played their parts). Rather, it will come mostly as the direct result of a specific set of beliefs embedded in civilization's working mythology. *The world was made for us. We are the crown of creation. Humans are separate from nature, an entirely unique order of creature. We are the masters of the world, and the world is here to serve us. In order to fulfill our birthright as humans we must* conquer *nature—subdue her and bend her to our needs in every respect. Only when our control is absolute will we have achieved our destiny.*

In his novel *Ishmael*, Daniel Quinn uses the fictional device of an extended telepathic conversation between a gorilla and a human pupil to draw out the outrageous absurdity of these propositions, which we have all been taught to regard as obvious truths. Ishmael, the gorilla, helps his student gradually to uncover and understand the story that civilization ceaselessly enacts. Somehow, we have decided that while all the rest of nature is subject to the evolutionary laws of life—which are centered around limited competition, mutual aid, balance, and moderation—we are immune. According to the "law," it is permissible for an organism to kill for food or to defend itself, but not systematically to kill its competitors, to deny its competitors access to food, or to destroy its competitors' food supply. Why? Because any organism that does these things reduces biological diversity and works against evolution—its own evolution included. A diverse ecosystem is always more resilient than a simple one: In one with thousands of species as opposed to dozens, more are likely to survive any climate change or diseases that might come along. Moreover, diversity implies more kinds of food (more kinds of berries, insects, flowers, etc.), and therefore more niches for survival. This is why ecologists regard biodiversity as one of the primary indices of the health of an environment.

But our aggressive styles of agriculture work against diversity: We've learned to kill "pests," which compete with us for food, and "weeds," which compete with our food crops. By doing so, we encourage the growth of a few domesticated varieties of plants and animals that we especially favor. As omnivores with few natural predators, we were already predisposed to biological success long before we started farming; but by flaunting the evolutionary law of limited competition we have ensured not only survival but domination—though probably only over the very short term. We are quite literally at war with nature. Whenever our population grows and food runs short, we solve the problem not by decreasing our numbers (which in wild species is accomplished not just through disease, famine, and predation, but by instinctive mechanisms that cause animals to lower their birth rates in such situations), but by increasing production. Expanded production permits further breeding, our population grows, we increase production again, and so on. It is a strategy not for survival, but for conquest. But every finite ecosystem prefers diversity to monomania, and so our dominance ultimately carries a high price.

Throughout the rest of nature, there are only rough parallels for humans' biological totalitarianism. In Australia, sugar cane farmers in the northeast decided a couple of decades ago that they could best cope with insect problems by introducing a voracious species of toad. The cane toads at first appeared to be a complete success: They were hardy, multiplied rapidly, and ate all bugs in sight. Unfortunately, however, it turned out that they had no natural predators in Australia; moreover they're poisonous, so that the animals that did feed on them died. And since cane toads can eat nearly anything—including birds and small mammals—there was nothing to keep them from spreading until they had taken the place of virtually every other small animal. Today in eastern Australia the cane toad is everywhere and native species are fast disappearing. But, then (a cane-toad philosopher might interpose), perhaps Australia was *made for* cane toads, and not for marsupial mice or bell birds or possums. . . .

THE HUMANITARIAN DILEMMA

Like cane toads, civilized humans are invaders. I don't know what the toads think about their new environment and their effect on it, but our own rationale is clear enough. We have a right—a *divine right*—to rule all of nature as benevolent monarchs. Many people would say that anthropocentrism is plain common sense. After all, every species looks out for itself first. And humans *are* clearly special: Only we of all Earth's creatures create elaborate cultural systems, design complex technologies, and preserve our ideas in writing for future generations. As the only *conscious* creatures on Earth (according to our criteria) we have not only the opportunity but the duty to tame the wilderness for our own benefit.

Of course, the loss of the spotted owl, the gorilla, the African elephant, the salmon, and the whales will be sad, says the voice of civilization. We should do what we can to save them. But, at the same time, we mustn't let sentimentality over mere animals deter us from our efforts to further the interests of the human race. Our foremost immediate concern must be to ensure that everyone is fed and that people in the poorest countries benefit from the kinds of economic development that have so dramatically lowered birth rates in the First World. Then, when world population growth levels off we can begin to pay more attention to the welfare of other species.

This is not merely the view of industrialists and rapacious land speculators; it is implicit in the plans of relief agencies, the proposals of visionary futurists, and the strategies of economists in every nation, rich or poor. It is a view rooted in religious tradition, and it carries all the moral authority of the Bible, the Qur'an, and other sacred texts. Who could argue with it? The apparent alternative, after all, is to consign hundreds of millions of human beings to a slow and agonizing death by starvation.

Unfortunately, however, this humanitarian worldview—to which all *good* people swear allegiance—seems to be leading to a biological holocaust from which humankind will be far from immune. We are faced, therefore, with a contradiction. If our premises lead to dire consequences, should we not question them?

BEYOND ANTHROPOCENTRISM

First, is it really true that anthropocentrism is *natural*? Yes, civilized cultures have always taken it as a given. Yet gathering and hunting peoples regard themselves not as regents of the Earth but as members of the community of life. And, since all human beings lived by foraging until only about ten thousand years ago, it would seem that civilized anthropocentrism is more an aberration than a rule among human societies. Yes, every species necessarily looks out for itself. But those that take over whole ecosystems do so at their own peril. The population of cane toads in Australia, for instance, if unchecked, will eventually crest and plummet until it finally achieves some sort of balance within a horribly impoverished environment. We know this through experience with other introduced species in Australia and elsewhere.

Are humans the only creatures on Earth to possess self-consciousness, and do we therefore have the moral right to decide the life and death of all other species? Descartes thought so: He regarded animals as mere automatons incapable even of feeling physical pain. That an otherwise intelligent person could hold this conviction is bewildering; that several generations should follow him in it would be inexplicable but for the fact that our anthropocentrism *predisposes* us to deny sentience to animals. Ancient peoples, by way of contrast, took it for granted that animals and even plants have feelings and preferences worthy of consideration. There is burgeoning scientific evidence for intelligence in other creatures, and recent experiments have demonstrated all known cognitive functions—in at least rudimentary forms, and in degrees equal to those demonstrated by human children—in many mammalian and bird species. That higher animals play, dream, and exhibit a wide array of emotional responses is a matter of immediate knowledge for anyone who takes the time to observe our fellow creatures sympathetically.

In short, anthropocentrism is based not in fact or common sense, but in tradition—a rather peculiar tradition that surely needs re-evaluation in the light of present circumstances. Actions based in the anthropocentric view will not ward off famine in the long run. Moreover, if pursued to the bitter end they will result in so great a loss of biodiversity that whatever humans survive will live in a world that is utterly ravaged—a world likely to be without songbirds (they're nearly all in decline), without cetaceans, with few large land animals, and with few trees and few *kinds* of trees.

THE COMMUNITY OF LIFE

What is the alternative? While the institutional and legal details might take a while to work out, the basis of the necessary alternative is already perfectly clear: It boils down to a simple but fundamental change of attitude regarding the role and status of humanity in the natural world.

First, we must recognize that we *cannot* violate the laws of evolution and of life. We may *seem* to be able to do so for a time—just as it seems the cane toads are doing—but eventually the results of our actions will catch up with us. Every manipulation of the ecological balance carries a price. We can defer payments, but the interest is high.

The truest test of intelligence is the ability to survive, and our survival is dependent on the health of the ecosystems of which we are members. The health of an ecosystem is measured in terms of diversity. Therefore, if we are truly intelligent creatures, we will do everything we can to maintain a maximum of biological diversity in our environments.

Ultimately, we can assure continued diversity only by rejoining the community of life—not as despots, but as reasonably good neighbors. Every community has its cranks, malcontents, deviants, geniuses, staid conservatives, wild partyers, etc. And every community experiences occasional conflicts. In a healthy community, there is room for everyone and there are ways to resolve conflicts before they build up and explode. No single faction dominates the community as a whole—at least, not for long.

If we humans are exceptionally talented in certain respects, there are surely ways to use these talents for the benefit of the entire community of life. And we should be humble enough to recognize that other members, who display talents different from ours, have as much of a stake in the community as we do.

This way of thinking is unfamiliar and will take some getting used to. We are accustomed to having our way regardless of anyone else. "Yes," I can hear someone saying, "It's picturesque to think of us humans sitting with the animals and trees in assembly, running the ecosystem as a democracy. But democracy is a human idea; the animals and trees do not spontaneously gather to reach consensus on issues. They don't even talk! In the anarchy of nature, human dominance is unavoidable."

Granted, the image of a community or assembly of beings is anthropomorphic, and I am not seriously proposing that we somehow induce a group of bears, badgers, and borage plants to sit in a circle and hammer out agreements on land use and water rights. I am suggesting instead that *a kind of* assembly is already in session, proceeding according to self-evident rules that we have studiously ignored. Every creature without exception makes its preferences known. If we want to know what those preferences are, we don't need a translator; we merely need to watch and listen.

LOOKING AHEAD; LOOKING DOWN

The practical implications of our adopting this attitude are of course enormous. We would need to reevaluate all human activities that threaten habitats—including large-scale industrial agriculture, cattle ranching, the building of dams and highways, mining, and (of course) the limitless proliferation of the human species. We would need to learn to live in downsized human communities, to feed ourselves by way of sustainable horticulture (until foraging is again possible on at least a small scale), and to make what we need through handcraft rather than mechanized manufacture. In the process of transition we would find plenty of outlets for our innate human creativity and intelligence—far more, I'd wager, than are available to the average modern city dweller.

Will such a transition avert disaster both for humanity and the rest of Earth's creatures? Tragically, the most likely answer is no. Even if the transition begins tomorrow, the human population will continue to grow for several decades as today's infants reach childbearing age. The implications of this fact alone virtually preclude an entirely desirable outcome, whether we pursue anthropocentric or biocentric projects.

Realistically, the choice that now faces us is not between catastrophe and no catastrophe; rather, it is between a catastrophe that leads to utter biological ruin and one that clears away the detritus of past human arrogance so that the web of life can repair itself and so that human beings themselves can eventually return to a sane and balanced relationship with their environments. If we are to achieve the latter outcome, then two factors are essential.

First, the global corporate leviathan must somehow be restrained from devouring every last tree, river, and cubic foot of living topsoil, and from enslaving every last indigenous tribe, before the inevitable collapse occurs. Second, sufficient numbers of people must desert the present insane civilizational system and pioneer new, democratic, ecologically sustainable communities so that when the system faces inevitable crisis large numbers will have alternatives at hand. Without these biocentric pioneers, chaos will likely breed only more chaos. With them, we may have the nucleus of a new culture that will in time provide human beings with a pattern of life that is truly meaningful and satisfying. The process of creating this new culture will be one that engages our creativity at every conceivable level. There is not one aspect of human thought, emotion, or activity that will not be examined and transformed in the crucible of necessity as we recreate human culture from the ground up.

One day, I tell you with all my heart, one day the white people and the Indians will change, like the dead things of winter change into the beautiful green and the flowers of springtime. And in that day, when a new spirit power comes, they will become brothers and make the whole earth beautiful!

—THE VISION OF THE GREAT
GREAT GRANDMOTHER
OF THE WISHRAM TRIBE
OF SOUTH-CENTRAL
WASHINGTON

 THE ENGLISH WORD *CULTURE* derives from the same root as *cultivate* and *cult*—the Indo-European base **quel-*, **quol-*, meaning "move around, turn." This apparently came to signify "be busy," which later branched in two semantic directions, "inhabiting a place" and "making a wild place suitable for crops." The Latin derivative *colere* means at once to "inhabit," "cultivate," and "worship."

The close etymological link between *culture* and *cultivate* is in some ways unfortunate, since the peoples of the world who do not cultivate—the plant gatherers and hunters—are, as we have seen, far from being cultureless. The problem is not merely that the word *culture* is soaked in neolithic Eurocentrism, but that by linguistically fusing *culture* with *cultivation*, we may unconsciously have helped sever our ties with wild nature. Ecologists tell us that agriculture has been the single greatest cause of environmental decline since the end of the Pleistocene epoch. Widespread destruction of topsoils, desertification, and loss of species diversity are all traceable to unsustainable farming practices dating to the invention of the plow. History is littered with the sad remnants of agricultural societies that ruined their habitats and then disintegrated or moved elsewhere, assuming all the while that theirs was the highest and best culture ever known.

The connection between *culture* and *cult* is equally problematic. Most people despise cults for their authoritarianism and quirky beliefs. But all religions are overgrown cults. And fundamentalist religion—which is (or claims to be) the attempt to preserve traditional beliefs and practices in the face of social change—appears today to be a primary source of intolerance and violence throughout the world.

If "cultivate" and "cult" comprise the semantic substrate for our ideas about culture, then our range of possible goals and directions for cultural renewal seems severely limited from the start. We might think instead of doing away with culture altogether. Yet this is hardly an option, at least for the foreseeable future: Human beings as they presently exist are nearly incapable of surviving without culture—without language, arts, or social conventions. Or, we might consider merely abandoning the *word* "culture." And yet the term has proven highly useful (especially to anthropologists, whom Roy Wagner once defined as those "who use the word 'culture' habitually"),[1] and there are no obviously superior alternatives.

Perhaps, then, the best approach in our current circumstances would be to rehabilitate both the word *and* that to which it refers. It is just possible that *culture*'s rebirth may come by way of new growth from ancient roots.

CULTIVATING DIVERSITY; WORSHIPING NATURE

While cultivation has ruined the land in the "breadbasket" regions of empires from the Euphrates to the Yangtze to the Mississippi, planting has not brought ecological disaster in all instances. A few horticultural or agricultural societies have managed to thrive continuously for centuries or even millennia in a state of relative harmony with their surroundings. Indeed, cultivation can in some cases actually promote genetic diversity. For example, the Peruvian Indians—who had the richest variety of domestic food crops of any cultures on record—grew hundreds of varieties of grains and vegetables that have yet to be investigated by scientists. Modern-day Peruvian farmers plant as many as forty-six varieties of potatoes in a half-hectare plot. Farmers in many primal cultures exchange seeds among villages in order to ensure continued vigor and pest resistance in cultivated strains. By comparison, industrial agriculture emphasizes the genetically weakened hybridized monocultures of a few basic staple crops.

Modern agricultural irrigation results in salinization of soils, but this is seldom true of small-scale indigenous horticulture. The Papago Indians of the southwestern U.S. and northern Mexico live in near-desert conditions, but have found ways to use intense seasonal rains to their advantage by locating their fields where they will naturally gather both water and nutrients from runoff. Deep-rooted nitrogen-fixing trees are left in fields for shade and fertilization. The Papago also rely on wild and semi-wild plants for much of their diet. The result is a system that is indefinitely sustainable.

Recent studies show that the swidden horticulture of indigenous rain-forest peoples is both more ecologically benign and more productive than modern commercial agriculture. "Green revolution" techniques are more efficient only when the hidden costs of fertilizers, pollution, pest control, long-range transportation, and soil degradation are ignored. The Kayapo of central Brazil, instead of planting in fixed plots, sow or transplant useful plants along their migratory trails. A single village may have upwards of 500 kilometers of such trails planted with edible yams, sweet potatoes, medicinal herbs, and fruit trees. Moreover, the Kayapo make little distinction between wild and domesticated varieties: They frequently transplant useful wild plants to accessible places, thus creating "forest fields"—a practice that works well for both people and nature. The people of Ladakh and Bali, and the Hopi of northeastern Arizona, all likewise evolved sustainable gardening practices suitable for their local soils and climates.

Nor has the compulsion to worship—*culture's* other root meaning—produced uniformly dire results. While some religions have glorified conquest and class privilege, others have done just the opposite. In the societies just cited—the Ladakhi, Hopi, Balinese, Papago, and Kayapo—religion was for the most part a force for social cohesion and environmental protection. The very word *Hopi* means "peace" or "the peaceful people," and this cultural self-image is rooted in a mythology that emphasizes the importance of following the Creator's instructions, of living in harmony, and of caring for the body of the Earth Mother. Among the Balinese, the distribution of fresh water for villagers' elaborate, sustainable irrigation systems—a potential source of friction between neighbors—is determined at the local temple, where religion serves to maintain economic equality throughout the society from generation to generation. And the Tibetan Buddhism of Ladakh teaches interdependence, tolerance, simplicity, and nonviolence.

Why has planting been an environmental disaster in many instances, but not all? *Why* has human propensity to worship been subverted to serve the interests of power and privilege in some cases, but not others? What secret have the Ladakhi, Hopi, Balinese, Kayapo, and Papago mastered, that others have not?

In their tilling, planting, and irrigating, the people of these cultures studied the land closely and regarded it as sacred. They sought to work with nature rather than dominating it. They took long-term effects into account. They kept their populations low relative to the carrying capacity of their ecosystems. And above all, they voluntarily restricted their economies to a small, local scale.

If there is one genuinely helpful characteristic that the religions of all these cultures seem to share, it is that they assist both the individual and the community in the cultivation of *empathy*—the ability to *feel with* another person, group, species, or being. When we open ourselves to feel what another is feeling, we find ourselves wanting for them what we want for ourselves—nourishment, happiness, freedom, and the opportunity for self-expression. Where empathy extends not only to other members of one's immediate group, but to animals, plants, and the land itself, culture is inherently ecological. And where empathy extends to future generations, culture becomes indefinitely sustainable.

In short, the cultures we are talking about seem for various reasons to have stepped off the steep slope leading toward the development of larger, more technologically intensive, and more stratified civilizations. They set up camp along the roadside, as it were, with no apparent intention of resuming the work of material "progress." Instead, they decided to spend their time and energy cultivating the human spirit and their relationships with the other beings surrounding them.

All of this suggests a new vision of what culture can be. And at the same time it calls us to reexamine common assumptions about cultural change and the meaning of "progress."

GOING FORWARD, GOING BACKWARD

Today the terms "forward" and "backward" as applied to culture are almost universally understood as relating to one aspect of society only: the development of ever more sophisticated technologies. "You can't stop progress," goes the saying. "Once the genie is out of the bottle, you can't put it back."

In *In the Absence of the Sacred*, culture ecologist Jerry Mander exposes these truisms to the light of day and offers an insightful critique of our society's mindless, quasi-religious fascination with technology for its own sake. "I suppose," writes Mander,

> that in order to be considered even minimally successful, a society must keep its population healthy, peaceful, and contented. All members should have sufficient food to eat, a place to live, and a sense of participation in a shared community purpose. Everyone should have access to the collective wisdom and knowledge of the society, and should expect that life will be spiritually and emotionally fulfilling for themselves and for future generations. This in turn implies awareness, care, and respect for the earth's life-support systems.[2]

Technology, says Mander, may have promised an improved standard of living, better health care, more leisure and convenience, and more consumer choices, but in many respects it has failed to deliver on those promises. And in terms of the minimum standards just outlined, modern technological society actually appears degenerate when compared to many traditional cultures. Mander's critique of technology calls into question our assumptions about what the terms "forward" and "backward" really mean.

But even if we convince ourselves that what we have thought of as "forward" is really "backward" in some sense, is it really possible to reverse the direction of cultural change? Going back in time is, of course, merely an exercise in imagination. We cannot turn back the clock; we cannot become literal children again, take back something we have said or done, or relive history. But if we take "going back" to mean moving *away from* civilization and *toward* a sustainable village culture, then there may be historical precedents. The Maya had an impressive civilization until seven or eight centuries ago, when it collapsed for reasons that are still unclear. As a civilization, the Maya were ruled by a wealthy, self-absorbed theocratic elite, they sacrificed their captives, and they farmed intensively and unsustainably. After the fall of their empire, the Mayan people took up smaller-scale farming and moved to villages that they still inhabit to this day. There is every indication that, for the people themselves, the collapse of their civilization was no catastrophe. Similarly, the period following the disintegration of the Roman Empire saw the birth and flourishing of medieval cities governed by democratic crafts guilds. While history textbooks still call this time the "dark age," some social philosophers have described it as a high point in terms of European cultural creativity.

Nevertheless, for us there would indeed be difficulties in returning to local, technologically modest, ecologically sustainable lifestyles. These are not necessarily difficulties of the kind usually imagined, however. Most people I talk to say that it would be hard to "go back" because it would be impossible to convince everyone to give up modern conveniences. No doubt it would be, assuming that we will always have the option of retaining them. But there is a much deeper and more serious problem. As civilization develops, it tends to undermine the very foundations of local, sustainable culture. Thus the real difficulty in going back is not just that it would be inconvenient, but that *we have nothing to go back to*. The practical skills, forms of decision making, songs, dances, and festivals that formerly bound people to one another and to the land have largely disappeared. And where some remnants of those patterns survive, they do so in ways that may not be particularly helpful in the process of cultural rebirth.

THIS IS NOT ABOUT NOSTALGIA

Recently an eighty-four-year-old friend told me of her early life growing up on a small farm in northeast Missouri with her parents and four siblings. They had no electricity or running water until as late as 1948. They grew popcorn, wheat, and watermelon as cash crops, but also kept a large vegetable garden, hogs, and a dozen milk cows. The only foods they bought were flour and sugar. They made their own soap and saved their seeds from year to year. They worked hard, my friend tells me—and I believe her. Certainly they worked harder than do many urban Americans today, and far harder than gatherers or hunters or people in most horticultural societies. But it was good, healthy work. Her eyes sparkle when she talks about life on the old farm (which the family sold in 1950 after her father had died and all the children had grown and moved on). When the conversation turns to the problems of the modern world (gang violence in the local high school in a rural town of seven thousand; the disappearance of small farms and farming communities; the junk-food eating habits of her overweight young employers), she looks sad and perplexed.

Many good people in America's heartland know that the industrial world is disintegrating around them. They see this as primarily a moral crisis and hope to stem the tide by clinging to the "old time religion" of fundamentalist Protestant Christianity. They can't see just how deep and ancient civilization's contradictions are; they don't understand that the "family" values they want to protect were common to generations that were already destroying land and culture on six continents—though in ways that seemed self-evidently good and necessary at the time. I feel these people's pain and I know that we must relearn much that they knew. But the path ahead toward sustainability does not exactly mirror the trail that brought us all here. Our grandparents' era was *relatively* more benign in many respects. But all the Christian virtue in the world won't bring back Eden unless we address and change the patterns of civilized life that were already beginning to undermine the biological integrity of culture even before Christianity got its start.

In some respects the path ahead may be a "great U-turn," as ecologist Edward Goldsmith puts it. We must learn to simplify our lives materially and curb our demands on the Earth. But these lifestyle transformations will be informed by a knowledge of implications and consequences of which our ancestors were oblivious. Now we *know* what happens when society mutates in certain directions. And increasingly, through the comparative study of cultures, we know of alternatives to the cancerous growth of civilized technics and economics.

CULTURE BEGINS AT HOME

The process of creating culture is literally all-encompassing from the standpoint of human interests and activities. It can therefore appear over-whelming at times. Our only recourse is simply to start where we are and put one foot in front of the other. A few general principles and directions seem clear enough. We might recall that the most ancient traceable root of the word *culture* means "to turn." The first essential step toward cultural sanity is a step in a new direction: We must turn away from mindless complicity in civilization's destruction of soil, life, and culture, and turn instead toward the universal sources of rebirth and renewal.

Probably the best place to start this turning is with regard to the material foundation of culture—how we get our food. Perhaps it is impossible now for many of us to feed ourselves by any means other than cultivation; if that is so, then we must personally engage in the discovery (or redis-covery) of methods of cultivation that are sustainable, small in scale, and that encourage genetic diversity—whether through gardening or merely purchasing organically grown foods. And perhaps the attitude with which we undertake this discovery should be one of worship—a worship of the land and of the principles and forces of regeneration. If there is any cult that would be worthy of our participation, it would be a cult of life, whose ritual is play and whose myth is the intimate biography of Gaia.

A significant root meaning of the word *culture* that we have neglected in this chapter until now is "to inhabit a place"—that is, to become psychologically and biologically attuned to the landforms, plants, animals, soil, and weather of the particular geographical region that we call *home*. Sustainable culture always grows out of the uniqueness of a given place, taking forms suitable to local availabilities and needs. It appears necessary and inevitable, then, that cultural rebirth begin at home.

Though it seems an immense task to reform an incomprehensibly complex pattern of collective thought and behavior held in common by countless people across scores of generations, we live at a time when that pattern is unraveling anyway. We may as well make the most of the situation. Traditional peoples such as the Hopi say that a chance like this comes along only once in a world age. It is the opportunity to regenerate culture not merely out of revulsion or fear, but in a spirit of discovery, creativity, and playfulness.

This may, however, be an opportunity of limited duration. As time goes on, our range of options may diminish to that of mere survival. It is horrifying to think that we might squander the present extraordinary chance to undertake personal and social transformation consciously, willingly, and artistically—and instead allow ourselves to descend without protest into what may become the worst of all possible worlds.

15 | HOW TO SAVE THE WORLD: A GLOBAL PERSPECTIVE

We see it like this: It is as if we are all in a canoe traveling through time. If someone begins to make a fire in their part of the canoe, and another begins to pour water inside the canoe, and another begins to piss in the canoe, it will affect us all. And it is the responsibility of each person in the canoe to ensure that it is not destroyed.

—AILTON KRENAK, BRAZILIAN
UNION OF INDIAN NATIONS

 THE NECESSITY OF GETTING to the root of our problems is perhaps best illustrated in the case of what may be the single most destructive symptom of cultural dysfunction—overpopulation. Unfortunately, while overpopulation represents a grave threat to our collective future, as a phenomenon it is intractable both politically and practically. Even if, through repressive legal sanctions, the world's annual births can be reduced below the one-to-one replacement rate, it will still be many decades before a significant decrease in total population occurs. And we simply do not have many decades of leeway before the weight of human numbers inflicts irremediable damage to the biosphere. Already, population pressure has led to overfishing, overgrazing, deforestation, pollution of ground water, and the catastrophic loss of topsoil worldwide.

The irresolvability of the population issue is largely due to the fact that it cannot be dealt with in isolation. Overpopulation is an effect of civilization: Historically, it has appeared in nearly every instance where people have adopted plows and built cities. And the most dramatic instances of overpopulation have occurred following the introduction of industrial modes of production. Overpopulation followed industrialization in Europe beginning in the eighteenth century, and the same cause and effect are now being forcibly exported throughout Asia, Africa, and Latin America.

If, in our analysis of global problems, we follow the chains of causation back to their sources, we always arrive at the same kinds of starting points—processes whereby economic, political, and technological power become progressively more concentrated. But the power structures that such processes build are resistant to change. Typically, when those at the helm are threatened, they deflect direct challenges by offering scapegoats, setting one economic, racial, or religious group against another. Today, liberals and conservatives, gays and homophobes, secular humanists and Christian fundamentalists, and tree huggers and loggers are at each other's throats, while those who profit from the present order, who wield the real power, and who thus bear the greatest responsibility for the suffering of people and planet, remain largely invisible.

In the last chapter I said that "cultural rebirth begins at home" and suggested an essentially personal and communal approach to solving the global eco-crisis. This is an approach explored further in the next chapter. However, it can be argued that the problems we face are institutional in nature, and that any solution must therefore include the reforming or dismantling of economic, governmental, and social institutions. While this is a necessary path of thought and action, it is not an easy one to tread. To be effective in working with public institutions, we must develop the skills of public life—persuasion, mediation, and dialogue. We must continually seek a clear understanding of the roots of problems, so that the institutional changes we pursue are ones that actually make a positive difference. And we must maintain a realistic view of the dynamics of power.

What institutional changes are needed in order to save the world? The following is my personal list.

RESTRAINING THE BEAST

Abolish secret government. It will be impossible for people anywhere to make changes in government policies unless they have a voice in how those policies are made. But presently many of the most important decisions affecting the lives of people around the world are made by unelected U.S. government officials who are carrying out policies that have never been approved by voters, and who are doing so according to procedures that are completely unknown to the vast majority of citizens. Historically, the Central Intelligence Agency has overthrown democratically elected governments, installed repressive dictators, and undermined free elections from Nicaragua to Iran to Chile to Indonesia. It also sometimes operates illegally within the U.S., financing many of its covert operations through drug running. CIA operatives literally have a license to kill, and routinely use assassination and sophisticated mind-control technologies to achieve their objectives. The CIA's job is essentially to prevent the redistribution of political power. This agency of government (together with other related departments and bureaus which together consume about $50 billion of American taxpayers' money yearly) simply has no reason for continued existence.

Reform or abolish corporations. Essentially, corporations are artificial legal entities that enjoy the rights of citizens, but that shield executives and stockholders from many responsibilities and liabilities. Today, transnational corporations constitute the real powers in the world. Each of the few dozen of the biggest global corporations has a yearly gross income that is greater than the GDP of all but the wealthiest nations. In the U.S., corporations funnel money through campaign contributions to buy the votes of politicians on critical legislation. Corporate money also effectively controls the dissemination of news and opinion via the main communications media (which are themselves giant corporations). Yet while corporations have the ability to overthrow governments (through cooperative arrangements with the CIA), influence the democratic process, mold public sentiment, and ruin whole ecosystems, thus directly or indirectly affecting the life of every living person, they are subject to vanishingly little democratic control. They are responsible only to their shareholders. Their function is to generate private profit, not to safeguard or benefit the public.

In *Taking Care of Business*, Richard Grossman and Frank Adams point out that early American colonists feared corporations and made every attempt to rein them in by democratic means. But over the past two centuries, as corporate power has steadily grown, legal restraints have fallen by the wayside. Nevertheless, in principle the American people still have the right to revoke corporate charters or to change the rules by which corporations are allowed to exist. State legislatures have the legal obligation to amend and revoke charters, along with the certificates of authority that permit corporations to do business outside their chartering state. They can also keep corporations from operating internationally. In principle, the American people could require that corporations be ecologically responsible if they are to maintain their charters. Automobile manufacturers, for example, could be required to reclaim and recycle their products when they are worn out. In addition to reducing waste, such a regulation would encourage manufacturers to end their policy of planned obsolescence.

Citizens should be better informed of these legal means of exerting democratic control over the corporate leviathan, and should take advantage of them.

Reform our economic system. Economic activity occurs when parts of nature ("resources") are extracted and turned into manufactured products, when elements of our common heritage are transformed into "property," and when human effort is exchanged for monetary symbols. The idea that economic *growth* should continue indefinitely—indeed, that it is desirable at all, even in the short term, given the present furious rate of economic activity—is sheer insanity. We must exchange the ideal of *growth* for that of *sustainability.*

Currently, the gross domestic product (GDP) is the primary measure of the health of nations. But the way the GDP is measured ignores the hidden costs of environmental degradation and social decay. It should simply be scrapped. As our primary gauge of economic health we need instead an Index of Human and Environmental Well-Being that would tell us whether the people are well nourished, whether more or fewer of them are committing suicide or turning to crime, how many songbirds are migrating this year, and how clean the air and water are.

In our current system it is possible for one individual to accumulate an unimaginably vast fortune while millions of others starve for want of bare necessities. The establishment by government of minimum and maximum incomes (perhaps according to a ratio such that the wealthiest individual could make no more than seven times what the poorest makes) is an obvious and necessary intermediate step in the transformation of the world economy, though our ultimate goal should be a reduction of the use of money itself to an absolute minimum so that such arbitrary rules would become meaningless.

Over the short term we must rescind GATT, which sets up a secret supragovernmental trade arbitration commission entirely controlled by corporations.

Decentralize government. Effective democracy requires face-to-face discussion, and therefore political units small enough for such discussion to take place. Nations are simply too large to serve as basic political units, because the only individuals who are able to make themselves heard in a polity of millions are those with the most powerful and strident voices. This is why national governments tend to be dominated by powerful economic interests. As we reduce the influence of corporations we should also minimize the role of national governments, eventually doing away with them altogether. We can replace them with autonomous, democratic, bioregional assemblies, where each individual has the opportunity to be heard.

Many political, economic, and environmental problems transcend borders, even bioregional ones; hence the need for something like a United Nations. But in practice the U.N. has served the interests of wealthy elites by everywhere promoting economic "development," which is increasingly showing itself to be merely a thinly disguised form of colonialism. Instead of an assembly of nations, we need a federation of bioregions. Each local bioregional assembly could appoint a representative to meetings of the federation, and delegates would be held accountable to express the will of the local group that elected them.

In addition, and organized along the same lines, there could be an assembly of *cultures*—one in which a representative of grass-roots organizations in European cultures (for example) would meet on equal terms with one from the Native American cultures and one from the Aboriginal Australian cultures. Subassemblies would include representatives from each of the scores of self-defined Native American cultural groups, each of the dozens of African cultures, the Pacific Island cultures, Southeast Asian cultures, and so on.

Reform agriculture. Everywhere in the world agriculture is ruining land and water. In the next twenty years, we will likely lose one-third of the world's remaining topsoil. Meanwhile there is immense pressure to increase production because of population growth. Corporate industrial agriculturists are responding with bio-engineered crops whose long-term safety for humans and effects on the biosphere are unknown; and by patenting seed stocks for future profit.

We need to encourage organic, small-scale, sustainable farming; break up giant agribusiness cartels and give land back to traditional owners; ban the patenting of any and all life forms; revive indigenous methods of cultivation; offer farmers subsidies to encourage soil conservation programs (which entail greater short-term costs); promote the growing of traditional and heirloom varieties of cultivars; and select food plants according to nutritional rather than standard commercial criteria. We must put a stop to foolish irrigation and plowing practices, drastically reduce the raising and grazing of cattle, and enforce *truly* humane standards wherever domesticated animals are still to be kept. All of this could be accomplished through regulation of corporate charters and by reversing existing government-imposed economic incentives.

These are examples of the kinds of systemic solutions that could indeed solve most of our global problems, given time and patience. But the implementation of even these few initial suggestions will require tremendous collective effort. Knowing that *this is what it would take to save the world as we know it* offers little cause for optimism: It tells us what kinds of change to work toward, but it extends little promise of success.

CAUSES FOR OPTIMISM

Sometimes it seems to me that the more one knows about the extent and causes of the ecological destruction and social injustice in the world today, the more bleak the overall picture looks. Pessimism, anger, and discouragement seem entirely justified.

It is only natural to want to see the future in terms of progress and opportunity, to look for causes for optimism. Unfortunately, in the present situation, some forms of optimism appear glib. Many people who are well off under the current system maintain a cheerful attitude by denying that serious global problems exist, and by focusing all their attention and effort on accumulating wealth, amusing themselves, and raising families. Others who have a budding social conscience reassure themselves with the belief that civilization can outgrow its difficulties if only each of us has a benevolent change of attitude and begins to recycle, contribute to worthy charities, and turn off dripping faucets. Still others look to some kind of extraordinary event to turn the tide—whether it be the Rapture, the arrival *en masse* of space aliens, the public disclosure of the presence of an Occult Spiritual Brotherhood, or vast Earth changes that send California sliding into the Pacific and ignite a spiritual awakening elsewhere. Of course, in principle any of these things *could* happen, but *expecting* them to do so is the equivalent of planning on winning a lottery. Whatever form it takes, foolish optimism tends merely to incapacitate us. For that very reason it is often actively encouraged by those interested in preventing fundamental social change.

Are there no causes for optimism that take into account the depth and severity of the situation facing us, and that would foster effective action and genuine cultural renewal?

One such cause can be seen in the fact that more people are becoming aware of the basic contradictions of civilization. Deforestation, pollution, racism, and poverty are hardly new; they have existed since the establishment of the first cities in Mesopotamia. Increasingly, however, we *perceive* these not as things to be taken for granted, but as problems that require solutions. As yet, few people understand the degree to which these problems stem from a few related sources. Nevertheless, for many that realization cannot be far away.

Other hopeful trends include the following:

Indigenous resurgence. While traditional cultures everywhere are threatened by economic predation, in many cases native peoples are showing extraordinary resilience, forming networks and alliances (such as the World Council of Indigenous People) that reach across tribal and national boundaries. While no one doubts that ancient ways of life will continue to change fundamentally in the wake of the intrusions of global technoculture, increasingly native peoples are insisting upon guiding the process of cultural change themselves, based on their own values and priorities, rather than accepting unquestioningly the agenda of industrial civilization. And in situations of blatant, long-term oppression (as in southern Mexico), indigenous populations appear willing to engage in organized resistance.

The flourishing of eco-ethics. As our natural "resources" dwindle, and as thousands of species disappear forever, many people are questioning the ethics of domination.

Less than a century and a half ago it was considered quite acceptable (in some places, at least) for one human being to own another as property to be sold or otherwise disposed of according to whim. Our ethics regarding slavery have changed. While *de facto* slavery unquestionably still exists, blatant forms of the practice are no longer officially tolerated in any country. Similar ethical shifts appear to be taking place today with regard to our attitudes toward animals and the rest of nature.

It is becoming clear that when philosopher René Descartes said that animals are mere automatons without any ability to feel or think, he made a hideous mistake that has caused untold needless suffering. Biologists have witnessed demonstrations of intelligence, learning, communication, and complex social behavior (including evidences of what can only be called compassion) in hundreds of species. In fact, it is becoming apparent—as primal peoples have always asserted—that all of nature is in some degree sentient. Thus the assumption that human beings have an inherent *right* to exploit other creatures without regard for their needs and feelings is beginning to seem as monstrous as the idea that some humans have the right to enslave others. To increasing numbers of people, the idea of buying and selling land, animals, and trees is starting to appear nearly as outrageous and absurd as the idea of buying and selling people.

Meanwhile the science of ecology is telling us that the health of ecosystems is a greater priority than any short-term human economic benefit, because as biological creatures we are utterly dependent on the web of life. We are not masters of that web; we are strands within it. Our ethics must therefore begin and end with the well-being of the entire biosphere.

Feminism. In virtually every civilization to date, men have dominated women. One half of humanity has colonized the other.

Feminism therefore potentially represents a social awakening of immense magnitude. In most instances it appears to be a force for peace, justice, and Earth-honoring. And while many feminists work for change in existing political and economic systems, the real impact of feminism may be a much deeper change of heart that emphasizes values based in nurturance and empathy over those that promote conquest and domination.

The rise of Earth-centered spirituality. Religion has played no small part in the destruction of nature and culture. The sky-god cults of the Near East, as transformed and forcibly spread by the civilizations of Greece, Rome, Europe, America, and the Islamic empires, have taught us to regard human supremacy over nature and men's dominance of women as divinely ordained. The widespread revival of Earth-centered, nonpatriarchal, non-hierarchical religions therefore seems a welcome antidote to the pious imperialism of the cross and the crescent.

Ecological spirituality is largely taking the form of an explosion of interest in European pagan traditions and native shamanic religions, which have always emphasized humanity's obligations to the powers of nature. However, "mainstream" Western religions have also tried to make themselves relevant to today's environmental concerns. Matthew Fox's Creation

Spirituality draws on the tradition of reverence for life represented by Hildegard of Bingen (1098–1179), Mechtild of Magdeburg (1210–1280), Meister Eckhart (1269–1329), and Julian of Norwich (1342-c. 1415). Meanwhile, John Cobb's Process Theology asserts that "the whole of nature participates in us and we in it";[1] the Eco-Justice movement of the United Methodist Church urges members to recycle and conserve; and ecological Judaism extends the Tikkun Olam, or the edict to heal the world, to the repair of the environment. There is even an Islamic ecological movement, which affirms that "The Qur'an teaches that the cosmos, nature, and the environment [are] full of signs of the Creator. . . . No religion on earth is so clearly evocative against destruction of domestic and wild life and against decimation of the God-granted natural wealth."[2]

Followers of Buddhism and Jainism, which have always held nonviolence and harmlessness as central tenets, might argue with that last statement. Indeed, Michael Tobias, the author of several books on ecology (the most recent of which is *World War III: Population and the Biosphere at the End of the Millennium*) has converted to Jainism precisely because of its implicit environmental ethic.

The current reshuffling of traditional religious ideas to make them pertinent to environmentalism may represent merely the warm-up phase of an historically significant development. It seems likely that, around the turn of the millennium, widespread apocalyptic expectations and their seeming fulfillment in the unfolding stages of global environmental, political, and economic collapse will lead to an epidemic of religious speculation. Amid the flood of crazed hallucinations of Armageddon, a new spiritual sensibility may surface and spread like wildfire—one based in a profound, shared experience of vulnerability and humility. As the century wears on, worsening global ecological and social crises may serve as the trigger for a deeply renewed sense of the sacred based in nature and the essential, intangible goods of human existence. Then perhaps spirituality may be able to accomplish what no amount of political infighting ever could.

OPTIMISM: PROGNOSIS OR STRATEGY?

Measured against the actions of a few backwoods eco-freaks, forest-dwelling natives, and urban radicals, the economic and political clout of huge transnational corporations is overwhelming. Any rational forecaster would therefore predict that the next few decades will see unprecedented suffering for humanity and the rest of nature.

That prediction is depressing in itself; it is even more so if we are convinced that the ultimate human good is defined by the survival and uninterrupted growth of civilization as we know it. Since it is difficult to imagine circumstances that would permit the continued existence, for more than another generation or two, of the present power system with its burgeoning appetites and unassimilable outputs, then *to the degree we are identified with that system there is no cause for optimism.*

However, there are still two good reasons for maintaining a hopeful attitude.

The first comes from the study of anthropology and history, which together reveal unequivocally that our present awesome global problems result not so much from flaws inherent in human nature as from historical circumstances, particular forms of social organization, and certain choices we have made in forging our covenants with nature. It *is* possible for human beings to live in peace. Therefore anyone who wants to do so can, in principle and in fact, start now.

The second reason for hope springs from a much deeper source. At the core of our being there is a part of us that transcends culture, that is coterminous with life in all its manifestations. To the degree that we are in touch with that dimension of ourselves, we are identified with what *will* survive; with what *always* survives. It is the part of us that knows that, even if the next few decades are utter hell for human beings, life will continue in some form and people will eventually learn and adapt.

This is an obdurate sort of optimism. It is more of a strategy than a rational predictor of outcomes. Pessimism, after all, creates only paralysis. The only effective tactic in any situation is simply to do the best one can with whatever one has to work with.

This is also a more satisfying form of optimism than it may sound like at first. Action in the cause of biological sanity is a generator of assurance. And best of all, it feels good. When *we are Life acting in the interest of its own survival, pleasure, and fulfillment,* then our actions are clear and strong. Our intention is undivided. And our means and ends are impeccable and harmonious. When we are in this sort of psychologically and spiritually integrated state, life is well worth living—no matter what challenges or odds we face.

16 | HOW TO SAVE THE WORLD: A PERSONAL RESPONSE

Current practice in United States economy called upon the person who had met his needs for necessaries to turn his attention forthwith to procuring comforts and conveniences, and after that to luxuries and superfluities. Only by such procedures could an economy based on profit accumulation hope to achieve the expansion needed to absorb additional profits and pay a return to those investing in new industries.

Our practice was almost the exact opposite for the current one. Food from the garden and wood from the forest were the product of our own time and labor. We paid no rent. Taxes were reasonable. . . .

Readers may label such a policy painfully austere, renunciatory or bordering on deliberate self-punishment. We had no such feeling. We felt as free, in this respect, as a caged wild bird who finds himself once more on the wing. To the extent that we were able to meet our consumer needs in our own way and in our own good time, we had freed ourselves from dependence upon the market economy.

—HELEN AND SCOTT NEARING

. . . [T]here is one way forward: the creation of flesh-and-blood examples of low-consumption, high-quality alternatives to the mainstream pattern of life. This we can see happening already on the counter cultural fringes. And nothing—no amount of argument or research—will take the place of such living proof. What people must see is that ecologically sane, socially responsible living is good living; that simplicity, thrift, and reciprocity make for an existence that is free and more self-respecting.

—THEODORE ROSZAK

THE SICKNESS OF CIVILIZATION is not merely abstract or general. It impacts each of us directly and specifically, turning—to varying degrees, depending upon the situation—what was potentially a free, creative, wild being into a slave or ogre. The nature of the impact partly depends on the socioeconomic stratum one happens to occupy: Participation in industrial-electronic mass culture tends to turn the wealthy person into a speculator, predator, and parasite; it makes the middle-class entrepreneur a frenzied, opportunistic competitor; it transforms the average worker into an obsequious wage slave; and it renders the jobless person a useless drone—a sort of social waste product, and perhaps a literal prisoner.

In the simplest analysis, the system reproduces various forms of authoritarianism and dependency. Toward anyone higher on the pyramid than ourselves, we are obliged to be obedient—whether the one who is "higher" happens to be a boss, a customer, a prison guard, or an IRS agent. Toward anyone who is lower in the pecking chain, we feel justified in acting as a demanding authoritarian—whether the individual concerned happens to be an employee, a store clerk, or a child. People at the bottom of the ladder have a tough time finding someone to boss around, but often have an intense psychological need to do so; hence spousal and child abuse, hierarchies within street gangs, and random violence. Ultimately, we are *all* helplessly dependent on the system itself, and we *all* take an authoritarian stance toward non-human nature. Individual personality differences may moderate the effect, but even inherently independent, generous people often find their natural inclinations compromised because dependency and authoritarianism are *built into the system* we all rely on for our food, water, housing, transportation, electrical power, clothing, entertainment, and so on. Because we are so dependent, we do things we otherwise wouldn't, or we curtail behavior that might jeopardize our continued participation in the system. And to the extent that the system itself is unfair or unsustainable, we thereby forfeit our moral integrity.

Meanwhile, we become ever more incompetent and alienated. Experts do nearly everything for us: Few of us can heal ourselves, produce our own food, or build our own houses. Thus out of necessity our attention is continually fixed on the human system. The non-human world, perforce, is either hidden from view (while it is turned into manufactured goods or waste products) or preserved in bounded enclaves as a therapeutic spectacle.

The strings of the net in which we struggle are usually almost invisible to us (so accustomed have we become to them), but they stand out in vivid relief when something goes wrong. Here in Sonoma County not long ago, we residents were the "victims" of a "natural disaster" that took the form of seasonal rains running off hundreds of square miles of pavement swelling local rivers, flooding houses that should have been built elsewhere anyway and causing widespread power outages. Temporarily, the system ground to a halt. Many people were prevented from showing up for jobs. Tens of thousands were without electricity. A local radio station set aside its usual programming to broadcast information immediately useful to the community. A local newspaper published an article describing the declining health of the Russian River watershed. People went out of their way to help strangers. Humans were forced to acknowledge nature on her terms, if only grudgingly and for a brief time. Of course, as soon as the rain let up, all of that changed. The human control system quickly repaired itself, the radio station resumed its soft-rock format, businesses reopened, and life returned to normal.

But to me this brief interlude in the otherwise smooth functioning of the social system only underlined the realization that what is *normal* for Sonoma County would look truly bizarre when viewed from any sane cultural standpoint. There are a lot of good people in this area—that's one of the things that makes it such a desirable place to live. They are, largely, people who would really like to see nature protected, who want to see the jobless and homeless somehow taken care of, and who disapprove of fascist trends in government. But business is business. It costs so much to live here that most people (those, that is, who don't happen to have sizable investments) have to work at something they don't much enjoy in order to pay the rent or mortgage. A little "fixer-upper" house on a tiny, undesirable lot costs a literal fortune. Many folks are chronically stressed, working two or three jobs and going into debt. Others seem to be in a perpetual medal-chasing sprint on the gilded treadmill. When my wife Janet and I fire up our twenty-year-old station wagon and putter out to the highway, we see an odd mix of sleek new Lexuses and BMWs (their cellular phones in continuous use) on one hand and ancient Volkswagens and Volvos (festooned with eco-activist bumper stickers) on the other. And, every few months, we see a new subdivision or shopping mall appearing. With the population rising, ever more demands are being put on rivers and streams as sources of water and as means of washing effluent out to sea. Here in this place of unusually high ecological awareness, the local watershed—the circulatory system of our bioregion—is dying, and few have the time or energy to do anything about it.

FINDING ALTERNATIVES

Today, as in most historical periods of civilizational decay and intense social change, new ideas are likely to come not from institutions, but from individuals and small groups acting without official encouragement.

But as one's life becomes a laboratory for cultural transformation, daunting challenges arise. Suddenly very little can be taken for granted. Choices that others make without thought become matters for careful scrutiny. For example, in a sane and stable culture, one doesn't worry about what one should eat; one simply eats what everyone else is eating. Today we know that the typical modern European-American diet is destroying both our own health and the world's topsoil, and involves practices that are inhumane and unsustainable. Alternatives must be found. Yet food choices are habitual, and changing eating habits requires willpower and effort.

Of course, we all know the easy answers to the eco-crisis: recycle, buy environmentally friendly products, turn the lights out when you leave the room, etc. These are undoubtedly helpful actions, but they hardly begin to address the core of the problems that confront us. As we start seriously to inquire about what it might mean to live lightly on the Earth, we get the feeling of swimming upstream. Our entire culture is based on consumption and growth, to which a life of voluntary simplicity is anathema. A thousand economic pressures—to say nothing of our own habits and preconceptions—seem to force us into lifestyle decisions that contribute to the destruction of nature.

There are no simple ways to avoid such contradictions. Each of us must find a personally acceptable way to navigate this period of cultural change. The choices are difficult. But perhaps the difficulty can be eased somewhat by sharing with one another our internal thought processes as we face the same or similar decisions.

Clearly, any genuine alternative to this insane status quo must begin by cutting our cords of personal dependence on the ephemeral human system of money and markets, bureaucracies and corporations, manufactured products and fossil fuels; and it must bring into greater clarity our fundamental personal dependence on the natural systems of land, water, weather, and living beings. It must provide a remedial education in the sorts of things every child in a sustainable culture learns—how to build one's own house and provide for one's health and nutritional needs with a minimum of time, materials, and environmental damage. From this modest beginning, one can envision a complete reorganization of society, including a profound mass psychological shift toward attunement with nature's rhythms and balances. But this society-wide transformation is likely to remain a mere pipe dream as long as we individually remain utterly at the mercy of the present regime.

So: How to make a beginning? How can individuals start to break out of the prison of corporate technoculture? Here are four strategies that seem extremely promising.

Join the second horticultural revolution. As I explained in chapter 1, if we know how a particular group of people gets its food, it is possible to infer how it comes to terms with nature in other respects as well. This suggests that food is at the foundation of culture, and that if we wish to renew human culture we should start by reexamining the way we obtain our food. If we wish to build a sustainable culture, we must begin by finding a way to feed ourselves in such a way that soil is not depleted or eroded, and the number of species in our bioregion is not reduced.

Fortunately, feeding ourselves sustainably can be enjoyable. The fact that backyard gardening is the most popular hobby in the civilized world gives some indication of the reluctance of urbanized humans to forsake entirely their connection with the Earth and with their basic means of production and sustenance. It takes only one or two hours a day to maintain a fine garden. And through composting it is possible to build topsoil rather than deplete it. Gardening brings many joys: In addition to offering the satisfaction of self-sufficiency, it supplies exercise, lowers blood pressure, and relieves stress. Even in a small apartment one can have a sprout garden, and it is usually possible to grow salad greens and herbs there as well.

Tending a garden may seem like a puny response to the world's immense problems, but it is an eminently practical one and it goes straight to the core of civilization's difficulties. Gardening is an act of cultural regeneration, especially if it is done with intelligence and care, and without use of chemical fertilizers and pest controls.

For growing food, I have yet to come across a better method than **Biointensive gardening**. Based on Alan Chadwick's blending of French intensive and Biodynamic techniques, Biointensive has been refined and taught in recent years by John Jeavons, author of *How to Grow More Vegetables than You Ever Thought Possible on Less Land than You Can Imagine*, and *Lazy-Bed Gardening: the Quick and Dirty Guide*. Jeavons's goal is to grow the maximum amount of nourishing food in a minimum of space, with a minimum of work, in a way that builds soil rather than depletes it. I've visited Jeavons's demonstration gardens in Mendocino County and was impressed with his scientific approach and clearly measurable results. Biointensive gardening relies heavily on composting, so it takes a little extra work to get started. But after the first two or three years, soil health, the nutritional content of the food, and the sheer quantity of yield more than repay the initial investment of time. The key to the whole process is to grow soil rather than vegetables (the veggies are a by-product).

Jeavons has a global vision: He is gearing his efforts not so much toward affluent American hobby gardeners, as toward people in Third-World countries where economic colonization and cash cropping have resulted in the loss of indigenous horticultural knowledge and self-sufficiency. And his efforts are having a noticeable impact: In Kenya alone thousands of gardeners have been trained in the Biointensive method and are diversifying and decentralizing food production throughout the country. Contact: Ecology Action, 5798 Ridgewood Rd., Willits CA 95490.

Permaculture, the brainchild of Australian curmudgeon Bill Mollison, is a comprehensive program for creating a sustainable way of life; in addition to gardening, it also involves house and landscape design, the channeling and storage of water runoff, aquaculture, and the strategic cultivation of perennial plants. The idea is to work intelligently with natural forces to create a happy and abundant existence that doesn't degrade the ecosystem. Permaculturists study water and energy cycles and design their landscapes and dwellings to minimize energy inputs and waste.

I recently attended a workshop given by Mollison and was impressed with his laziness. I'm lazy, too, and any scheme toward self-sufficiency that required constant hard work would scare me off quick. Where would I find time to play the violin, read, or just sit and think? Mollison replaces brute force with observation and intelligence. Permaculture is flexible and evolving, and its basic principles can be applied in almost any situation. Janet and I visited a Permaculturist's home in southern California a few years ago and were charmed by the beautiful practicality of the place. It was essentially a diverse, purposeful, miniature ecosystem: We picked and ate an exotic lunch as we walked along a jungle pathway just outside our friend's house, which was as space-consciously designed as the cabin of a sailboat. For information contact: *The Permaculture Activist* (journal) c/o Peter Bane, Route 1 Box 38, Primm Springs TN 38476; (615) 583–2249.

Eat lower on the food chain. While I respect the way tribal hunting societies treated the wild animals they depended on for food, it seems clear that hunting *per se* cannot be carried over into the present context. With a very low human population, hunting may be practical; given our current overpopulation, it is capable of supplying only an infinitesimal portion of humanity's nutritional needs. The keeping of domesticated livestock, as an alternative, is both cruel (as anyone who's been to a stockyard knows) and ecologically disastrous. The tragedy currently being played out in the rainforests of Central and South America—where trees, native cultures, and entire animal species are being traded for a few years' production of fast-food beef—is merely the latest performance of a script that is familiar to nearly every country on every once-forested continent. Moreover, food production per acre from domestic animals is only a tiny fraction of that available from plants. *Today, therefore, one of the most effective and practical single steps anyone in an industrialized country can take both to benefit the natural environment and to serve the long-term welfare of the global human population is to eat less meat.*

My own opinion is that the simplest and best solution to the moral dilemmas posed by the meat industry is to become a vegetarian. While this is an alternative that many people seem to regard with distaste, it offers considerable personal benefit. Nearly all of the relevant medical research of the past twenty years points to the desirability of a diet low in fat and cholesterol and high in fiber. Statistically, vegetarians live longer than meat eaters, and vegetarianism need represent no nutritional compromise. As for food enjoyment, I can report (after about twenty-five meatless years) that I find eating far more pleasurable knowing that no animal suffered and died merely to satisfy my conditioned carnivorism.

Bring ecology home. A growing (though still marginal) number of people in industrial countries are discovering ways to disengage from power networks. They are exploring, for example, natural building techniques (including straw bale and rammed earth), and solar energy and heating. Excellent sources for solar power information and supplies are: **Real Goods** (555 Leslie St., Ukiah CA 95482; (800) 762-7325) and **Home Power Magazine** (P. O. Box 520, Ashland OR 97520; (916) 475-3179).

The Earthship is a living system that provides for basic human needs (food, water, shelter, and energy) with minimal dependence on external inputs from civilization and with minimal disruption of the natural environment. Earthships are houses that are relatively cheap and easy to build, using natural or recycled building materials. The main structural element is a wall made of discarded tires (which can usually be obtained free) filled with rammed earth. This thick, heavy wall provides thermal mass, which means that the finished structure will tend to maintain a constant temperature. Photovoltaic panels provide electricity, a solar oven cooks food, and a solar or composting toilet safely returns human excrement to the soil. Water is collected from the roof and stored in an indoor cistern; gray water is cycled through an indoor tank that grows plants (including garden veggies). No waste water leaves the building. The inside of an Earthship is part cave, part jungle. All necessary water can be obtained from roof runoff, provided the house is sited in an area that has a minimum of eight inches of precipitation per year.

Earthships are described in detail in three books (*Earthship* volumes I–III) by Michael Reynolds, the originator of the Earthship concept. Reynolds and colleagues have pioneered two Earthship communities in New Mexico and in *Earthship* volume III describe the process of buying land, drafting a Land Use Code, Articles of Association, and by-laws. For information write: Solar Survival Architecture, P.O. Box 1041, Taos NM 87571.

Some eco-pioneers advocate **building with straw bales** instead of rammed earth. The latter provides more thermal mass, but straw is quicker and easier. This is important because the main obstacle to be overcome in building one's own eco-shelter seems to be sheer inertia ("Where do I find the time, the money, the expertise?"). Straw is an agricultural waste product—so the bales are cheap—and it is annually renewable. Straw is also a superb insulator (R40), and straw-bale houses are highly resistant to fire and earthquakes. The real beauty of straw-bale building, though, is that a few friends working together can put up the walls of a house in a weekend. In essence, one simply piles up the bales like big building blocks, adds a roof, cuts holes for doors and windows, stuccos the outside, and plasters the inside. Earthship components (photovoltaic cells, cistern, solar toilet, solar oven, and so on) can be incorporated at the builder's discretion. Several straw-bale structures built nearly a century ago in Nebraska are still standing. Janet recently attended a straw-bale discussion workshop with an enthusiastic group of local architects, of whom one was heard to exclaim, "This is so easy, it could put us out of business!" Recommended reading: "A Straw Bale Primer" ($10) by S. O. MacDonald, P.O. Box 58, Gila NM 88038. For information contact: Matts Myhrman, Out On Bale, 1037 R. Lynden St., Tucson AZ 95719; (602) 624-1673 (publisher of the journal *The Last Straw*).

In some cases, natural homebuilding efforts are being undertaken communally. For example, Jarlanbah Permaculture Hamlet in New South Wales,

Australia, is a community-in-progress sited on a 22 hectare portion zoned for rural residential development. It consists of 43 freehold lots ranging from a half to three quarters of an acre in size, situated in hamlet clusters and surrounded by common land. The commons is to be managed collectively by residents for reforestation, sustainable agriculture, and water catchment, and as a wildlife corridor, woodlot, and orchard. A community center will serve needs defined by residents. Structures are being designed to meet the following criteria:

❧ Houses must be integrated with the surrounding land in terms of aesthetic, climatic, ecological, and lifestyle factors.

❧ A pleasant indoor microclimate is attained through the use of passive and active solar design and technologies; appropriate placement of verandahs, pergolas, and solar screens; and insulation, ventilation, and use of appropriate building materials and thermal mass.

❧ Homes are designed for high energy efficiency and, through the use of solar technology and energy-conserving appliances, will be independent of grid electricity.

❧ Materials are selected for environmental and climatic stability, are of earth tones, and are recycled and/or locally produced.

❧ Roofs are designed for rain-water collection and angled for maximum solar gain. Each house has rainwater storage tanks, uses water-conserving fittings, and recycles graywater for garden irrigation and flush systems. Sewage treatment is by way of dry composting toilets or an aeration treatment plant.

Revitalize democracy. Of course, living together isn't merely a matter of intelligent engineering; our present dilemmas are as much social as technological or environmental.

How can we manage our collective affairs without authoritarianism, domination, and inequality? In mainstream political discourse the word *democracy* is used to describe systems of government that purport to mitigate these social ills. But democracy as it is actually practiced in many countries is a farce.

It is important to realize that the practice of grass-roots democracy is not an innovation; rather, it is extremely ancient. Most tribal peoples (such as the Iroquois) kept decision-making powers dispersed among the people. It is centralized government that is relatively new. The *idea* of democracy (as conceived by the Greeks or the American colonists) was actually a throwback: It proposed a way for people to regain power over their lives—power that had been usurped by kings, bureaucrats, and other elites. Unfortunately, the elites have since discovered innumerable ways to co-opt, manipulate, or paralyze the democratic process. Thus the people need continually to reassert their primal authority.

Despite encroachments by power elites, millions of people worldwide are now practicing basic and effective forms of democracy that involve them in solving their common problems and prioritizing their common values. And this is the case not only for traditional peoples, but for many urban industrialized people as well. As Frances Moore Lappé and Paul Martin du Bois point out in *The Quickening of America*, hundreds of citizens' environmental, labor, and health networks have sprung up in the U.S. in the past two decades. Increasing numbers of businesses are owned by workers, neighborhood mediation teams resolve conflicts that might otherwise end up in the legal system, and organizations like the Industrial Areas Foundation teach citizens how to organize, set common goals, and lobby for their common interests. Lappé's and du Bois's Institute for the Arts of Democracy has identified and teaches the basic skills of public life, which include active listening, mediation, positive conflict, the effective expression of anger, public dialogue, public judgment, reflection, and evaluation.

Start a local currency. While the reform of our global economic system is beyond the ability of any one of us to accomplish single-handedly, anyone *can* start a local currency. The advantage of local currencies is that they give communities greater control over their economies. Local currencies foster self-sufficiency and face-to-face exchanges of goods and services, instead of a growing dependence on distantly-headquartered multinational corporations.

Local currencies are nothing new. In ancient Greece, each city minted its own coins. More recent times have seen "labor notes" of nineteenth-century English socialist Robert Owen, and the "time store" of nineteenth-century American anarchist Josiah Warren. During the Great Depression, the mayor of Worgl, Austria, decided to print notes ("tickets for services rendered") to pay people working on a bridge and drainage project. The town council decided to accept the scrip for all local taxes, and soon each note was changing hands an average of twenty times a month. Other towns began to take up the idea, and within three months whole areas of the country were transforming themselves from poverty to prosperity. Unfortunately, the Austrian central bank, afraid of losing control, took the matter to court, where the local currencies were declared unconstitutional.

Several contemporary local currencies have withstood legal challenges. LETS (Local Economic Trading System), started by Michael Linton in Vancouver in 1983, has gained a foothold in Australia, New Zealand, and Britain. Essentially a computer barter system that trades green dollar credits, LETS entails a centralized accounting system. If Jeff wants a cord of wood from Jim, but doesn't have anything Jim wants in exchange, Jeff calls up the central computer and asks it to credit Jim's account and debit his own by an agreed-upon amount. Each month everyone gets a statement in the mail. Today, in Britain, Manchester has its "bobbin," Warminster has its "link," and Tomes its "acorn"—all names for local LETS units of currency.

While the computerized LETS system works well, some local-currency advocates prefer the issuing of an alternative paper currency. In 1991, community economist Paul Glover founded the Ithaca HOURS system in Ithaca, New York. Since then, over $50,000 of local currency has been issued to nearly one thousand participants (including over two hundred businesses), which means that hundreds of thousands of dollars' worth of trading has been transacted. Each HOUR received is counted as ten dollars of taxable income. Glover says: "We printed our own money because we watched Federal dollars come to town, shake a few hands, then leave to buy rainforest lumber and fight wars. Ithaca's HOURS, by contrast, stay in our region to help us hire each other. While dollars make us increasingly dependent on multinational corporations and bankers, HOURS reinforce community trading and expand commerce which is more accountable to our concern for ecology and social justice."[1] Currency systems similar to Ithaca HOURS have been started in Santa Fe, New Mexico; Kansas City, Missouri; Boulder, Colorado; Paradise, California; and Conyers, Georgia. Glover markets a Hometown Money Starter Kit for $25 (2.5 HOURS option in NY), available from Ithaca Money, Box 6578, Ithaca NY 14851.

Become a bioregionalist. Globalization initially sounds like a good idea, in that it seems to imply an end to regional and ethnic rivalries and a broadening of parochial perspectives. In practice, however, globalization means that every place is beginning to look like every other place, and people everywhere are being transformed into interchangeable economic units. As we become increasingly mobile we tend to see local variations in the landscape merely as curiosities or potential commodities; meanwhile, vital local communities dissolve into automobile-dominated suburbs (islands of wealth) or slums and shanty towns (seas of poverty).

More and more people everywhere are realizing that the world cannot be saved by government decree; it can be protected and brought back into wild harmony only locally by people who know, love, and care for the area they call home. This requires the rediscovery of a sense of *place*—as defined not by political boundaries, but by natural, topographic, biological ones; by watersheds, mountains, and forests.

The word *bioregionalism* refers to a social movement dedicated to counterbalancing the excesses of globalization. Anyone can become a bioregionalist by learning about local plant and animal species, natural history, and native peoples, and by becoming involved in the local political process. Efforts to save forests, rivers, and endangered species through laws and regulations at the national level have produced important victories, though currently many laws are being rolled back. Often, local efforts meet with greater success. By making their voices heard in their communities, bioregionalists can help remind their neighbors of the interest they share in protecting the health of the land and water that all depend on. *Dwellers in the Land: A Bioregional Vision,* by Kirkpatrick Sale, offers valuable guidance on the bioregional path, as does the **Planet Drum Foundation** (Box 31251, San Francisco CA 94131).

WHAT IF CIVILIZATION THREW A PARTY AND NO ONE CAME?

None of these strategies is an end in itself, nor can any—or all of them used together—yield a truly sustainable culture. That could arise only from generations of people living in a given place, playing and working together, and building shared symbol systems for the investment of meaning in the elements of daily life.

However, we must begin somewhere. And where else but with the way we choose to live here and now? We may not personally be capable of reining in the corporate leviathan (though we can exert some influence by way of political activism), but we *can* refuse to let our lives be controlled by it, *if* we are willing to opt out of the commercial culture. The strategies mentioned above are designed to enable us to do just that with a minimum of stress and strain. They promise a personally satisfying existence and, what is more important, an existence that if widely replicated would result in a society very different from the one that currently prevails. How so?

If large numbers of people lived in Earthships, corporations would lose their labor pool. Who would choose to work in a factory or office if the basics of life were available freely (after a small initial investment) to everyone? Michael Reynolds complains that he has a hard time motivating his employees (who live in Earthships) to work full time, since they have only limited needs for cash. As more people became self-sufficient, they would likely spend their time doing what was inherently satisfying, rather than frittering away their days on the consumer treadmill. The market for useless products would disappear as people examined more closely their real needs. Cities would empty out and society would reorganize itself from the grassroots upward. The industrial system would wither, and with it all of its horrific effects on people and planet. So would the military machine: soldiers would naturally rather stay at home. Because they were building and maintaining their own homes, and because necessity demanded it, people would give more attention to inputs and outputs and the effects of their actions on the local environment. Craftwork would flourish, and with it a basic sense of competence and self-worth. Money would recede in importance. Poverty would disappear, as would obscene wealth—since wealth requires that some people accept lives of material dependency so that others can maintain economic advantages. Authoritarian control systems would dissipate. People's energy and creativity would be devoted to finding ever more elegant ways of integrating human life with the rest of the biosphere, and with evolving ever more satisfying participatory forms of artistic expression.

Of course, as with all utopian plans it is one thing to *say* "if only everyone thought or did such and such" but quite another to get everyone to think or do it. Unlike most other utopian schemes, however, this one can be implemented in its essence virtually immediately by anyone anywhere, acting alone or with a few friends. Even if my building a straw-bale house doesn't result in the immediate conversion of the Pentagon into a Global Peace Institute, the world of my personal experience—the world for which I am directly responsible—will be altered from its very foundations upward. Moreover, the sustainable cultures of the planet will gain one free human and the megamachine will lose a cog.

Another objection to this utopian vision: If enough people were to desert the system so that it felt threatened, it would take all necessary steps to defend itself by coercing humans into continued participation. This is extremely likely. However, the system is much better equipped to deal with a direct frontal assault than with defection from within. It may be possible for large numbers of people to leave quietly by the back door before those in power realize what is happening. They have already created a surplus labor pool which they are finding difficult to control (hence the frenzy for building new prisons). They might initially regard the desertion of a portion of the population as a practical benefit, since it would reduce the clamor for jobs and government relief.

Still another objection: Didn't millions of people attempt to desert the system in the 1960s and '70s, and didn't their efforts end in utter failure? As a participant in some of those ventures (I helped start a rural commune in 1973 and have lived in a half-dozen intentional communities in the years since) I know first-hand the challenges of trying to wean oneself from the megamachine. Yes, we faced enormous personal and interpersonal hurdles. Still, having spent the last few years back in the "normal" life of rent, credit, jobs, and taxes, I can say without qualification that I would rather face the challenges of countercultural life deliberately and willingly than acquiesce to passive participation in a vast, heartless social machine over which I have vanishingly little control.

I heartily disagree with those who characterize the communal experiments of the '70s as uniformly failed. Clearly many mistakes were made and some efforts were more successful than others. Many of us were immature and unrealistic (this was certainly true in my case), and it seems inevitable, in retrospect, that most of us would eventually succumb to the corrosive influence of the mainstream consumer culture. However, I believe that whatever setbacks we experienced should not deter further experimentation that is more deliberate and better informed.

All objections pale when we take into account the apparent fact that the megamachine is presently in a final stage of disintegration, and that its painful dissolution will likely only accelerate in the decades ahead. In addition to being a visionary project, defection from the megamachine is also a survival strategy. If civilization slowly fizzles, we will be spared some of the agony of those who remain dependent upon it to the bitter end. If civilization implodes suddenly rather than incrementally (as could happen in the case of some spectacular environmental disaster), people in Earthships or eco-villages will fare far better than those in the cities. In either case, the former will be in an ideal position to act as seeds of a new, sustainable culture.

NEW CULTURE

Perhaps, when the new Bible of Science is written, one may read of man as the prodigal son of Mother Nature, flouting for a time her admonition and her wisdom, spending his heritage in riotous living; but at last reduced to the husks upon a barren waste of his own making, he crawls back to his Old Mother's fireside and listens obediently to the story of a certain wise man whose name was Ecology.

—CLARK WISSLER, SPEECH TO
THE ECOLOGICAL SOCIETY,
DECEMBER, 1923

 IN THE PRECEDING CHAPTERS I have sought to offer a rational explanation for how humankind arrived at its present ecological and social crises, and suggestions for how we might create a new, sustainable culture by individually and collectively adopting a new covenant with nature. But when dealing with cultural change on a massive scale, rational explanations and prescriptions are of only limited use. When societies undergo fundamental change, they usually do so on the basis of motives that transcend rationality.

I have long been fascinated by Carl Jung's suggestion, made over seventy years ago now, that part of the dilemma of the modern world is that its myth is dying. He said that we need a new myth in order to revive our sense of purpose and to save our world from collective suicide. But what would this new myth be?

The myths Jung was talking about aren't, of course, merely tales invented by unscientific primitives to explain natural phenomena; they are the stories that constellate the meanings of a culture. According to Jung, we in the modern West have every bit as deep a need for vital myths as ancient or tribal peoples ever did. But somehow now, as we witness the final links being forged in the first global civilization in history, the stories that formerly made sense of the world have ceased to do so.

The decaying remnants of old myths are to be found not only in the tales of the Greek pantheon but (more significantly) in the religious literature of the East and West, North and South. These stories of saints and saviors, of migrations and wars and floods and culture heroes, which shaped the worldviews of scores of generations on every inhabited continent, still hang about like ghosts, inspiring the occasional outburst from this or that fundamentalist sect but having little of relevance to say to the vast majority of people whose lives are shaped far more by the modern reality of an all-consuming market economy powered by furiously evolving technologies.

For the dominant culture, the old stories serve to articulate the mythic themes of *disobedience, woundedness, guilt,* and *conquest.* God has given us, his people (note the pronoun), dominion over the land, plants, and animals, and it is our destiny to subdue not only these but also any alien tribes of human beings who happen to be in our way.

In its most prevalent form, this myth says that the world began as a garden presided over by a male deity and inhabited by the first man and woman, who were naked and innocent. The garden was filled with trees and animals, so that everything needed for life was abundantly available. But, because the first people disobeyed their God, they were expelled from the garden and forced to till the soil.

The bulk of the ensuing story has to do with the achievements and tribulations of a singular tribe that believed itself to have been granted a unique covenant with God. Sometimes the tribe flourished by laying waste to cities that stood in the way of its expansion; at other times, it was itself persecuted nearly to extinction. But eventually a great and long-promised leader appeared, who was none other than the only Son of the Creator of the Universe. He offered a message of simplicity, humility, peace, love, and forgiveness, which his followers went about spreading, at first by preaching, healing, and martyrdom, and later by threats, bribes, and torture.

The myth, having begun in Paradise, ends there too; but now it is an entirely different Paradise. Formerly a garden, it has become a city—the New Jerusalem; one which is entirely symmetrical, measured, crystalline, and metallic (its streets being lined with gold). The world has been utterly transformed, so that nature is nowhere evident; only the spiritually perfected works of God and his elect remain.

It was a powerful myth in its time, though not entirely self-consistent. In any case, it has nearly run its course: We have subdued just about everything that moves, and the garden of Earth's wilderness is indeed fast becoming one huge city. But rather than being paved with gold, its streets are paved with homeless people, fast-food restaurants, and, overwhelmingly, with concrete. At the end of time we expected to be caught up in a cloud of glory, but it turned out to be carbon monoxide fumes instead.

No wonder so many people have stopped believing in the old myth. Still, some cling to it with a vengeance. Nearly everyone waits in apprehension, sensing the end of an age.

MYTH AND SCIENCE

Myths make sense in (and of) a cultural context. When the context changes, the old myths stop making sense. That's what happened to the Greek myths over twenty-five hundred years ago, when philosophers like Xenophanes began to question the reality of the traditional gods and goddesses. In a similar spirit, our own philosophers have been chipping away at the Judeo-Christian mythos for the past couple of centuries, attempting to replace it with a secular substitute.

In *Myth and Philosophy: A Contest of Truths*, philosopher Lawrence J. Hatab of Dominion University has argued that myth cannot and should not be reduced to other modes of expression (such as rational explanation in philosophy, mathematics, or science), and that in its own way myth offers truths as real and important as those of rational discourse. Moreover, according to Hatab, when philosophy tries to break completely with myth, it loses its way; and it is this attempt on the part of modern science and philosophy to demythologize human consciousness that has weakened our ties with the deepest truths of our cultural heritage.

The materialist philosophers that Hatab opposes say that we should get rid of myths altogether, become more rational, and wean ourselves from superstition. Myth, they say, should retire in favor of science. But science, though it is formulated in a way quite different from traditional myths, still serves a mythic function: It tells us how the Universe began, where the first people came from, and how the world came to be the way it is. This suggestion that we do away with mythology is based on a fundamental misunderstanding of myth and of the human psyche. Myth in some form is inevitable and necessary. Our knowledge is always finite, and is always overlapped by our need for meaning. Our thoughts and aspirations seek some symbolic language through which we can talk about, and participate in, what we otherwise cannot see, touch, or taste. What is our goal, our meaning, our purpose as human beings? These are the questions a myth can answer.

Virtually every thinking person sees the need for dramatic global renewal if our world is to survive; and, as the greatest politicians, artists, spiritual leaders, and even scientists know in their bones, only a new myth can inspire creative cultural change. But where will this bolt of inspiration come from?

Ironically, while many scientists have sought to undo myth altogether, it is science itself that seems to me to be serving as a primary source for a new myth. Science's great strengths are its continual checking of theory with experience and its ability to generate new theories in response to new discoveries. While it is still a very young enterprise, and capable of generating its own irrational dogmas, science is in principle malleable and self-correcting. Currently, it appears that elements of a new myth are emerging through quantum and relativity physics (despite the fundamental theoretical problems mentioned in chapter 11), though more directly and powerfully through the findings of anthropology (which is "discovering" the wisdom of native peoples), psychology (which is only beginning to develop a comprehensive understanding of human consciousness), sociology (which offers a comparative view of human economies and lifestyles), and ecology—as well as through the profound, nearly universal human response to the view of planet Earth from space, an image that owes more to technology than to theoretical science.

THE NEW STORY

Each of these sources is, I believe, contributing to the formulation of a myth whose general features are becoming clear enough that it can be articulated in simple story form. We could call it the myth of *healing and humility*. It starts out somewhat like the old myth, but diverges rather quickly:

Tens of thousands of years ago, human beings subsisted by gathering wild plants. These ancestors of ours were nomadic and lived in a magical interdependence with their surroundings; The animals and trees were their friends and spoke to them. To be sure, they faced challenges—sickness and accidents, for example—but generally enjoyed good health and a stable and rich communal life.

While other creatures' adaptations to their environment were physical and instinctual, human beings had developed large brains that allowed them to adapt and develop socially, spiritually, and linguistically in ways that were unique. This capacity for inner development and thus for cultural invention allowed people to respond quickly to environmental changes. And the environment did change—ice ages following warm periods; floods following droughts—sometimes over the course of millennia, other times in the space of hours or days.

The most dramatic climate shifts were brought about by occasional massive comet or asteroid impacts. On at least one occasion, still tens of millennia ago, the planet's atmosphere was darkened for years by dust raised from such a collision. So many plants died out during those years that humans resorted to hunting animals for food. Later, they retained the habit.

Then, between ten thousand and twelve thousand years ago, another series of catastrophes inspired more human adaptations. Up to this time, wild game had been plentiful—so much so, that the human population had burgeoned. But now many of the big game animals were being hunted to extinction. In addition, climates everywhere were fluctuating rapidly and sea levels were rising, drowning densely populated coastal areas. Suddenly the world had changed, and people would have to change too in order to survive.

The tribes that had been most deeply traumatized by these events tended to live in a perpetual state of emergency, to blame themselves for provoking the gods, and to pass their felt trauma on to their children in the form of abusive discipline. Whereas before human groups had been egalitarian, this new crisis seemed to call for stern leadership. Men—especially the strongest and most driven ones—became dominant. Tribes began to fear and fight one another, and to fear the sky and the elements.

One further social adaptation to catastrophe had to do with the basic ways in which people related to their environment. Every creature, and every culture, must survive both by adapting to its environment, and by altering its environment to suit itself. But there are relative degrees of compromise between these two courses of action. In the case of our crisis-ridden Paleolithic ancestors, some apparently chose the former, deciding to learn more about the natural world so that they could accommodate themselves better to it. They dreamed myths that encoded meanings having to do with protecting populations of wild animals, with keeping the numbers of humans within bounds, and with honoring the diversity and interconnectivity of the web of life.

Other people, however, decided to concentrate on adapting the environment to themselves. They domesticated plants and animals; they cleared and plowed the land. They chose the best places and built permanent settlements. The populations of these groups continued to grow unchecked. As settlements increased in size, social arrangements became more stratified and classes developed. A few individuals became wealthy and powerful; the rest tried to make themselves useful. As their territory expanded, they came into conflict with other settled groups, with whom they fought or formed alliances; or with food gatherers and hunters, whom they killed or enslaved.

Wherever they settled, they exhausted the land. After a few generations, famine would strike and they would move on. Eventually, however, their populations and territories grew so large that there was nowhere else to go. Meanwhile, virtually all of the peoples who had taken the first option were now absorbed within the lands of the planters and herders. Huge cities sprang up, and devices were invented for every imaginable purpose—for communication, transportation, manufacture, cooking, cleaning, personal hygiene, and mass killing. The feeding of the masses in the cities and the production of all these new devices required increasingly intensive farming and mining, and the ruthless regimentation of human labor.

As the whole Earth began to cry out in fatigue, as cities began to disintegrate in factional warfare, and as hunger gripped the poorer classes of the planting-and-herding groups, the youth of the latter began to seek out the few remaining peoples who had learned to adapt themselves to the land. The planters, who had been so arrogant, began to humble themselves before their cousins, from whom they had departed so long ago and whom they had butchered and enslaved at every opportunity. They began to humble themselves before the wild things and the wild places of the Earth. They vowed to heal and renew the land and to forge sacred ties of mutual respect and aid between species and cultures. And they vowed to remember, so that they would not make the same mistakes again.

All together, gradually, they came to understand and release their ancient fears. They began to use the wisdom and knowledge they had accumulated and preserved through the previous millennia to begin to build a new way of life, different both from their primordial food-gathering ways and from their later planting-and-herding ways. Realizing now that they were all deeply wounded, they together resolved to heal the deep effects of trauma, and to renounce violence. They learned to limit their population, and to satisfy their basic needs by ever-simpler means. Their social groupings became smaller and more democratic. The crisis they had just been through had deeply impressed them with a new sense of morality: Whereas before they had celebrated unbridled consumption and accumulation, now they knew the perils of excess size, speed, and sophistication. They had learned that it was only by respecting all life that they could live again in magical interdependence with their natural surroundings. Now, as long ago, they began to see the land as sacred, and to hear the voices of the trees and animals. Once again, life was good.

IS IT TRUE?

It is fair to regard this new myth with a degree of skepticism. After all, myths can be used to manipulate people. On many occasions individuals or groups have simply engineered a new myth by studying the requirements and tailoring one for the occasion. Quite of few of our culture's current myths came into being this way—national myths, economic myths, myths about war enemies and beloved political leaders. But the truest and most genuine myths aren't manufactured: they are dreamt and sung and danced and lived.

In writing this story, I am keenly aware that I am to some extent "manufacturing" it, in the sense above, but at the same time articulating it from some source beyond myself. I am convinced that the basic outline of the story has a life of its own and is true, both in the sense that it is factual and in the sense that it is *true to life*. Of course, no myth is entirely true, any more than is any scientific theory entirely true. But if it helps us see ourselves and our situation from a more inclusive viewpoint, then we may perhaps profit by holding it lightly for a time and seeing how it affects the way we see and be.

One way in which I'd suggest testing the genuineness of this (or any) new myth is by asking the question, *whom does it serve?* Does it serve the interests of powerful people and institutions—the sort who are in the habit of manufacturing myths? Or does it serve a larger constituency?

Assuming this story *is* in some sense a new myth such as Jung was calling for, what should we do about it? Should we advertise it? In a sense, that's what I'm doing by writing it down and publishing it. If I didn't think that there is some usefulness in the exercise, I wouldn't bother. But it is a limited usefulness. This story is, after all, only one articulation of the new myth. Other people at different times and with differing perspectives will doubtless cast it in other, perhaps truer or more compelling terms. Some would tell the story in theological language, whereas I have chosen not to. Also, there are many related sub-stories that I have omitted from this rendition—ones having to do with the return of the Goddess; with the rediscovery of gentle, honest manhood; with the details of our real or potential renewed bonding with the animals, the herbs, and the stones.

More important than broadcasting the story, however, is living it. We can discover its truth only by testing it in the laboratory of our behavior and perceptions. Of course, such an effort only makes sense if one already has some intuitive sense of the new myth's truth and necessity—which, I believe, many people have. Those of us who see the need to limit population growth and to foster economic equality and democracy; who are seeking ways to honor natural cycles, energies, and balances and to nurture the feminine principle in the world and in our own consciousnesses—are all already drawn to the invisible outline of this new vision of human purpose and meaning.

As the old myth crumbles, taking with it institutions, economies, and lives, perhaps we need a story to make sense of the deepening chaos and to guide us toward a more coherent and sustainable pattern of existence. But that new story will serve us well only if it draws its power from the depths of our being, where culture, nature, and spirit all converge. Is it a fact, or is it only wishful thinking?—that as the cement facade of civilization grows more impressive it also becomes more brittle. Cracks continually appear. And through those cracks we see the human vulnerability and woundedness of those who inhabit the edifice. Deeper still, we occasionally catch a glimpse of light—a flame blazing at the core of humanity, a fire that burns at the heart of creation. This fire is the source from which new cultures and new species spring; it is the generative potential of life itself. And here lies our hope: In the heat of world destruction and world renewal, can we but learn to dwell in that flame.

NOTES

CHAPTER 1: OUR COVENANTS WITH NATURE

1. W. E. H. Stanner, *White Man Got No Dreaming: Essays 1938–1973* (Canberra: Australian National University Press, 1979), 157–158.
2. *Ibid*, 162.
3. *Ibid*, 162.
4. Jack Weatherford, *Savages and Civilization: Who Will Survive?* (New York: Crown, 1994), 54.
5. John Reader, *Man on Earth* (New York: Harper & Row, 1988), 60.
6. Weatherford, *op. cit.*, 176.

CHAPTER 2: FATEFUL CHOICES, THEN AND NOW

1. William Eckhardt, *Civilizations, Empires and Wars: A Quantitative History of War* (Jefferson, N. C.: McFarland, 1992).
2. Duane Elgin, *Awakening Earth: Exploring the Evolution of Human Culture and Consciousness* (New York: William Morrow, 1993), 12.
3. *Ibid.*, 19–20.
4. Melvin Ember and Carol R. Ember, "Prescriptions for Peace: Policy Implications of Cross-Cultural Research on War and Interpersonal Violence." *Cross-Cultural Research*, Vol. 28 No. 4, November, 1994, 343–350.

CHAPTER 3: CATASTROPHE AND CULTURE

1. Victor Clube and Bill Napier, *The Cosmic Winter* (Oxford: Basil Blackwell, 1990), 33.
2. *Ibid.,* 138.
3. *Ibid.,* 34.
4. Georg Feuerstein, Subhash Kak, and David Frawley, *In Search of the Cradle of Civilization* (Wheaton, Ill.: Quest Books, 1995), 94–95.
5. Quoted in Immanuel Velikovsky, *Earth in Upheaval* (New York: Dell, 1968), 256.
6. Clube and Napier, *op. cit.,* 42.
7. Mircea Eliade, *Patterns in Comparative Religion* (New York: New American Library, 1963), 39.

CHAPTER 4: COLLECTIVE TRAUMA AND THE ORIGIN OF CIVILIZATION

1. Robert Jay Lifton, *Survivors of Hiroshima: Death in Life* (New York: Random House, 1967).
2. Alice Miller, *For Your Own Good* (New York: Farrar, Straus, Giroux, 1983), 16.
3. Quoted in Susan C. Roberts, "Multiple Realities: How MPD is shaking up our notions of the self, the body and even the origins of evil," *Common Boundary* May/June 1992, 29.
4. Morris Berman, *Coming To Our Senses: Body and Spirit in the Hidden History of the West* (New York: Bantam, 1990), 22.
5. Colin Turnbull, *The Mountain People* (New York: Simon & Schuster, 1972), 31.
6. *Ibid.*, 287.
7. *Ibid.*, 157.
8. *Ibid.*, 134.
9. *Ibid.*, 291.
10. Lewis Aptekar, *Environmental Disasters in Global Perspective* (New York: G.K. Hall, 1994), 84.
11. *Ibid.*, 86.
12. *Ibid.*, 115.
13. *Ibid.*, 115.
14. *Ibid.*, 113.
15. *Ibid.*, 56.
16. *Ibid.*, 158.
17. *Ibid.*, 77.
18. William Calvin, *The Ascent of Mind: Ice Age Climates and the Evolution of Intelligence* (New York: Bantam, 1990), 88.
19. *Ibid.*, 69.
20. Julian Jaynes, *The Origin of Consciousness in the Breakdown of the Bicameral Mind* (New York: Houghton Mifflin, 1976/1990), 117.
21. *Ibid.*, 66.
22. *Ibid.*, 209.

CHAPTER 5: WHAT ARE OUR OPTIONS?

1. *The New Republic*, "Lip-Flop," editorial, July 23, 1990.

CHAPTER 6: TOWARD A REBIRTH OF CULTURE

1. Tr. Walter Clode, quoted in Goldian VandenBroeck, ed., *Less Is More:*

The Art of Voluntary Poverty (Rochester, Vt.: Inner Traditions, 1991), 146.

2. Stanley Diamond, *In Search of the Primitive: A Critique of Civilization* (New Brunswick, N.J.: Transaction Books, 1974), 1.
3. *Ibid.*, 2.
4. John Perrott, *Bush for the Bushman* (Greenville, Pa.: Beaver Pond Publishing, 1992), 102.
5. Robert S. Rattray, *Ashanti Law and Constitution* (London: Negro University Press, 1929), 286.
6. Diamond, *op. cit.*, 6.

CHAPTER 7: THE ARTS: BRINGING SPIRIT DOWN TO EARTH

1. Quoted in Duane Preble, *Man Creates Art Creates Man* (San Francisco: Canfield Press, 1973), 9.
2. Quoted in Margie K. C. West, ed., *The Inspired Dream: Life as Art in Aboriginal Australia* (Brisbane, Australia: Queensland Art Gallery, 1988), 25.
3. Franz Boas, *The Mind of Primitive Man* (New York: Macmillan, 1938), 216.
4. Stanley Diamond, *In Search of the Primitive: A Critique of Civilization* (New Brunswick, N.J.: Transaction Books, 1974), 148.
5. Quoted in Howard Zinn, *A People's History of the United States* (New York: Harper Perennial, 1990), 353.

CHAPTER 8: ECONOMICS: IS MONEY EVIL?

1. Norman Angell, *The Story of Money* (Garden City, N.Y.: Garden City Publishing, 1929), 17–18.
2. Helena Norberg-Hodge, *Ancient Futures: Learning from Ladakh* (San Francisco: Sierra Club Books, 1991), 101.
3. *Ibid.*, 85.
4. *Ibid.*, 102.
5. *Ibid.*, 104.
6. *Ibid.*, 141.
7. *Ibid.*, 141.
8. *Ibid.*, 114.
9. *Ibid.*, 157.
10. John H. Bodley, *Victims of Progress* (Menlo Park, Calif.: 1986), 152.

11. International Society for Ecology and Culture/Ladakh Project, P.O. Box 9475, Berkeley, CA 94709, (510) 527–3873.

CHAPTER 9: GOVERNANCE: FREEDOM, NECESSITY, AND POWER

1. Dale Van Every, *Disinherited* (New York: William Morrow, 1966), 65.
2. Jerry Mander, *In the Absence of the Sacred* (San Francisco: Sierra Club Books, 1991), 229.
3. Lucy Mair, *Primitive Government* (Harmondsworth, England: Penguin, 1962), 162.
4. Quoted in Stanley Diamond, *In Search of the Primitive: A Critique of Civilization* (New Brunswick, N.J.: Transaction Books, 1974), 180.

CHAPTER 10: SPIRITUALITY: RAW OR COOKED?

1. Lewis Mumford, *The Myth of the Machine, Volume One: Technics and Human Development* (New York: Harcourt Brace Jovanovich, 1966), 258.
2. Morton Smith, "The Historical Jesus," in R. Joseph Hoffman and Gerald A. Larve, eds., *Jesus in History and Myth* (New York: Prometheus, 1986), 50.
3. Burton L. Mack, *The Lost Gospel: The Book of Q and Christian Origins* (San Francisco: Harper Collins, 1993), 247.
4. Smith, *op. cit.*, 51.
5. Mack, *op. cit.*, 115.
6. John Dominic Crossan, *The Historical Jesus: The Life of a Mediterranean Jewish Peasant* (San Francisco: Harper Collins, 1991), 421.
7. *Ibid.*, 422.
8. Mack, *op. cit.*, 203.
9. *Ibid.*, 203.
10. *Ibid.*, 204–205.

CHAPTER 11: SCIENCE: MORSELS OF KNOWLEDGE, BANQUETS OF IGNORANCE

1. Tom Van Flandern, *Dark Matter, Missing Planets & New Comets* (Berkeley: North Atlantic Books, 1993).
2. Claude Lévi-Strauss, *The Savage Mind* (Chicago: University of Chicago Press, 1966), 15.

3. Quoted in Lévi-Strauss, *op. cit.,* 4.
4. *Ibid.,* 22.
5. *Ibid.,* 19.

CHAPTER 12: A DIFFERENT KIND OF PROGRESS

1. Quoted in Scott Peterson, *Native American Prophecies* (New York: Paragon House, 1990), 188.
2. Quoted in Peterson, *op. cit.,* 190.
3. Quoted in Peterson, *op. cit.,* 189.

CHAPTER 14: THE ROOTS OF CULTURE

1. Roy Wagner, *The Invention of Culture* (Englewood Cliffs, N.J.: Prentice-Hall, 1975), 1.
2. Jerry Mander, *In the Absence of the Sacred* (San Francisco: Sierra Club Books, 1991), 25.

CHAPTER 15: HOW TO SAVE THE WORLD: A GLOBAL PERSPECTIVE

1. Carolyn Merchant, *Radical Ecology: The Search for a Livable World* (New York: Routledge, 1992), 128.
2. Quoted in Merchant, *op. cit.,* 124.

CHAPTER 16: HOW TO SAVE THE WORLD: A PERSONAL RESPONSE

1. Paul Glover, *The Boycott Quarterly,* Spring, 1994.

READING LIST

Aptekar, Lewis. *Environmental Disasters in Global Perspective.* New York: G.K. Hall, 1994.

Berman, Morris. *Coming To Our Senses: Body and Spirit in the Hidden History of the West.* New York: Bantam, 1990.

Boas, Franz. *The Mind of Primitive Man.* New York: Macmillan, 1938.

Bodley, John H. *Victims of Progress.* Menlo Park, Calif.: 1986.

Calvin, William. *The Ascent of Mind: Ice Age Climates and the Evolution of Intelligence.* New York: Bantam, 1990.

Clube, Victor, and Bill Napier. *The Cosmic Winter.* Oxford: Basil Blackwell, 1990.

Crossan, John Dominic. *The Historical Jesus.* San Francisco: Harper Collins, 1991.

Diamond, Stanley. *In Search of the Primitive: A Critique of Civilization.* New Brunswick, N.J.: Transaction Books, 1974.

Dominguez, Joe, and Vicki Robin. *Your Money Or Your Life: Transforming Your Relationship with Money and Achieving Financial Independence.* New York: Penguin, 1992.

DuBois, Paul Martin, and Frances Moore Lappé. *The Quickening of America.* San Francisco: Jossey Bass, 1994.

Eckhardt, William. *Civilizations, Empires and Wars: A Quantitative History of War.* Jefferson, N. C.: McFarland, 1992.

Eliade, Mircea. *Patterns in Comparative Religion.* New York: New American Library, 1963.

Feuerstein, Georg, Subhash Kak, and David Frawley. *In Search of the Cradle of Civilization.* Wheaton, Ill.: Quest Books, 1995.

Glendinning, Chellis. *My Name Is Chellis and I'm in Recovery from Western Civilization.* Boston: Shambhala, 1994.

Grossman, Richard L., and Frank T. Adams, *Taking Care of Business: Citizenship and the Charter of Incorporation.* Pamphlet available for $5 ppd. from Charter, Ink., P.O. Box 806, Cambridge, MA 02140.

Hatab, Lawrence J. *Myth and Philosophy: A Contest of Truths.* Chicago: Open Court, 1990.

Heinberg, Richard. *Memories and Visions of Paradise: Exploring the Universal Myth of a Lost Golden Age.* 2nd ed. Wheaton, Il.: Quest Books, 1995.

Highwater, Jamake. *The Primal Mind.* New York: New American Library, 1981.

Hoffman, R. Joseph, and Gerald A. Larve, eds. *Jesus in History and Myth.* New York: Prometheus, 1986.

Hoyle, Fred. *Ice: The Ultimate Human Catastrophe.* New York: Continuum, 1981.

Jaynes, Julian. *The Origin of Consciousness in the Breakdown of the Bicameral Mind.* New York: Houghton Mifflin, 1976/1990.

Kramer, Joel, and Diana Alstad. *The Guru Papers: Masks of Authoritarian Power.* Berkeley: North Atlantic Books, 1993.

Lévi-Strauss, Claude. *The Savage Mind.* Chicago: University of Chicago Press, 1966.

Lifton, Robert Jay. *Survivors of Hiroshima: Death in Life.* New York: Random House, 1967.

Mack, Burton L. *The Lost Gospel: The Book of Q and Christian Origins.* San Francisco: Harper Collins, 1993.

Mair, Lucy. *Primitive Government.* Harmondsworth, England: Penguin, 1962.

Mander, Jerry. *In the Absence of the Sacred.* San Francisco: Sierra Club Books, 1991.

Meadows, Donella, Dennis L. Meadows, Jørgen Randers, William W. Behrens, III. *The Limits to Growth: a report for the Club of Rome's project on the predicament of mankind.* New York: Universe Books, 1972.

Meadows, Donella. *Beyond the Limits.* New York: American Forum, 1992.

Merchant, Carolyn. *Radical Ecology: The Search for a Livable World.* New York: Routledge, 1992.

Miller, Alice. *For Your Own Good.* New York: Farrar, Straus, Giroux, 1983.

Morgan, Elaine. *The Aquatic Ape: A Theory of Human Evolution.* New York: Stein and Day, 1982.

———. *The Scars of Evolution: What Our Bodies Tell Us About Human Origins.* Oxford: Oxford University Press, 1994.

Morris, Desmond. *The Biology of Art.* New York: Knopf, 1962.

Mumford, Lewis. *The Myth of the Machine, Volume One: Technics and Human Development.* New York: Harcourt Brace Jovanovich, 1966.

———. *The Myth of the Machine, Volume Two: The Pentagon of Power.* New York: Harcourt Brace Jovanovich, 1970.

Norberg-Hodge, Helena. *Ancient Futures: Learning from Ladakh.* San Francisco: Sierra Club Books, 1991.

Perrott, John. *Bush for the Bushman.* Greenville, Pa.: Beaver Pond Publishing, 1992.

Peterson, Scott. *Native American Prophecies.* New York: Paragon House, 1990.

Quinn, Daniel. *Ishmael.* New York: Bantam, 1992.

Radin, Paul. *Primitive Man As Philosopher.* New York: Dover, 1957.

Raup, David M. *Extinction: Bad Genes or Bad Luck.* New York: W. W. Norton, 1991.

Roszak, Theodore. *The Voice of the Earth.* New York: Simon & Schuster, 1992.

Sale, Kirkpatrick. *Dwellers in the Land: A Bioregional Vision.* San Francisco: Sierra Club, 1985.

―――. *Rebels Against the Future: The Luddites and Their War on the Industrial Revolution.* Reading, Mass.: Addison-Wesley, 1995.

Sessions, George, ed. *Deep Ecology for the 21st Century.* Boston: Shambhala, 1995.

Shepard, Paul. *Nature and Madness.* San Francisco: Sierra Club, 1982.

Smith, Morton. *The Secret Gospel.* New York: Harper & Row, 1973.

―――. *Jesus the Magician.* 2nd ed. New York: Harper & Row, 1981.

Suzuki, David. *The Wisdom of the Elders.* New York: Bantam, 1992.

Turnbull, Colin. *The Mountain People.* New York: Simon & Schuster, 1972.

Van Every, Dale. *Disinherited.* New York: William Morrow, 1966.

Van Flandern, Tom. *Dark Matter, Missing Planets & New Comets.* Berkeley: North Atlantic Books, 1993.

Velikovsky, Immanuel. *Worlds in Collision.* New York: Macmillan, 1950.

―――. *Earth in Upheaval.* New York: Dell, 1968.

―――. *Mankind in Amnesia.* New York: Doubleday, 1981.

Wagner, Roy. *The Invention of Culture.* Englewood Cliffs, N.J.: Prentice-Hall, 1975.

Weatherford, Jack. *Savages and Civilization: Who Will Survive?* New York: Crown, 1994.

Wilson, Edward O. *The Diversity of Life.* Cambridge, Mass.: Belknap, 1992.

Zerzan, John. *Future Primitive.* Brooklyn, N.Y.: Autonomedia, 1994.

Zinn, Howard. *A People's History of the United States.* New York: Harper Perennial, 1990.

INDEX

QUEST BOOKS
are published by
The Theosophical Society in America,
Wheaton, Illinois 60189-0270,
a branch of a world organization
dedicated to the promotion of the unity of
humanity and the encouragement of the study of
religion, philosophy, and science, to the end that
we may better understand ourselves and our place in
the universe. The Society stands for complete
freedom of individual search and belief.
For further information about its activities,
write or call 1-800-669-1571.

*The Theosophical Publishing House
is aided by the generous support of
THE KERN FOUNDATION,
a trust established by Herbert A. Kern
and dedicated to Theosophical education.*